301
CRAZY
Property Management Stories

J. N. BENNETT

This is a work of fiction. Names, characters, businesses, events, locales, and incidents are either the products of the author's imagination or used in a fictitious manner. Any resemblance to actual persons, living or dead, or actual events is purely coincidental.

ISBN13: 978-1-0917-1273-7
ISBN10: 1-0917-1273-5

Contents

1. The Christmas Wreath

The tenant hung a Christmas wreath from her front door knocker. It was too thick to allow the storm door to close. The storm door was left unlatched and open a few inches. It was an HOA violation because the wind might rip it off its hinges and toss it in the air, down the street, causing property damage or injury. The HOA inspected it, sent a violation notice, and threatened fines. The property manager called the tenants.

"Hello. We got an HOA notice that your wreath is keeping the storm door from closing."

"Yes. No big deal. Right?"

"Those busybodies at the HOA have a rule against it. The storm door has to close."

"It's not gonna happen. My wreath is too thick."

"Can you take it down?"

"What about religious liberty? It's a Christmas wreath."

"Oh. Hmm. Can you hang it somewhere else? Like on the lamp?"

"That would look stupid. It belongs on the door."

"Please? I just want to get the HOA off my back."

"No."

"What if I did it?"

"Did what?"

"Made it fit. Made that wreath fit."

"You can try. As long as it stays where it is on the front door."

They agreed. The property manager went to the house while the tenants were at work. He took the wreath off, laid it flat on the sidewalk, and stomped on it. He hung it back up and closed the storm door. Perfect fit.

2. Anything Else?

The landlord who owned the rental property called the property manager.

"Has my house has been cleaned yet?"

"The cleaning is done." He didn't know if it was done.
"Have you seen it?"
"Yes. It looks great." He hadn't seen it.
"Good. I was worried."
"Anything else?"
"Did the painters finish?"
"Yes. It looks great." He had no idea.
"What a relief."
"Anything else?"
"Was the lawn mowed?"
"It looks great." He forgot to have it mowed.
"I'm so nervous. I want everything just right."
"Anything else?"
"Can I drive by and look for myself?"
"No. Don't. The tenant is moving in. He's stressed out and mean as a snake."
"I guess you know best."
"Relax and let me do my job." He wasn't doing his job.

3. Garage Door Opener

The tenant moved in and immediately called the property manager.

"Hey. There's no garage door opener."
"I know. It never had one."
"Every house has a garage door opener."
"Not some older houses."
"I've never seen a garage without an electric opener."
"I grew up without one. I didn't have color TV either."
"So you're old. I'm not. I'm asking for a standard house."
"We didn't advertise or offer a standard house. It's old. It's one of a kind."
"I want a garage door opener."
"We said the house was quaint."
"I don't want quaint."
"You said it had character."
"I did?"
"You saw the house before you rented it, right?"

"Twice."

"The garage door has a handle. You pull it up. The old fashioned way."

"This is the twenty-first century."

"I really hate to tell you this, but your house doesn't have a dishwasher either."

"No? Why not?"

"It's not required by the lease or the law. All this stuff was in the advertising."

"Who reads the advertising?"

"I grew up in a house without a dishwasher. When I was young my sister washed the dishes by hand and I dried them. I have fond memories of those days. We're still close."

"Idiot."

4. The Mailbox

The tenant ran over the mailbox. The neighbors saw him do it. One of the neighbors was the landlord who owned the house. The property manager called the tenant.

"You need to pay for a new mailbox."

"Why me?"

"You ran over it."

"No, I didn't. I came home from work and found it like that."

"The neighbors saw you."

"The neighbors don't like me."

"The owner of the house was out walking his dog and saw it."

"The owner is spying on me?"

"No. He lives on your street."

"I didn't do it."

"It made a loud cracking sound. Everybody heard it. They looked out their windows. You ran over it again just getting out of the driveway."

"How do you know?"

"I drove by. Your fender is cracked. There's paint from the mailbox on your bumper."

"You're spying on me."

"Come on. Even the dog saw it. Give up. Own it."

"The mailbox was too close to my car in the first place."

"I have no comeback for that."

"How will I get my mail now?"

The tenant used a bungee cord to strap the mailbox to a lawn chair at the end of the driveway. He got his mail, including a thirty-day notice from the property manager.

5. Spirits Convey

A hundred-year-old house in a small town was advertised on the rental market. When the house was shown by realtors to potential renters, some of them claimed to see and hear ghosts. The property manager asked the homeowner if the house was haunted. The homeowner confessed that there were two ghosts. He had seen them. He claimed to have talked with them.

The property manager was not required by the law or by his industry's ethics guidelines to disclose non-material defects. Ghosts, were not real, everyone knew that. But if the spirits, or rumors thereof, were detrimental to marketing they could cause a delay in leasing and a loss of income for the owner. He called the owner.

"We're not getting rental applications on your house. It's in a great location and the price is below market. May I disclose this ghost issue in the advertising?"

"Won't that keep people from wanting to see my house?"

"Maybe. Maybe not. It may spur interest, get more traffic, more showings."

"You think so?" asked the owner.

"What do you have to lose? The ghosts, if they are real, have kept people from applying so far."

The owner agreed. "Give it a try. For one weekend."

The house was advertised the same as before, with one change. Added to the property description were the words "Spirits Convey." It made renters and realtors curious. The house was shown twice as often. Three rental applications were received. The house was rented to an acupuncturist and her husband, a mystery writer. They had stayed at a famous haunted hotel in New Orleans. He was writing a book about haunted houses. It was perfect.

After a month of living in the house the tenants called the property manager. They were disappointed. The ghosts were appearing less frequently. They were fading. The tenants said it might be deceptive advertising.

6. You Call This Clean?

The property manager did a check-in inspection with a new tenant to document all pre-existing wear and tear and the condition of the property.

The tenant said, "You call this clean? It's not clean to me."

"The owners cleaned the house yesterday, after they moved out."

"Aren't they required to have it professionally cleaned?"

"It's not required in your lease."

"I want it professionally cleaned. Look at the foyer ceiling lamp. There are dead bugs in the globe."

"The owners spent three days cleaning up. They may not agree with you."

"Well maybe they have lower standards than I do."

"I'll remove the globe and rinse the bugs out."

"What about the kitchen floor?"

"It looks pretty clean."

"It doesn't shine. It should shine."

"It's clean though."

"It should shine, right?"

"No. It's twenty-year-old vinyl. I can mop it with Quik-Shine. It will shine for a while."

"What about that toilet. It has a ring of dirt or something."

"That's a circle of mineral deposits at the water line. It's normal."

"Minerals? I don't think so."

"Water has minerals. Magnesium. Sodium. Calcium. Read a water bottle. Minerals."

"I want clean toilets."

It just hasn't been flushed for weeks. Watch. I'll flush it. See? All gone."

"I expect cleaning. Is that unreasonable?"

"How about I give you a fifty dollar compensation?"

"Fifty? Where do you get fifty?"

"When we first showed you the house, you hated it. When we gave you a lease to sign, you hated that. No one in my office wanted to meet you here today because you argue about everything. I said I'd do it for fifty bucks. They all pitched in. I have the money right here. You want fifty bucks?"

"This is crazy. Very unprofessional."

"Sixty?"

7. The Cold Kitchen

A tenant moved into a condo. After a few weeks she called the property manager.

"There's a cold spot in the kitchen."

"What? A spot?"

"A corner. A corner of the kitchen is cold."

"How cold?"

"Just cold."

The property manager said, "I never noticed that before."

She asked, "Do you think it could be the insulation?"

"It's a newer building. Made by a good builder."

"Maybe a draft from a leak?"

"Probably not. Your kitchen is against an interior party wall."

"What can you do about it?" asked the tenant.

"I can bring you a thermometer and we can compare the temperatures in different rooms."

"Maybe it's not that kind of cold. Maybe it's not a temperature thing."

"What do you mean? What kind of thing is it?"

"It's like a cold spot in one of those houses on Ghost Search. The TV show."

"I don't watch that show. What do the actors say about cold spots?"

"It's usually cold where somebody died. Did anybody die in my condo?"

"No. I mean I don't know. How would I know?"

"Can you come and stand in the kitchen with me and feel it?"

"I'm available Monday morning."

"No, it only happens late at night, a little after ten o'clock."

"What time is Ghost Search on?"

"From nine to ten."

8. The Dead Dog Deposit

The tenant called the property manager and said his dog had died.

The property manager said, "Oh, no, I'm so sorry. You must feel terrible."

"Yes, but I'm wondering if I can get my pet deposit back."

"Well, no, your security deposit and pet deposit are in an escrow account until the end of the lease term."

"But I don't have a dog anymore. I should get it back."

"We really can't assess damage until the house is empty."

"How can a dead dog hurt the house?"

"Hmm. Let's say the dog chewed up a carpet before he died. That would be a deposit issue."

"He didn't. You're not listening. He's dead."

"In theory, what if the dog ate the azaleas? That could come out of the deposit."

"I don't have azaleas."

"I can't return the deposit now. There might be latent damage."

"What does latent mean?"

"I think it means hidden."

"My dog is dead. What's so complicated about that?"

"I feel bad about your dog. How are you coping with the loss?"

"I'm getting a puppy."

9. Twenty-Some Occupants

A family of four tenants moved in. Then they moved their parents in. Then they moved some friends in. When the property manager found out, he called the landlord and told him there were twenty-some occupants.

The landlord asked, "Are they paying rent?"

"Like clockwork."

"Are they taking good care of my house?"

"They are, surprisingly."

"Do they ask for a lot of repairs?"

"None yet."

"Are the neighbors complaining?"

"No. The neighboring houses are mostly overcrowded too."

"Then why are you calling me?"

10. The Tenant Disappeared

The tenant disappeared. His furniture was gone. His closets were empty. The power and water had been turned off. Newspapers piled up in the driveway. The neighbors said he had been gone for a month. The property manager put a notice on the door, changed the locks, turned on the utilities, and sent contractors in to fix things up. Weeks later the tenant returned. He couldn't get in. He called the property manager.

"I'm locked out. I can't get in."

"You disappeared. I changed the locks."

"I was just out of the area visiting friends."

"You stopped paying rent. You stopped paying electricity."

"I need to get in."

"I can meet you there, if you give me a forwarding address."

"Why?"

"I need to know where to send a subpoena."

"Why?"

"You owe rent and a lot more."

"But I need to get in. It's my home."

"Not anymore. But tell me where you live now."

"Then can I get in?"

"First please admit in writing you broke the lease."

"Wait a minute."

"And pay back rent, late fees, attorney fees, repair costs."

"Why are you being that way?"

"You left without saying goodbye. What was I to think? I was hurt. I've moved on."

11. Sue Me

The rent was late. The property manager called the tenant regularly asking when the rent would be paid. He sent her emails and letters requesting rent payment.

The tenant called back. "Stop harassing me!"

"I'm not harassing."

"You're not allowed to harass me."

I'm following the federal collections practices guidelines."

"You're harassing me. I'll sue you."

The property manager was weary of tenants threatening lawsuits. He said, "Go ahead. Sue me. I get to wear my new suit in court. I get to sit in landlord-tenant court and watch all those landlords win and all those tenants lose. I get to testify about your debts and threats. Then, after I win in court, my attorney will take me to that little cafe across from the courthouse where all the attorneys have lunch and brag about who beat the stupidest tenant that day. Sue me."

12. Creepy

A tenant called to report a homeless woman in the woods behind his house. She squatted there and smoked cigarettes. She had trash bags full of clothes or something. She could be seen there at odd hours, just squatting on her haunches. Neighbors talked, but did nothing.

The tenant insisted the property manager come to the house and see for himself. The woman was fifty feet behind the house on someone else's land. He asked what the property manager would do about it.

"I can look into it."

"Can you do anything?"

"Maybe not. Those woods are not ours."

"But it's creepy."

"We don't manage the woods."

"My children won't play in the back yard now."

"Have you called the police?"

"No. Will you?"

"Have you called social services?"

"We didn't think of that."

"I wish I could help but I have no jurisdiction."

"Can't you do anything? Please. Anything? It's creepy."

"Okay. I'll look into it."

"You'll look into it?"

"I promise I'll look into it."

"Thank you."

He didn't look into it. He couldn't do anything. He didn't care. As he drove away the woman in the woods was lighting up again. Maybe the fire department would get involved.

13. The Masseuse

A tenant applied to rent a condo. She was a masseuse. Being self-employed, she had no current employment reference. She submitted her previous year's tax returns and bank statements to demonstrate ample income. She was qualified and moved in.

One property manager did the move-in inspection. Another did the annual mid-term inspection. A third went to the house and met her when she had a maintenance complaint.

They talked about her in the office.

"Did you see her massage table?"

"Yes. In the bedroom?"

"No. It's in the den. Where she works."

"It looks like a bedroom."

"The place smells like incense."

"I thought she was really good-looking."

"I know. I wasn't going to say it but yes."

"She told me she does evening appointments."

"I've never had a professional massage."

"I don't think we should be talking about her."

"Why not?"

"You know. I know what you're thinking."

"I'm not thinking at all."

"That's what I mean."

14. Military Transfer Clause

A tenant was transferred out of state by his employer, a defense contractor.

"I've been transferred. I need to terminate my lease."

"You can't just terminate unilaterally."

"But there's a military transfer clause in the lease."

"For active duty uniform military."

"I'm a defense contractor."

"I know."

"I work for the Department of Defense."

"I know."

"The law says you have to let me out of the lease."

"The SCRA?"

"What's that?"

"The law. The Servicemembers Civil Relief Act."

"I never heard of that."

"It's the law for active duty uniform military, to break a lease."

"I qualify for that, right?"

"Maybe. If you do, give us your PCS."

"What's that?"

"Permanent Change of Station orders."

"Where do I get that?"

"From your CO."

"What's that?"

"Commanding officer."

"I don't think I have one of those."

"Then call your JAG officer."

"What's that?"

"Judge Advocate General."

"Who's that?"

"Your military legal rep."

"I never heard of that."

"Then talk to your military superiors, or the Pentagon I guess."

"I don't work for them."

"Now we're getting somewhere."

15. My Girlfriend Sleeps Over

During the annual inspection at a one-bedroom condo rented by a single male, the property manager saw a closet full of women's clothes.

"Do you have a roommate? It looks like you've added one."

"Yes. I can have a roommate, can't I?"

"Yes. But she has to apply to be added to the lease."

"Why?"

"Liability. All occupants have to be liable for debts and damage incurred by all."

"No. Where did you get that?"

"All occupants are jointly and severally liable."

"Joint what?"

"It's in your lease. You read the lease, right?"

"She's not a roommate. She's my girlfriend. She just sleeps over sometimes."

"Oh. That's different. You can have guests. No problem."

"What's the difference?"

"The difference is between what you told me the first time, and what you told me the second time."

"It's really none of your business."

"It's my business. I snoop around and ask questions. Sorry."

"I bet you've had girlfriends sleep over too."

"When I was your age. Those were the days."

16. I Want a Gay Tenant

A client told the property manager "We'd love to have a gay tenant."

The property manager said, "We don't ask about sexual orientation."

"But I think gay people are neater."

"We can't discriminate against straight people."

"I'm just saying if a gay tenant comes along, I want them."

"We have no way of knowing who's gay."

"I have two gay friends. Their apartment is immaculate."

"I get it, but we comply with Fair Housing laws."

"What does the law say?"

"Race, color, religion, sex, national origin, familial status, disability. And now sexual orientation. These are protected classes. We can't consider these things in providing housing."

"Oh. But I would rather have gays than right-wing Christians, wouldn't you?"

17. I Prefer an Asian Tenant

The homeowner asked the property manager if he could find an Asian tenant.

"I would prefer an Asian tenant if you can find one."

"We don't consider national origin, because of the law and all."

"But can't you try to find Asians?"

"We don't go looking for them. All people are welcome."

"But it's a heavily Asian neighborhood. Don't you think we'll get some Asians?"

"No idea."

"Aren't Asians neater?"

"I don't know."

"Don't Asians have better educations?"

"I really can't talk about it."

"Of course, I'll still take regular white people."

"I think we're breaking the law just talking like this."

"I'm not asking you to break the law."

"You should talk to an attorney about this."

"When you find a tenant, just tell me what kind of people they are."

"Then, what kind of people are you?"

"What do you mean?"

18. Where Are They From?

An applicant was accepted to rent a house. When the landlord received the lease he saw the tenants' names on the lease and called the property manager. He asked about the new tenants.

"Where are they from?"

"What do you mean?"

"Their names look Arab or Indian or something."

"I don't know."

"You didn't tell me everything about them."

"I told you everything I'm allowed to."

"Wouldn't you tell me if they were from Iran, or North Korea?"

"National origin is a protected class."

"Since when?"

"Maybe it was the 1964 Civil Rights Act, or the 1968 Fair Housing Act."

"I think the decision should be mine."

"It is. You can go rogue on your own, but I can't. A realtor like me can lose their license."

"Find out where they're from. Just for my information."

"Let me look into it and call you back."

The property manager did not look into it. He didn't call the tenant or otherwise inquire.

He just ignored the landlord's request, waited a couple days, and then called him back.

"I found out where the tenant is from."

"Good. Where?"

"Baltimore."

19. Waive the Late Fee

The rent was late. The property manager called the tenant.

"Good morning. Our records show we have not received your rent payment this month."

"I know, I know. I'm trying. How much do I owe you?"

"Two thousand rent and a hundred dollar late fee."

"Oh, I can get you the money tomorrow, but can you waive the late fee?"

"I might waive the late fee after you pay the rent."

"That's what I said."

"No, you asked me to waive the late fee now, *before* I have your rent payment in hand."

"What's the difference?"

"If I waive the late fee now, you get a discount for no reason. If you pay tomorrow, I might waive the late fee *afterward*, but I won't waive it in exchange for a promise."

"I don't get it."

"Hmm. Let's see. You go to a restaurant. Dessert is free with any meal. You say you want the free dessert now, then you might buy a meal later."

"I don't get it."

"Bingo."

20. The Early Fee

The tenant always paid his rent a week early. He called the property manager to make sure payment was received.

"Did you get my rent?"

"Yes thank you. You always pay early. We appreciate it."

"I just worry that you might get confused and think it was for a different month."

"No, we keep records, we write things down, and we use those fancy computers that everyone's using these days."

"Funny guy. But I am very organized and I don't want any late fees."

"Okay, but what about an early fee?"

"What's that?"

"Like if you pay too early and we charge an early fee."

"You're shitting me."

"Yes I am. No such thing as an early fee."

"So, we're good."

"Yes, unless you want me to get a legal opinion."

"Come on. Now you're making fun of me."

"I'm kidding. It's Friday. I'm about to go home. The perfect tenant, you, calls me to make sure I am happy that you're making my job easy by paying early. So I start joking around. I joke. That's all."

"So no early fee."

"No. But we do charge for unnecessary phone calls now."

"Funny guy."

"Lighten up, it's Friday."

21. I'm a Woman

The property manager got a new client. Her name was Joey. His assistant sent Joey a welcome-new-client letter that started with "Dear Sir." Joey called the office and said, "I'm a woman. Don't address me as 'Dear Sir'"

After a tenant was accepted and a lease signed, the lease was sent to the landlord. It was addressed to "Mr. Joey Smith." She called the office and said, "I'm a woman. Please put that fact in my file."

Months later an inspection report was sent to the landlord. The cover letter began with "Dear Sir." Joey called the office and said she wanted to be addressed as a woman. She told the property manager he should stop forgetting she was a woman. "Please get it straight. Woman, woman, woman."

He said, "I'm sorry for the mix-up. I met you but not everybody here knows you."

"Can't you put it in my file? Or in your software?"

"It's in there. But some of our employees send hundreds of documents out each day and don't take the time."

"Please tell them. Tell them all. Bring it up in a meeting."

"I will. Good idea. I apologize in advance if this mix-up happens again."

"Not comforting."

The property manager brought it up in a meeting. It had happened with other clients. One named Bobbi and one named Morgan. The boss asked for ideas.

"We could use a gender neutral prefix."

"How would we do that?"

"We could write 'Dear Mx.'"

"What?"

"It's a genderless honorific. Google it."

"What about 'M.'? Just M."

"Never heard of that. A little too cute. Our clients wouldn't like it."

"What if we just address communications to 'Joey Smith' and drop Mr., Miss, and Mrs. altogether?"

"Like Dear Joey Smith. Dear Bobbi Smith. Dear Morgan Smith. No more 'Dear Sir.' I like it."

"Why didn't we think of this twenty years ago?"

"What about that word 'Dear'? Do we really need that word 'Dear'?"

22. A Good Listener

The tenant was moving in and was not happy.

"The house smells musty. Did you have the ducts cleaned?"

The property manager answered, "I'll check our records and let you know when it was last done."

"Whose bags of trash are those on the street?"

"Those were left by the owner yesterday when he moved out. Trash pick-up is tomorrow."

"Are you going to replace the toilet seats?"

"What's wrong with the toilet seats?"

"Think about it. I don't want to sit on used toilet seats. It's gross."

"I'll spray Lysol on them."

"Someone left a bottle of wine on the counter."

"The owner left that as a housewarming gift. They were glad to get a highly qualified tenant."

"It's a cheap wine."

"Here, take my clipboard and do your own move-in inspection. You'll be more thorough than me."

"What if I see something that you should fix?"

"Write it down and tell me at the end of your inspection. I'll listen."

"And if there's something I don't like?"

"At the end of your inspection I'll listen to all your complaints."

"I expect action."

"I hear you."

"Don't you do anything?"

"Not at first. First I listen to you. Then I make phone calls and write emails."

"So you really don't do anything."

"People say I'm a good listener."

23. House Painting Not Included

The property manager listed the house as "Spacious. Near shopping. New appliances. No pets."

A prospective tenant submitted an application. After she was approved, she asked if the interior would be painted.

"I expect you will paint the house."

"We didn't offer painting in the advertising. Your offer didn't require painting."

"But it needs painting."

"It's as-is unless you have contingencies. Your agent should have told you."

"She said she thought it needed painting."

"Rental applications have a section for contingencies. You left it blank."

"I thought it was the law you have to paint."

"There is no such law. I Googled it."

The tenant refused to sign the lease unless the house was painted. The property manager rescinded the acceptance and voided the deal. The tenant's agent called.

"You can't deny my client. She was already accepted."

"She won't sign the lease without painting. That's a voidable counteroffer. The deal is voided."

A second application was received. The contingency field was blank. The property manager called the agent and asked if he understood that no painting would be done, that the property was as-is.

"The listing didn't say as-is."

"It doesn't have to. If you make an offer to buy or rent a house, you can't say later that you want a deck built too. Or you want painting. Or new appliances. It's common sense."

"I'll talk to my client. She loves the house."

A third application was received. The applicant filled out the contingency field, requiring that the living room be painted as a condition of the application. Just the one room. The landlord found it a reasonable request and accepted the application. A lease was signed.

The first agent called. "You pulled the rug out from underneath us."

"There was no rug."

"Smart ass."

The second agent called. "You cheated us. My client wants that house."

"You mean your client wanted that house plus two thousand dollars of painting."

"I'll report you."

"Oh my."

The third agent called. "Thank you for agreeing to painting the living room. My client feels like she wheeled and dealed and won."

"She did. The landlord also enjoyed that little bit of wheeling and dealing. He feels like everybody won. He said he'll throw in the dining room painting too."

24. House Painting Not Included 2

The tenant wanted the condo painted before moving in.

"When will the unit be painted?"

"The owner has no plans to paint the condo."

"Don't they have to paint?"

"No. You may request it and they may agree or deny your request."

"I'm paying a pretty penny for this place."

"The list price was fifteen hundred. You countered fourteen hundred."

"So?"

"We agreed. You won. So that's one hundred a month you save."

"So?"

"One hundred a month equals twelve hundred a year. That's the cost of painting."

"In my old apartment they always painted between tenants."

"This is not an apartment. This is a condo."

"What's the difference?"

"Management, marketing, ownership, laws, regulations, prices. Everything."

"Nobody told me. You should have told me."

"I just met you. I can answer all your questions now."

"Why won't you paint? It's common sense."

"This is not common sense. This is property management."

25. How Much Do Your Services Cost?

The property manager took a call.

"Good morning. How may I help you?"

The caller, a prospective client, asked, "How much do your services cost?"

"Would you like to see a brochure of our prices and what services we offer?"

"No. Just how much you charge."

"I can come to your house and evaluate how much rent you might get for it."

"I'm not ready for that yet. I'm shopping price."

"Well I can tell you that the cheaper firms offer fewer services than we do."

"Please. Just my costs."

"Okay. Our leasing commission is equivalent to one month rent and our management fee is ten percent of rents collected."

"What if I find my own tenant?"

"Then we might discount the commission."

"What if I do all my own maintenance?"

"We do not recommend that. You'd have to respond to midnight emergencies."

"Can I set the rent price?"

"If you can do all these things, why do you need property management?"

"I'm retired. I live next door to the rental. I'm handy. But I might need help."

"Give me your address and I'll mail you our brochure."

"No thanks. I've got a bunch of those from a bunch of property managers."

"Well, thanks for your time. Call us if you have any more questions."

"Okay. I have to fire my current property manager first."

"Who's that?"

"Property Management Services."

"That's us."

"Oh. Shoot. Never mind."

26. My Dog is Sick

"Hello? Property Management Services."

"Hi, I'm the renter in the house on Shawn Drive. I'm calling to tell you my dog is sick."

"I'm sorry, that's terrible. How can I help?"

"Well, he got sick after we noticed mold in the family room."

"What color mold?"

"What does that matter?"

"Was it spotty, or streaky?"

"It's just mold."

"Can you send me a picture?"

"You don't get it. The mold is making my dog sick."

"I'm so sorry about your dog. What did the vet say?"

"We haven't gone to the vet."

"You better take him to the vet. And get me the doctor's opinion. I'm worried."

"What are you doing? Are you doubting me?"

"No. But I see myself as sort of an amateur mold expert. I have to verify if it's really mold."

"If? We need to move out. We can't live here."

"Let me come to the house and take a mold sample from the family room to the lab. I can also take the furnace filter out and have it tested for airborne spores."

"You don't have to come to my house. I just want to terminate the lease."

"Well, if we test the mold and it's positive, and the vet says its mold related, then our attorney can give direction based on state law and EPA rules. The government determines your rights and our responsibilities in these cases. This is a sensitive situation and we must do this the right way."

"Why can't I just move out?"

"You can move out while we look into this. Go to a hotel and keep your receipts. But you have to continue paying rent."

"I can't pay rent for a house I don't live in."

"Okay. I have an idea. You can file a Tenant's Assertion at the courthouse and pay your rent into escrow until the issue is settled in court."

"My kids are going to get sick next. I'll sue you."

"If they get sick, take them to the doctor. And let me know what the doctor says."

"That's private. Doctor-patient privilege."

"That's your privilege, at your discretion. You can waive it any time, for any reason. HIPAA law just gives you options."

"You're rude. I want to talk to your supervisor."

"There's no one here. They left me unsupervised."

27. That's Not Mold

The tenant thought he saw mold.

"Look at that mold on the baseboards."

The property manager said, "That's not mold."

"How do you know?"

"I Googled it. Black or gray mold might be Stachybotrys. Cladosporium is green. I don't think orange mold has a name. Mildew is green. White mold is usually not mold at all. Your baseboards are just dirty, that's all."

"Well, I Googled it too. Black mold is toxic."

"Black mold, or Stachybotrys, is an allergen, not a toxin."

"Stocky Botris?"

"It's pretty rare. My mold contractor says it only grows in chronically dark, wet places."

"Bullshit."

"In our region the most common mold is Penicillium Aspergillus. Do you want me to have your baseboard tested?"

"I want you to fix it now."

"Let's test it first to make sure it's not just dust or soot."

"My brother-in-law is an attorney."

"I always say test first, sue later."

"I think a judge will see it my way."

"Let me just take some pictures of your baseboards."

"What for?"

"Judges love pictures."

"Don't take any pictures in my house."

"Okay. I'll stop taking pictures. I only took four."

"Don't you have something better to do than deny responsibility all day?"

"I have two more houses to go. Today is mold day. Busy, busy, busy."

28. Due Process

The landlord called. "I got your email about the late rent. Has the tenant paid up yet?"

The property manager answered, "No. I talked to them. They are waiting for their paychecks to come in."

"They're ten days late. I want them out."

"Okay we can file Unlawful Detainer. The attorney will need a retainer of four hundred dollars and a letter of engagement."

"No. I want them out NOW."

"So do I, but it takes a month or two to evict, if there are no continuances or delays."

"No, no, no. The lease says after five days we can take possession."

"This isn't Texas. We have to do that due process thing."

"Are you an attorney?"

"No."

"Well I am, and the contract is the contract. I want you to go in and change the locks."

"I am no legal expert, but I'm pretty sure taking possession of the house requires the presence of a sheriff and a licensed locksmith."

"I want my house back now."

"We could be sued, lose our license, or get shot for trespassing."

"If you won't do it, I will."

"I will send you an email stating my objection to your approach. If you want to proceed on your own, our state's landlord-tenant law calls that 'Self-Help.' It's actionable. I don't want to be held responsible."

"I don't need your help. I know the law and the contract. I can take my house back."

"They stopped doing it your way over fifty years ago. Fair Housing Act and all."

"Don't lecture me. What's your name?"

"Joe Smith. That's spelled J-O-E…"

"Goodbye."

29. Don't Fix the Stairs

The stairs were cracked. The tenant fell down the stairs. The property manager sent a carpenter, who said repair would cost a lot. The landlord said no. The property manager got a cheaper estimate. Still too high. A couple days later another person fell down the stairs, a child this time. The landlord said the tenant was making it up. The tenant stopped paying rent. The landlord sued the tenant for rent. The tenant sued the landlord for personal injury. The judge asked the property manager if he managed the property. He said, "No, not anymore." He had tried to negotiate a compromise and failed. He had warned the landlord of his liability, and advised the tenant to pursue a remedy on her own. When that failed, he gave the landlord and tenant notice that he was terminating management. He asserted he never took sides, he always acted properly, and he denied any and all liability. He appeared in court solely as a witness. The judge offered the landlord and tenant mediation by a court appointee. The landlord and tenant refused. They would not sit at a table together. They both wanted to win. The judge dismissed both suits and told them to hire lawyers next time. The tenant moved out. The landlord super-glued the stairs. They both lost.

30. Don't Fix the Leak

The toilet overflowed.
>The bathroom flooded.
>The dining room ceiling below collapsed.
>The dining room furniture was ruined.
>The carpets were ruined.
>The wood floors were ruined.
>The tenant demanded it be fixed.
>The landlord said it was the tenant's fault for clogging the toilet.
>The landlord wouldn't fix it.
>The tenant sued.
>They went to small claims court without attorneys.
>They had no witnesses or evidence.
>They spoke out of turn.
>They interrupted each other.
>There was no evidence of tenant neglect.
>There was no evidence of landlord neglect.
>The judge ruled for the tenant.
>The landlord had primary responsibility for the property.
>The landlord had to fix everything.
>The landlord paid for all repairs.

Everything was fixed.

The tenant went back to flushing disposable diapers down the toilet.

The toilet overflowed again.

The property manager arrived with the plumber and a camera.

The plumber snaked a diaper and a Beanie Baby out of the toilet.

The tenant said they weren't his.

31. The Missing Key

When the landlord got her monthly statement there was a two-dollar charge for a new house key. She called the property manager.

"What is the key charge for?"

"I bought a new key after the move-in."

"Why? I gave you four keys, as you requested. Two for the tenant and two for you."

"After we had repairs done I didn't get a key back from the handyman."

"So where is that key? A stranger has a key to my house? Who? What guarantee do I have that my house is secure? What will I do when I move back?"

"I'm sure he returned it. I'll look around."

"I'm not very confident."

"It's around here somewhere."

"Listen. Change the locks at your expense. Please."

"I'll check around. The key probably fell to the bottom of our key cabinet. I'll look again. Sorry for the mix-up."

"Mix-up? I want new knobs and deadbolts. Free."

The property manager called the contractors and cleaners who had entered the house. No luck. He checked the key cabinet and his desk. Nothing. He called the tenant. Nothing there. The key was definitely lost. He called the landlord back the next day and lied.

"I found the key. Sorry for the mix-up."

"Mix-up? Where was it?"

"It was in the lockbox on the door. I forgot all about it."

"Are you kidding me?"

"No. I'm very sorry."

"I'm still very angry. I don't know if I can trust you anymore."

"The extra key is on me. I'll refund two dollars to your account."

"Two dollars?"

32. The Thank-You Hug

A young woman applied to rent a condo. The property manager pulled her credit and found a very low credit score. The property manager told her she was not qualified based on her poor score. The applicant showed up at the property manager's office and met with him in the conference room. She really wanted the condo and wanted to explain her credit problem. She had gotten divorced. Her ex-husband left town and stopped paying rent. She took on a second job but could not pay both her divorce attorney and the rent. Her child fell ill and she had to quit one of her jobs and stay home more. In recent months things improved. Her ex-husband shared custody and expenses, she got a better job, she paid off her credit cards, then caught up on other bills, but could not erase her significant credit issues. She said she wanted a new start, a second chance to prove she could be a dependable and reliable person. She promised the property manager she would be a good tenant and the landlord would be happy if he would just give her a chance.

The property manager wrote the applicant's whole story in an email to the landlord, just as the prospective tenant had described it. The landlord was impressed, having dealt with dishonest tenants in the past. Her forthrightness paid off. The landlord accepted the offer, the property manager informed the tenant, a lease was signed and a move-in was scheduled.

Two years later the tenant moved out. She had paid her rent on time and never called with a repair or complaint. She was such a perfect tenant the property manager had forgotten all about her. After she moved out she arrived in the office and asked to meet with the property manager in the conference room again. The property manager entered and did not recognize her. She had lost weight. Her hair was redder. She was wearing a sharp business suit. She hugged the property manager and thanked him for having faith in her. She would always appreciate it. She was buying a home. When she left the property manager told his co-workers about it. They couldn't believe it. They never got hugged.

33. You Can't Increase My Rent

At the end of the lease term the tenant asked to renew the lease for another year. The property manager said he would call the landlord. The property manager asked if the tenant would pay a twenty-five dollar a month rent increase, to keep up with current market prices. The tenant said it was not fair to raise the rent. The property manager replied that he would convey her sentiment to the landlord. The tenant found the landlord's phone number on the internet white pages and called the landlord first, before the property manager could. She asked the landlord if he had authorized a rent increase. He had not. The landlord then called the property manager and asked why the tenant should pay a rent increase that the landlord had not requested. The property manager explained that the management agreement signed by the property manager and the landlord required the property manager to look out for the best interest of the landlord and maximize the landlord's profits. The landlord said he was uncomfortable being confronted by the tenant and unhappy with the property manager for not checking with him first. The landlord said the tenant had also complained about a repair request that had been ignored for three months. The property manager said he had received the same repair complaint three months ago, and had sent the landlord an estimate for three hundred dollars, but that the landlord had not authorized the repair. The property manager pointed out that the extra twenty five dollars a month in increased rent would have added up to three hundred dollars over the span of a year, would have been just enough money to pay for the repair. The landlord was quiet for a minute, and said he would think it over.

34. The Rottweiler

The property manager performed an annual inspection at a rental property while the tenant was at work. He knocked loudly, waited a minute, entered with his key, and yelled out, loudly announcing his presence, his name, and the name of his firm. He waited a minute. No one was home. He inspected the bedrooms first and then the hall bath. When he walked out of the bathroom a growling Rottweiler confronted him in the hall. The property manager backed up into the bathroom and shut the door. Every few minutes he opened the door a crack and peered into the hall. The dog stood his ground and stared and growled each time. He called his office and asked for help. The other property managers laughed. They were busy cleaning up after a flooded basement and a kitchen fire. They would call him back shortly, maybe. After fifteen minutes the property manager climbed out the bathroom window and dropped ten feet onto the patio. He hurt his ankle. His paperwork flew off in the wind and into the neighbor's yard. The property manager limped to his car and called his office again. He said there was no problem, everything was under control. After he returned to his office, he called the tenant and told him he should have mentioned the dog. The tenant said, "Too bad. No more inspections. Right?"

35. The Dog's Ashes

When the tenant vacated the rental property she moved her most important possession last. It was an urn containing the ashes of her dead Mastiff. She was moving out because the house held too many memories of Mister Big. At the move-out inspection she showed the urn to the property manager and started to cry.

She said, "I don't know what to do. He was my best friend."

"I understand. I lost a cat."

"Stop. It's not the same."

"Sorry."

"This place has so many memories of Biggy."

"I don't mean to be insensitive, but there was no dog on the lease."

"So?"

"The owner said that no dogs were allowed. It's in the lease."

"Why does it matter at a time like this?"

"It's just those chew marks on the door frame. And the carpet is clawed off of those steps."

"You can't be serious."

"They'll come out of your deposit."

She started to cry again. "Get out. Get out!"

"I'm not leaving. The house is empty. Your movers are about to pull away. Give me the keys. Please."

She stomped out with tears in her eyes. She drove away. The property manager pulled the shades, set the thermostat, locked the doors, and went back to his office. Mister Big was still sitting on the kitchen counter.

36. Mom's Ashes

The tenant moved out and left behind an urn. The property manager called the tenant.

"You left an urn in the house."

"That's my mother's ashes. I forgot to pack her."

"What do you want me to do with her?"

"Can you mail her?"

"There must be some kind of regulations about mailing human remains."

"Can you keep her until I'm back in town?"

"No, your mom can't stay with me."

"Doesn't your office have storage?"

"Not for remains. Listen. I left the urn in the house, in the garage, on the shelf with the old paint and cleaning supplies.

I'm done with her. I'll let you into the house to pick her up, that's the best I can do."

"Sheez. Relax. I'll have someone come get her."

"Where's your father?"

"In an urn on my sister's mantel."

"Maybe you should call your sister and have her pick up your mom."

"I don't call her anymore. We're not what you call a close family."

37. Sex Toys and Guitars

When a group of young male tenants moved out they left behind a large collection of sex toys, some musical instruments, and a tiny amount of marijuana. The house was filthy and the refrigerator door was missing. The landlord asked the property manager, "What will you do about it?"

He replied, "We have to demonstrate damages in order to recoup losses."

"How do you do that?"

"I called the cleaners first. Next I'll call a handyman. We get prices."

"Are you going to punish them?"

"Punishment is iffy. Punishment is for crimes, not breaches of contract."

"Then what good are you? What did I hire you for?"

The property manager said, "You know, fixing leaks, collecting rent, inspecting the house."

"What a rip-off."

"The tenants left behind a vintage Gibson guitar and an old Stratocaster in the basement."

The landlord asked, "Those are mine now, right?"

"Technically, we should store them for thirty days before taking possession of them."

"I would like to pick them up today. Do you know about how much they're worth?"

"I know exactly how much they're worth."

"How much?"

"Don't jump the gun. Give me a day to see if the guitars have been reported stolen. I'll consult an attorney about the possession thing, about waiting thirty days, or giving the tenants notice of our intentions. Converting their personal property to cover your losses should be done by the book. Then we should go in the house together."

The landlord said, "I'll wait twenty-four hours. No more."

The property manager said, "We should carry the guitars out wrapped in tarps or trash bags so neighbors don't see them. Sometimes nosy neighbors take the tenants' side."

"Have you done this before?" asked the landlord.

"Yes. Do you play?" asked the property manager.

"I have a Martin. I play a little bluegrass."

"You're gonna love that Gibson."

38. Tenant's Losses

A tenant called and demanded, "You have to pay for my groceries."

"Why?"

"The freezer stopped working. I lost five hundred dollars in groceries."

"Did you report the freezer broken?"

"It's not broken. The power is out."

"Did you call the power company?"

"Who's that?"

Another tenant asked the property manager to replace a microwave oven that didn't work. The property manager asked, "Did you check the breaker box?"

"What's a breaker box?"

Yet another tenant called and said, "My diamond ring is missing."

"Oh?"

"It disappeared."

"Did you call the police?"

"Why would I call the police?"

Another tenant complained, "I can't find my saxophone."
"Okay. And?"
"Did your plumber steal it?"
The property manager asked, "When did you last see it?"
"A year ago, before I moved in."
"Did you call the movers?"
"Why would I call the movers?"

Another tenant asked the property manager to pay for a new lamp.
"Your handyman broke my lamp."
"I'll have him fix it. He's a handyman."
"I just want the money."
"How much?"
"Make an offer."

Another tenant moved out. Six months later a package was delivered to the house for him. The property manager picked it up. He called, emailed, and wrote to the tenant to tell him about the package. There was no reply. He threw the package away. After a year the tenant called and asked for the package.
The property manager asked, "What did it look like?"
"It looked like a cardboard box."
"What was in it?"
"None of your business."
"Did you get postal insurance for it?"
The tenant said, "You can do that?"

39. Calling Frank

"Hello Frank? I'm from Property Management Services."
"I got your message. I didn't appreciate it. It sounded threatening."
"It was, sort of. You're not letting realtors show the house."
"I just got out of the hospital."
"You're still moving out at the end of the month, right?"
"I'm not well."

"You're never well. You've been saying that for six years."

"It's true."

"You agreed to let us show the house during the final month of your lease."

"No, I didn't."

"You agreed in writing."

"Did not."

"It's in your lease. You signed your lease."

"I didn't sign anything. I didn't read anything."

"Prospective new tenants are waiting to see the house."

"I won't let them in."

"I can come over and let them in for you."

"No, you can't. I'll call the cops."

"Good idea. I'll call them too."

"My dog will bite you."

"I'm good with dogs. I'll get treats."

"Leave me alone."

"I could come over and hang out."

"That's illegal."

"Oh, I'll obey the law. I'll give you proper notice and all that."

"I have pepper spray."

"Frank, just let me in the damn house."

"You never fixed the toilet."

"You wouldn't let the plumber come in either."

"The house is falling apart."

"It was pretty nice when you moved in."

"I'll sue you."

"Frank, you're stealing from the owner of the house. He needs to find a renter."

"I'm sick. I just got out of the hospital. I'm dying."

"I'm sorry. I don't mean to harass you. It's just business."

"Stay away. Please."

"Can I come over now? Frank?...Frank?...Hello?"

The property manager went to the house. He put a lockbox on the door knob and a For Rent sign in the front yard. He returned a day later to find the sign removed and the lockbox sawed off. Frank's car was gone and he no longer answered his phone. Weeks later the property manager got a call from Frank's brother.

"My brother Frank died."

"Oohh, no, I feel terrible."

"Can I have his security deposit?"

40. Icicles

The tenant left town for the winter holidays to visit family. He didn't notify the property manager. The lease required the tenant provide notice if they left the house unoccupied for over fourteen days.

After a couple weeks a neighbor called the property manager. She had been walking by and saw icicles on the house. Icicles usually form on the eves, but these icicles were everywhere: on the siding, on window sills and door frames. The property manager grabbed a key and hurried to the house. Newspapers were piling up on the driveway and mail was overflowing the mailbox. Upon entering he found the heat turned off at the thermostat. The interior was below thirty degrees. The tenant was nowhere to be found. The property manager turned the heat on and called a plumber. The plumber wouldn't be able to find the leak until the ice melted. He turned off the water main and arranged to meet the plumber when the temperature got above thirty-five.

Days later the plumber found frozen, burst pipes in the bathrooms and kitchen. The basement was flooded. All the carpets were soaked. Three ceilings had caved in. Cleaners, carpet installers, plumbers, drywallers, carpenters and painters were called in.

A month later the tenant returned to find notices all over the front door declaring abandonment, hazardous conditions, work-in-progress, and eviction. The locks were re-keyed. The tenant called the property manager.

"What's going on with my house? I can't get in. This is outrageous."

"You disappeared. The heat was off, the pipes froze, the neighbors called. The inside of the house was destroyed by all the ice and water."

"That's not my fault. That's the house's fault."

"We have written statements from neighbors and contractors. We have a dozen witnesses. We can get affidavits if you want."

"I didn't turn the heat off."

"I took a picture of the thermostat. The heat was off, off, off. I couldn't get it fingerprinted. The police laughed at the idea. But the owner of the house is going to war over this. You were subpoenaed and missed your hearing. You can appeal but it will be expensive. This is a very big deal."

"It was Christmas. I was with my parents in Florida. Everyone wants to be with family at Christmas. You can't do this."

"Do you have anywhere to stay? Do you need help finding a place? I might be able to get you a discount at a hotel for a while."

"I want to see inside the house. I have rights."

"You're right. I couldn't get a restraining order to keep you out. But we could meet you at the house. You can meet the contractors and the owner of the house. The neighbors asked if they could be there too. There were rumors you had died in the house. Your house was the subject of a lot of speculation and gossip. Everyone called it the 'Ice House.' People want to see you. They want to talk to you. You're famous around here. Do you read the local paper? You're in it."

41. The Rooming House

The landlord asked the property manager to find tenants and collect rent for him. The property manager got all the papers signed, listed the house on the rental market, found and screened three tenants. At the move-in inspection the property manager and tenants found one of the bedrooms furnished and apparently being lived in. They found the owner in the kitchen making lunch. The property manager was mystified.

"We're here for the check-in inspection. Why are you still here? Is something wrong?"

"No, I'm okay. Are these my tenants? How do you do?"

"Wait, wait. You're supposed to be out. They move in today."

"I know. You can put them in the upstairs bedrooms. I'm living in the basement bedroom. We will share the kitchen. I pay the utilities but the tenants can pay for the mowing or newspaper subscriptions and whatnot."

"You're staying? That's not the deal."

"I didn't tell you I'm staying here? I must have told you."

"You signed over possession of the entire property as of today. You're sort of trespassing. No offense."

"I'm sure we can all get along. I'll stay out of the way. I'm very quiet. I read a lot.

Sorry for the mix-up."

42. May I Speak to Your Manager?

"Hello? Are you my property manager?"

"Yes. May I help you?"

"I'm a little short on cash this month. Can I skip a month rent?"

"I'm sorry, but the rent is due on the first of each month per the contract."

"But my hours were cut back. It's not my fault."

"How much can you pay now?"

"I can't. I have unexpected medical costs."

"But the lease stands. What are your prospects for the near future?"

"Can I use the security deposit for rent?"

"The deposit is in escrow until the end of the lease term."

"But that's my money."

"It's for damages."

"I haven't damaged anything."

"Damages can be physical, or financial losses you cause."

"Sheez. You're so picky. Can I talk to your manager?"

"I'm a manager."

"Can I talk to your superior?"

"We don't have a top-down system, it's kind of horizontal. You know what I mean?"

"What about your boss, the owner of the business. Let me talk to him."

"He's a hands-off guy. He knows nothing about this kind of situation."

"How do I reach him? I'm your customer. You work for me."

"Okay. Call our front office and ask for Alisia Banekker. She's my boss."

"Got it. You are going to be sorry."

The tenant hung up. The property manager hit the receptionist's intercom button on his phone.

"Alisia, you'll be getting an angry call from a tenant about me. I told him you're my boss, so fake it, and tell him you'll get to the bottom is this. Tell him I will be disciplined or something."

43. I Got a Dog

A tenant called the property manager.

"I got a puppy. Do I need to do anything? Paperwork?"

"If you didn't have a dog on your application or lease, you can't have a dog. You need written permission from the owner first."

"Oh. Well I don't really have a dog just yet. I'm thinking of getting one. What do I do?"

"Put your request in writing. Include the breed, age, and weight of the dog. If the owner accepts there will be a pet deposit."

"How much is a pet deposit?"

"Sometimes it's two hundred and fifty dollars. But if you already have a dog, the owner may want five hundred, considering the breach of lease and all."

"That's a lot. Maybe I won't get a dog."

"I can hear barking in the background. What's your dog's name?"

"I don't have a dog yet. I'm just thinking about it."

"Is it house trained? The carpets are new."

"Never mind."

"I can hear it barking. Hello? Hello?"

44. Hiding the Dog

The property manager was on the road inspecting properties. He arrived more than an hour early to his fourth inspection of the day. He parked across the street from the house and wrote up inspection reports. After fifteen minutes the tenant came out the front door with a beagle. He didn't notice the property manager. The property manager checked the file and lease. There was no dog documented. The listing said No Dogs. The owner did not allow pets of any kind in his property. The property manager took a photo of the tenant with the beagle. The tenant walked the dog to the neighbor's house and knocked. The neighbor took the beagle inside and the tenant walked back to the rental property.

At the appointed hour, the property manager knocked on the tenant's door and entered. They walked through the house together. There was no evidence of the dog. No smell, no hair, no dog food or bowls, no chewed up furniture or clawed carpets.

When the inspection was done and the property manager was about to leave, he stopped and turned toward the tenant. He sniffed the air, pretending to smell something.

"What's that smell?"

"What smell?"

"Not sure. Do you have a dog?"

"No. I've never had a dog."

"Well I'll just write down that I thought I smelled a dog."

"What do you smell? I don't smell anything."

"It's ten percent dog and ninety percent air freshener."

"Maybe the last tenant had a dog."

"The owner lived here last. He's allergic. No dog ever."

"Well I don't have a dog, that's for sure."

"It smells a little like a beagle. Maybe a mixed breed, but part beagle."

"I said I don't have a dog."

"Maybe I'm just smelling that beagle next door."

"What?"

"Your beagle. Next door. Gotcha."

"So there's no smell?"

"No smell. I made that part up."

45. The Trespassing Inspector

Tenant: "Your honor, the inspector from the property manager's firm entered our house without permission."

Judge: "How does the defendant respond?"

Inspector: "We emailed the tenant and made an appointment to inspect after he moved out. We entered when the house was empty."

Tenant: "We had an appointment later in the day for the inspection. The inspector entered two hours before we gave up the keys and surrendered possession of the property."

Judge: "Is this true?"

Inspector: "Yes, your honor, but the house was empty."

Tenant: "The inspector entered two hours before the appointment. So the notice was not proper or reasonable."

Inspector: "Your honor, the house was empty."

Judge: "Is that true? Was the house empty?"

Tenant: "Yes, your honor."

Judge: "Then what are your losses?"

Tenant: "We claim the inspector trespassed, which is against the law."

Judge: "This is not a criminal complaint. It's not a criminal court. It's a civil court, a lawsuit for damages. What is your loss?"

Tenant: "We lost our right to possession several hours early."

Judge: "I will grant you one dollar for suffering a loss of two hours possession of an empty house."

Tenant: "Thank you, your honor."

Inspector: "Thank you, your honor."

46. Was the Grass Cut?

Tenant: "Your honor, the property manager charged eighty dollars to our security deposit for mowing. We mowed the lawn before we moved. The grass was not long."

Property Manager: "Your honor, the grass was six inches long. It's in our inspection report."

Tenant: "Your honor, I have a photograph of the lawn taken that day."

Judge: "Let me see the picture. Thank you. I can only see the edge of the lawn in this picture. It's not clear."

Tenant: "If you look closely you can see the grass appears to be short. Way down in the right corner of the picture."

Judge: "Yes. Maybe."

Tenant: "The eighty dollar charge seems high. We believe it could have been cut for thirty dollars."

Property Manager: "We didn't have time to shop around. A new tenant moved in the next day and demanded the lawn be cut immediately."

Tenant: "But eighty dollars?"

Property Manager: "It was a big yard. The grass was long. Eighty dollars is fair."

Judge: "I'm going to disallow the eighty dollar security deposit deduction. You can refund that to the tenant. The other deductions are not contested. They stand. I find for the tenant in the amount of eighty dollars."

The two parties left. The judge hung his head and shook it slowly from side to side. He missed criminal court—assaults, break-ins, and the occasional manslaughter.

47. The Ghost

"Hello. Property Management Services."

"I'm calling to report a ghost in my house."

"A ghost? Are you sure?"

"Every morning I make my bed. When I come home my pillows have moved."

"That's weird."

"Yes. And sometimes my shoes are moved from my bedside to the hallway."

"Wow. I don't know what to say. Do you have a roommate?"

"Yes. My boyfriend."

"Do you two get along?"

"Yes. I told him there's a ghost. He thinks I'm crazy."

"What do you want? Do you want to move out?"

"No. We like it here. Did you know about the ghost and conceal the fact?"

"I never heard about ghosts in your house."

"But aren't you responsible?"

"There's nothing in the lease or the law about the supernatural. It's not covered."

"My boyfriend says we should be compensated somehow."

"He's not on the lease. You're the only tenant. Does he pay rent?"

"You mean my boyfriend or the ghost?"

48. Compost

The tenant and the property manager did a move-in inspection in a one hundred and fifty-year-old row house. The floorboards were worn and creaky. The walls had little insulation. The windows leaked air. The kitchen was forty years out of date. The pipes banged.

The tenants said, "We love this house. We love the old town. The restaurants and bars. The arts and music scene."

The property manager said, "I'm so glad you like it. It's so old, it takes special tenants to appreciate it."

"There is one thing. That compost heap at the back of the lot. Can you get rid of that?"

"Compost is supposed to decompose and recycle. You know, back to nature. It's not like trash you haul away."

The tenant said, "It's our house now, but it's not our compost. It's ugly. It might attract rats. We're going to have barbecues out back. We want it gone."

"It's just grass clippings."

"It's gross. We feel it should go."

The property manager said, "But everything else is okay?"

"Yes, we love everything else."

The property manager went to his car and opened the trunk. He picked up the compost in big armfuls and piled it all into his trunk. When he was done his white shirt was covered with green grass stains, completely ruined. He walked toward the tenants and offered a wet and grassy handshake. The tenants retreated a half step. The property manager joked, "No hug?"

He handed them the keys. It was such an old house. He was so relieved they never asked him about the lead paint and asbestos linoleum.

49. The Twenty-Five-Pound Dog

The rental house advertisement and listing said "No dogs over 25 pounds" because there was new hardwood flooring throughout. Bigger dogs would scratch right through the finish into the wood. The tenant's application included a "Twenty pound terrier."

At the annual mid-term inspection the property manager saw a dog that looked like it was forty pounds.

"That's not the little dog on the application."

"Yes it is."

The property manager did not believe him. He asked, "May I pick up your dog?"

"Don't touch my dog."

"Do you have bathroom scales? We could weigh him."

"No. And it's her, not him."

The inspector said, "It's a breach of the lease."

"Prove it."

"Don't worry. We would never take your dog away. We would take the house away."

"You can't do that."

The property manager said, "You are in breach of the lease. Your pet exceeds the weight limit agreed upon. I'm giving you thirty days to comply with the lease. A notice and demand letter will be delivered to you, in writing, by the close of business. Then I will return in thirty days, re-inspect, determine if the breach persists, and if it does, provide notice to vacate. Then we will file Unlawful Detainer to pursue eviction for possession of the premises."

The tenant opened the front door and told the inspector to leave. The inspector looked back at the dog as he left. It was peeing on the dining room floor.

50. The Cat on Facebook

The owner of a rental property was allergic to cats. The property manager's advertising said No Pets. The listing said No Pets. The lease said No Pets. After the tenant moved in the owner looked at the lease to find the tenant's name and he Googled it. He found the tenant's Facebook page. It showed a picture of a black cat sitting on the window seat in the breakfast area in the owner's rental house. The owner called the property manager and raised hell. The property manager called the tenant and accused him of breaking the No Pets clause. The tenant accused both of invasion of privacy. He said his Facebook page was private. The property manager sent the tenant a Cure or Quit Notice threatening eviction if the breach of lease was not cured. The Facebook picture was taken down. The property manager called the tenant. "We want to terminate the lease because of the cat."

"I got rid of the cat."

"Nobody gets rid of their cat. Nobody."

"I did."

The property manager continued. "I bet you have a box of kitty treats on your kitchen counter."

"What?"

"I bet you have a litter box in the laundry room."

"Excuse me?"

"I bet you wanted a dog and your wife talked you into a cat."

"Who do you think you are?" asked the tenant.

"I'm a cat owner."

51. The Chicken

The tenants' neighbors called the HOA and the property manager and complained of a chicken in the yard. Chickens are livestock, not pets, and were prohibited by the county. The property manager called the tenant. She did not speak English very well.

Property manager: "No puede tener un pollo in su casa." (You may not have a chicken in the house.)

Tenant: "No hay problema. Vamos a comerlo esta noche." (No problem. We are going to eat it tonight.)

The next day the property manager went to the house and walked around the yard. He found a rusty short-handled axe stuck in a stump in the yard. There were feathers in the grass. He took the axe back to his office and hung it on the wall above his desk. He inscribed the handle with the words: "No puede tener un pollo en su casa." His co-workers did not believe his story. They did not believe any of his stories. Stuff like that never happened to them.

52. Mold Panic

A tenant called the property manager. He claimed to have found mold in the unit and had moved out. He stopped paying rent and demanded his security deposit back.

The property manager said, "Would you like to have a professional mold test performed?"

"No thanks," said the tenant.

"Can we meet at the house and take a look?"

"No thanks. I moved out."

"Maybe it's just dirt."

"No, it's mold. I moved out."

"Maybe a good cleaning will get rid of it."

"Not good enough. I said we moved out."

"What does it look like? Do you have pictures?"

"No," said the tenant. "My children are sick. The doctor said it's asthma. Asthma is caused by mold."

The property manager said, "Asthma is *exacerbated* by mold. Not caused."

"Says who?"

"The EPA and CDC websites."

The tenant said, "I can Google too."

The tenant threatened to sue the property manager.

The property manager asked, "Did the doctor diagnose your kids with asthma?"

The tenant said, "What doctor?"

"You told me the doctor said it's asthma."

"My family's medical conditions are none of your business."

The property manager said, "Exactly."

53. The Assault Rifle

The property manager and the tenant did a final move-out inspection. The house looked good but the property manager said he would consult the homeowner before releasing the security deposit. The tenant proudly produced a gun case and opened it. Inside was an AR-15 semi-automatic rifle, a copy of a military issue weapon. The property manager froze. His heart pounded. Then the tenant handed the gun to the property manager. The property manager oohed and aahed and aimed the rifle at an imaginary distant foe. He felt the heft of it and pretended to admire it. He had seen guns in rental properties before, but not one so menacing. He handed it back to the tenant, who put it in its case and locked it up. The property manager asked why he had not packed it in the moving truck with everything else. The tenant said he always kept the gun at hand. He never knew when there would be a breakdown in law and order, or a race war, or some other disaster. He grinned with a wild look in his eyes. The property manager faked a smile and did a quick handshake and goodbye. The property manager left the home, went to his office, got on the phone, called the landlord and recommended they promptly refund the security deposit in full.

54. The Trash Can

The HOA notified the tenant and property manager that they were violating community rules regarding trash cans. All trash cans had to be concealed in the back yards of the townhouses except on trash pickup days.

The property manager called the tenant, who said she was in the middle unit in the row of townhouses. There was no outside access to the back yard. Trees and thick undergrowth grew all the way up to the rear fence line. The gate could not be opened because of all the overgrowth. She could not comply, as it was impossible to put the can in the back yard. He asked if she could move the trash can through the house on trash days. She said the community cans were too big to fit through the door.

The property manager called the HOA and told them of the tenant's dilemma. The homeowner's association could not offer a solution. The property manager asked if the trash could be hidden in the front shrubs. The HOA could not agree to it. He asked if the tenant could purchase a trash can camouflaged as a shrub, as advertised on the internet. The HOA could not say. He asked if other residents had the same problem. They could not say.

On a non-trash day, the property manager drove through the community and made note of twenty-three visible trash cans in violation of community rules. He called the HOA and asked if those twenty-three were being notified and fined for violations as well. They could not say.

The property manager talked to some of the townhouse community neighbors. He learned that the HOA board president lived in the end unit of the tenant's townhouse row. He walked around back, behind the president's house. There he found a stack of lumber laying on the common ground, being used to build a deck. The deck and house displayed no building permit. A small storage shed was also behind the unit, on the common area, another rules violation. The property manager took photos of the house and the violations and sent his report and photos to the HOA. He pointed out that the biggest violator was the association president. He requested an extension of the time period allowed to resolve the trash problem. There was no reply or further notice, no hearing or fines, until the next year when a new community HOA board president was elected.

55. The Missing Cat

The tenant was despondent at the move-out inspection. In all the chaos of moving, her cat had disappeared. She had alerted the neighbors and posted signs in the neighborhood, to no avail. She asked the property manager to keep an eye out for the cat.

A week later the property manager went to the house to show it to a prospective new tenant. Arriving early, he opened the windows and doors to air it out. It still had a cat smell.

While showing the house, he opened up rooms and closets, showing off the condition of the house, which had been cleaned and touched-up. When he opened the closet under the basement steps, the cat ran out of it and dashed upstairs and out the front door. It was thin and mangy. The closet was soiled extensively. He chased the cat, only to see it run away down the street and into the sewer.

A few days later the former tenant called and asked if he had seen any sign of the cat. The property manager lied and said he had not. He said he had looked for it in vain. He was sorry.

He consulted his fellow property managers and asked if he should have told the truth. One said yes, the truth is always best. Another said the truth would only give false hope. A third said that admitting to seeing the cat would only obligate the property manager to spend more time wasting precious company time searching. It could lead to blame being placed upon him.

The property manager brought it up at his firm's Tuesday staff meeting. A vote was taken. Truth won. The property manager made the call. At the tenant's tearful request, he posted signs in the community and talked to neighbors. The cat was never found, but one neighbor at the end of the street was evasive under questioning. The property manager suspected the cat had found a home there, and was given sanctuary. He kept it to himself.

56. Normal Wear and Tear

A landlord returned to live in his townhouse after five years abroad. He walked through with the property manager. The house was okay, but the paint job was marked up. There were nail holes and scuff marks.

"Is the tenant going to pay for repainting?"

"It looks like normal wear and tear."

"Not to me. I had these walls painted. I expect them returned the same way."

"Normal wear and tear is nail holes and scuff marks. Neglect or abuse would be holes requiring drywall repair, or ink marks, shelf brackets, molly bolts."

"Where did you hear that?"

"Books, mostly. Trade publications. Websites. Our industry's association conferences. Some we learn in court when judges order us to give the deposit back to the tenant."

"Well I wouldn't take the tenant to court."

"No, the tenant would take you to court. The deposit is theirs unless we can prove otherwise. It's hard to believe, I know."

"I thought the deposit was for repairs."

"Only for repairs due to abuse and neglect. But at the end of the day, I know I work for you. Give me written instructions to deduct painting from the security deposit and I'll do it."

"Why written instructions? Can't you just do it?"

"A judge will cut me to pieces charging for scuffs and nail holes. I want to be able to say it wasn't my idea."

"I think a judge would see it my way."

"Judges have rental homes. They have to paint them and clean them between tenants. They know the drill."

"Well. I don't know the drill."

"I should have told you more about this process when you hired us. We met in the house here for three hours. I couldn't cover everything. Maybe I concentrated more on the positive stuff."

"How much will repainting cost?"

"How much did you spend last time it was painted? How much is your loss?"

"My wife's brother painted it for nothing. He owed me a favor."

57. Scratches on the Wood Floor

A landlord was moving back into his rental property. The house looked good except for scratches on the wood floor in the living room, about two square feet of damage. The owner asked the property manager to deduct the cost of refinishing the wood floors.

"The whole living room?"

"The dining room too. It's all one floor."

"How about a pro-rated cost based on the amount of damage?"

"That won't pay for much."

"How about just the living room, or half the total cost of refinishing? A compromise?"

"That doesn't make sense. It cost us about two thousand to refinish it last time. We still have the bill. That's what I want."

"Okay, you're the boss."

Two thousand dollars was deducted. The tenant lost his entire security deposit. He sued the landlord. The property manager represented the landlord in small claims court.

The tenant spoke first. "Your honor, they took my whole security deposit for a small scratched area on the wood floor. I have pictures of the scratches on the floor."

The judge asked the property manager, "Do you dispute his claim?"

"Yes, the landlord asked me to deduct the entire cost. I have a bill here for refinishing the floors."

The judge looked at it. "This bill is from five years ago. Did you refinish the floors after the tenant moved out?"

"No, sir, but the damages are damages. The lease says the cost of the loss may be deducted, but it doesn't require the work be done."

The judge said, "The picture shows a couple square feet of damage. The bill shows four hundred square feet of refinishing. I'll allow a deduction of ten dollars for the damaged area. Next time work this out together, not in court."

Later the landlord asked the property manager, "How did we do in court?"

"The tenant won one thousand nine hundred and ninety dollars. You won ten dollars. The judge pro-rated the damaged area versus the undamaged area."

"What do we do now?"

"Pay the tenant nineteen hundred and ninety dollars."

"Can we appeal?"

"You can appeal, bump it up from small claims to General District Court and hire an attorney. It will cost money."

"It doesn't seem fair."

"Are you going to refinish the floors?"

"No. It's a small area. You can hardly notice it."

58. Ten Years with No Repairs

The landlord returned to live in her home after ten years of renting it to one tenant, with no repairs, updating, painting or cleaning. The tenant had never requested a repair or complained about anything. Rent had been paid on time for ten years. The total rent paid over time was $250,000. The owner had bought the house for under $200,000 twenty years before. The rent paid her mortgage, and then some.

She had little or no expenses for the duration of the lease.

The landlord and property manager walked through the house together. It was dirty and needed painting. It would need new towel bars, mini-blinds, carpets, light bulbs, vinyl floors, and appliances. Everything appeared to be original, dated and decades old. When she saw it she broke down crying. Her home was not the same. She fell to her knees in the living room. The property manager had never consoled a crying landlord before.

He sat beside her on the floor and wrote down all the facts of her landlord experience for her: the profits, the costs, the age and value of the household components, the depreciation of fixtures and appliances, and especially the increased value of the house and lot. He explained that no client of his had ever received such a high income to expense ratio. He told her she had gotten the perfect tenant performance. All of her repairs now would pale in comparison to the total rent she had received of a quarter of a million dollars. She got up off the floor and asked him how much it would cost to fix her house up. He said he would get her estimates for everything. She asked how much of it would be covered by the tenant's security deposit. "None of it," he said. "Not a penny."

59. The Wrong House

The prospective tenants flew in from out of town and were shown eight houses in one weekend by their realtor, a friend of a friend. They flew home and applied by email for the house they liked best. They had seen so many houses at once; their memory did not serve well.

They applied to rent the property and were accepted. They signed and returned a lease attached to an email. A month later they arrived and met the property manager for the move-in inspection. They looked around curiously. After a few minutes, they told the property manager it was the wrong house.

The property manager showed them their application, the address, and listing details. Still, they said, it was the wrong house. The property manager showed them the address on the lease contract they had signed. It was still the wrong house, they insisted. They thought they had chosen the split-level colonial. Instead, they got the brick rambler.

The tenants asked him what he could to. The property manager asked them who had shown them the house, who had given them the application? They said they had worked with a local realtor, who was a friend of a friend. A realtor with a good track record.

The property manager suggested they call the realtor who had shown them the house. The property manager himself had made no mistakes, but someone had. There was no backing out of the lease now, without significant losses on all sides.

The tenants asked the property manager why he was not taking responsibility. He replied that it was not the wrong house, to his knowledge. He had gone by the book. He suggested it was just a slip of memory on their part.

They bit the bullet and moved in. The property manager called their realtor and asked if she knew about the mix-up. She said the tenants had seen eight houses and applied for two of them. They were turned down by their first choice, and signed a lease for their second choice. They were tired and confused after all that house hunting. She accepted no blame.

The property manager didn't want the blame either. He asked her to call them and explain why they thought they had the wrong house. As their agent, who made a commission on the deal, she should set them straight. She said, "No, thanks." They had wasted her whole weekend looking at houses they didn't like. They were both picky and indecisive. She only worked with them because they were friends of a friend.

60. The Catalytic Converter

A tenant moved into a condo. He got a parking permit from the condo association, allowing him to park in the condominium parking lot. He called the property manager several days after he moved in with an unusual problem.

"Property Management Services. How may I help you?"

"I just moved into the condo on Blake Lane. Last night someone stole the catalytic converter from my car."

The property manager said, "Oh, I read an article about that. They sell them, for the copper I think. What did the police say?"

"I don't know. I didn't call the police. Are you going to pay for a new one?"

The property manager was puzzled again. "We don't cover theft of cars or anything you own. Your personal property is at your risk, your responsibility."

"But it's in your parking lot."

The property manager disagreed. "We don't manage the parking lot. We manage the condo. The condo association manages the lot. But they don't cover crime. You should call the police. If you file a police report your insurance may cover it."

"What insurance?"

"Your car insurance? Your renter's insurance? I don't know. I can't really give you insurance advice."

"But it's your parking lot."

"No, sorry, it's not ours."

"Someone is responsible."

"Please call the police. Get a police report for your insurance firm. I'll send you a copy of the lease and the condo addendum you signed, explaining that your property is your responsibility."

The tenant said, "This is crazy. No one is taking responsibility for my car."

"That's exactly what I'm saying," replied the property manager.

61. The Missing Door Stop

After a thorough move-out inspection with the tenant, and a subsequent walk-through with the landlords as they moved back in, all was well with the property, except one missing doorstop.

"Where is my doorstop?"

"It's gone I guess. I guess we missed that on the inspection."

"Very unprofessional. I want a new doorstop."

"I buy them for about two dollars at Home Depot. Can I buy you a new one?"

"No. The tenant should pay. They should have respected my house."

"Come on, the house looks great."

"Don't patronize me. I want it taken out of the security deposit."

"I can get a doorstop myself and install it today. Okay?"

"That's cheating. The tenant should not get away with this."

"I can call the tenant now and get him over here to replace it."

"No. I want to pick it out myself."

"Okay. Let's look at the other doorstops in the house. We should get one that matches."

"Are you nuts? I'm going to get a nice one. Brass maybe. I'll pick it out. And I'll charge for my time and labor."

"Time and labor? Okay. Have it your way. Send us the receipt for the doorstop and an invoice for your labor. We'll deduct the costs from the deposit, write you a check, and return the rest to the tenant."

"How long will this take? Did the tenant skip town?"

"No. He moved a block away. He loves the neighborhood. He is very close with all of your neighbors. He wants to keep his kids in the same school. You'll probably meet him at the annual block party. Good luck with that."

62. The Missing Hedge Row

The landlord moved back into his home after renting it out for several years. He called the property manager and complained that the hedge row between his yard and the neighbor's yard was missing. He wanted it replaced.

The property manager looked at his marketing photos of the house. He confirmed that there were hedges when the owner moved out. He drove to the house to meet the owner. The owner pointed to where the hedge row had been. There were bare spots in the grass where the plants had been removed. The property manager went out to the street and looked down the property line.

"It looks like the shrubs were on the neighbor's yard."

"They were my shrubs. I trimmed them. I owned them."

The property manager went next door and talked to the neighbor. She said they were her shrubs. She'd had a landscaper remove them because they were dying.

The property manager said, "It really looks like they weren't in your yard. Look at the grass line and the rear fence line."

The landlord said, "They were mine and I want you to replace them."

The property manager went back to his office and Googled the satellite photos of the neighborhood. The photos online were several years old so they still showed the hedges. They showed the hedges were apparently on the neighbor's property. He called his client.

"I looked at the satellite photos of your lot. It looks like they were the neighbors' plants."

"What does a picture prove? I want proof."

"I can apply to the county property records for a plat. That might prove it."

"What's a plat?"

"It's like a surveyor's drawing. You probably got one when you bought the house, to verify your property lines."

"I never heard of that. I watered those plants. I loved them. Tell that to the neighbor."

"The neighbors are very nice. They got you a housewarming present. They're going to come over and introduce themselves. You can talk it out with them. That's what neighbors are for."

63. Ten Thousand Dollar Pet Deposit

A rental house's advertising included the words No Dogs Allowed. The owner hated dogs. A potential tenant applied to rent the house, but he had a dog. He asked if he could rent the house anyway. The owner said no. The applicant asked if he would reconsider if he offered to replace all the carpets when they moved out at the end of the lease. "No, no pets," said the owner. The applicant offered to pay a ten thousand dollar pet deposit. That's how much he wanted that house and loved that dog. The big fenced-in backyard was perfect for a dog. No, said the owner, No pets.

The property manager turned down the applicant and asked the owner why he had turned the offer down.

"That was a generous offer. You must really hate dogs."

"I do. A lot."

"Why, is it the way they scratch up floors?"

"No."

"The dog smell?"

"No."

"The dog hair?"

"No."

"I give up. I guess you never had a dog."

"I've had lots of dogs."

"Then what is it? What is it about dogs that you hate?"

"My old dogs tore up my gardens. I lost all my flowers and plants. I lost my vegetable garden."

"But your house doesn't have any gardens."

"Exactly."

64. Eighty Dollar Light Bulb

The tenant moved out. The house was inspected. It was in perfect condition, except one light bulb was burnt out in the hall bath. A new tenant moved in and demanded the light bulb be replaced. The lease held the former tenants responsible for replacing light bulbs. The new tenant reasoned that if he would be responsible later upon move-out, the previous tenant should be responsible now. The property manager called a handyman who was sent to the house to replace the bulb. The property manager received a bill for eighty dollars for the light bulb and deducted that amount from the previous tenant's security deposit. The old tenant called the property manager and screamed bloody murder. "Eighty dollars for a light bulb? Ridiculous!" The property manager retrieved the handyman's bill and sent it to him. It read:

Bob's Handyman Service
September 5, 1999
Job location: 2341 Main Street
Invoice #7565
Job description: Replace light bulb
1. Received call from property manager.
2. Warned property manager of trip charge.
3. Called tenant and scheduled work.
4. Arrived on time for appointment.
5. No one home.
6. Called tenant and re-scheduled.
7. Arrived on time.
8. Waited ten minutes while tenant secured dog in utility room.
9. Replaced light bulb with 75-watt soft white bulb.
10. Tenant demanded 100-watt bulb instead.
11. Rescheduled and returned with 100 watt bulb.
12. Waited for tenant to secure dog.
13. Replaced bulb.
14. Tenant pointed out other repairs not on work order.
15. Returned to shop.
16. Wrote up bill.
17. Sent bill to property manager.
18. Waited for property manager to call and complain about eighty-dollar light bulb.
Charges
$35.00 Trip charge
$35.00 second trip charge
$5.00 box of four 75-watt bulbs
$5.00 box of four 100-watt bulbs.
$80.00 total
Suggested action: Next time replace all light bulbs in house: $135.00.

65. A New Counter

The tenant moved out and left a burn mark on the formica kitchen counter top. It was a round, dark ring the size of a pot or pan. The move-in inspection report showed it did not pre-exist the tenancy. The owner of the house expected the tenant to pay for a new counter.

"I want a new counter."

"Your counter is twenty or thirty years old."

"So?"

"So you're not owed the cost of a new counter, you should get the depreciated value."

"But I want a new counter."

"A formica counter only has a depreciable life of ten or fifteen years."

"What are you saying?"

"Or you should get a prorated amount for just the area damaged."

"How much are we talking?"

"Less than a hundred would be fair."

"I want a new counter."

"A new formica counter would cost maybe five hundred, maybe more, not sure."

"I want a granite counter. What about that?"

"That's a couple grand. That's the whole security deposit."

"Then that's what I want."

"You really should charge a depreciated or prorated amount."

"Where do you get this stuff?"

"Books, trade magazines, lawyers. It's what I do."

"I want a new counter."

"I can get you some estimates, if you like."

"I can get my own estimates, and they will be higher than any you get, I'm sure."

"Why don't you just buy a new granite counter yourself? If that's what you want. And charge the tenant a reasonable amount. If I were you I'd charge fifty dollars. Your counter was pretty beat up to start with."

"I don't want a new counter. I want the money."

66. A New Refrigerator

The tenant had a bad day and kicked the refrigerator, leaving a dent three inches long by a half-inch deep on the refrigerator door. The landlord demanded a new refrigerator. The property manager said the refrigerator was beyond its depreciable life. The landlord didn't understand.

The property manager said, "The refrigerator is over twenty five years old."

"But it still works, right?"

"It's lived a long and happy life."

"I want a new one."

"Its time was up anyway, before the dent. It was rattling and humming."

"How much is my refrigerator worth?"

The property manager said, "Well, Let me ballpark it. If it cost a thousand dollars twenty-five years ago, and it has a depreciable life of twenty-five years, it's worth nothing. Sorry."

"But it works."

"And if it costs fifty dollars to haul it away, that's fifty more dollars below nothing, below zero."

"But it still works."

"And since it uses the old CFC coolant banned in the great ozone debate twenty years ago, it's worth even less. Maintaining it would be a waste of money."

"Why can't I just have a new refrigerator?"

"The tenant just dented the door. A new door is less than a hundred dollars."

"So that's all I can get?"

"I say let it go. You'll be glad you did. Get yourself a nice new refrigerator."

"Who's your supervisor?"

67. A New Sink

When the tenant moved out, the house was perfect, but for some hairline scratches in the stainless steel kitchen sink. Since the house was new at move-in, the landlord demanded a new sink, at great cost. The property manager Googled "How to fix scratches, stainless steel sink." After looking at a few websites, he bought fine steel wool and stainless steel polish, went to the house, and scrubbed the sink, with the grain, for five minutes. The sink looked like new. The landlord was pleased with it, but asked him if he could still deduct something from the security deposit to punish the tenant. The property manager said that rental leases generally do not carry punitive damages, especially when there are no material losses. Punitive damages were more likely to be found in lawsuits involving loss of money, property, or life and limb, but that he could force the tenant to pay for the steel wool pads and polish he already bought. Less than eight dollars. The landlord said, "Nevermind."

68. No Dog on the Lease

The property manager called the tenant.

"We have reason to believe you have a dog. There's no dog allowed on the lease."

"I don't have a dog."

"I saw a dog in your back yard when I met the contractor who was fixing the fence."

"It's not my dog. It was visiting."

"Please. There's no dog on the lease."

"Maybe it was the neighbor's dog."

"All the same, there's no dog on the lease."

"Why can't I have a dog?"

"Sorry, but it's not on the lease."

"Then I don't have a dog. Can I get one?"

"It's not on the lease."

"What's wrong with dogs?"

"The owner's allergic."

"Then tell him not to get a dog."

"We advertised NO DOGS. The lease says NO DOGS. I told you at move-in NO DOGS after I saw the dog cage in your moving van."

"You're spying on me."

"No, I'm enforcing the lease."

"What are you going to do about it?"

"I'll keep calling. Write you letters. Email you."

"That's harassment."

"I'll keep it friendly. I'll say please and thank you."

"What if I get rid of the dog?"

"You won't. Nobody ever gives up their dog."

"Maybe I'll get more dogs. A whole bunch of dogs."

"Okay, you win. The landlord wanted me to evict you but I told him I could talk sense to you."

"Well you can't."

"The dog can go, or you can go. Either way."

69. Weeds Versus Rosebushes

The landlord rented her house. She had square boxwoods lining the sidewalk, crepe myrtles in the four corners of the lot, and gorgeous rose bushes on the sides of the house. The tenant had no interest in yard work. Weeds multiplied, mulch dissolved, flowers dried up and dropped their petals.

The landlord got photos from the property manager with the annual inspection report. The rose bushes were out of control, and being choked by wild vines. She called the property manager and cried over the phone. Her roses were her babies.

The property manager called the tenant and told him that the lease required him to mow the grass and remove weeds. Could he save the rose bushes? The tenant said he didn't know a rose bush from poison ivy. He could cut it all down or do nothing.

The property manager called the landlord again and explained that the lawn care was over the tenant's head. Would she hire a service to do lawn and garden care? She agreed.

The gardener arrived on a date agreeable to the tenant. He methodically saved good plants and killed bad plants. When he looked into the back yard he saw what appeared to be a garden, mulched and fertilized, bordered by neat garden timbers, with six straight rows of cannabis, a plant prohibited by state law. He called the property manager.

"I did the work in the front and side yards, but the back gate was locked. I didn't enter the back yard, but from the fence-line I think I saw an 'herb garden' back there. I have no problem with him growing that stuff, I just thought you'd want to know."

The property manager thanked him and called the tenant.

"The gardener weeded the front yard but the gate to the back yard was locked so he didn't do any weeding back there."

The tenant said, "I'll take care of the back yard myself. I keep it locked. For privacy."

The property manager said, "Privacy. Sure. And if you have *weeds* back there you should *weed* them yourself, even if you don't *weed* in front you should *weed* in back. Understand?"

"I'll mind the back yard, you mind the front. Okay?"

"One other thing" said the property manager.

"What's that?"

"If you get caught I'll have to take your house away. Nothing personal."

The tenant asked, "Can you do that? Is that legal?"

70. The Shadowy Wall

The property manager showed a vacant rental house to a picky couple. While standing in the dining room, the prospective tenants pointed to a shadowy pattern on the wall. The wall appeared to have vague white lines on it, in a geometric pattern. They asked if it would be painted over. The property manager said no, it would not. They protested that it was unsightly. The property manager said paint wouldn't fix it. They asked why not. He walked to the center of the dining room and grabbed the chandelier by the base and turned it. As it turned, the pattern on the wall turned. He turned it the other way and the pattern moved back with it. He began to explain to them shadows and light, prisms and refraction. He sarcastically explained how the owner had painted that wall with two coats of paint already but the chandelier effect kept coming back. They called him a smartass and moved on to the living room.

71. No AC

The tenant called the property manager and complained she and her family had no AC. The property manager said he could get an air conditioning mechanic to her house in a day or two. She said it had to be today, because she had asthma, her kids had asthma, they were all going to die from heat exhaustion, or stroke, or something. It had to be today.

It was the first scorcher of the summer. The maintenance department already had all of the AC companies on calls. They were all backlogged, just like they were every summer in mid-June.

The property manager suggested the tenants to go to the basement, lay on the cool concrete floor, and cover themselves with wet towels. He got the idea from a science fiction movie about global warming. He would fix the AC as soon as he could. She took her kids to the hospital instead, where they were kept overnight for observation. While waiting for the AC to be serviced, they spent two nights at a hotel and demanded compensation. She complained to the property manager's boss about the ordeal, who confronted the property manager. The property manager protested that he was tired of tenants who waited until the first heat wave in June to test their AC. They were asking for trouble. They were idiots. The property manager was fired. It became a legendary humorous story among his colleagues. AC Armageddon. Swelter in Place. The firm paid the tenants' hospital and hotel bills. That week they held a staff meeting on customer service. The boss hired a new property manager and upgraded the training procedures.

72. As Is

The rental property was advertised "As Is." The landlord offered no painting, no cleaning, no decorating or upgrades, just normal maintenance during the lease term. The owner had zero cash flow. Comparable houses in the neighborhood rented for twenty-three hundred dollars a month, so it was advertised at two thousand per month—a bargain, priced to move. A perfect house for a handy fix-it person, or a bargain hunter who is not choosy.

A rental application was received. It had two contingencies: painting and cleaning. The application was denied by the landlord. Another application was received. It was contingent upon removal of the bright wallpaper and replacement of the antiquated harvest gold refrigerator. The landlord denied the application because he could afford no upgrades. A third application was received contingent upon painting, cleaning, and new screens to replace the torn ones. It was also denied.

A fourth application was received accepting the AS IS condition and it even asked for an immediate move-in. The landlord accepted instantly. A week after the tenant moved in, the thirty-year-old hot water heater burst and flooded the basement. The HVAC blower motor died. The costs would total well over two thousand dollars.

The property manager called the owner with the bad news. The owner said he couldn't afford to replacements. The house was As Is. He wouldn't repair anything. The property manager said the state laws regarding habitability required heat and hot water. Without them, the house could be deemed uninhabitable, or violate zoning rules, or be condemned outright. In all three of those scenarios, the tenant could break the lease unilaterally. The owner said, "As Is means As Is." The property manager called the tenant and said the owner had no money for the two thousand dollars worth of repairs. The tenant asked where his two thousand dollars a month in rent was going?

73. Counting Toothbrushes

When tenants were accused of over-occupancy, like moving twelve people into a three bedroom house, or subletting the rec room to a family of four, or having ten cars parked on the street, the property manager would make an appointment to meet the tenant at the house and get their side of the story. When he arrived he would inevitably find the house transformed. Beds had disappeared. Closets were over-stuffed and shut tight. Cars were moved away for the day. A smiling little family of four would stand in the kitchen and say they didn't know what he was talking about. He would walk through the house seeking evidence. His last resort was to count the toothbrushes in the bathrooms. He would usually find ten or twenty toothbrushes. Sometimes there would be twenty bath towels or a dozen different types of shampoo. A dozen bicycles in the back yard. He would describe the discrepancies to the little family. They would say they had friends, they had guests, they had family members visit. Didn't everybody?

74. Crying in the Kitchen

The property manager got a complaint from the tenant's neighbor. He was told of possible lease violations like over-occupancy, illegal subletting, a boarding house business, overcrowding, fire hazards, and health department violations. He met the tenant at the house. They stood together, talking in the kitchen. He questioned her as politely as possible for a half hour. She confessed it was all true, but didn't know there were so many rules. Tears ran down her cheeks. She had recently moved out of the rental and moved back to her parent's house and had sublet the property to friends from work. They had no lease. She didn't want to give up their names or personal data. The property manager would have a hard time serving them with subpoenas if he didn't know who they were. He told the tenant all the violations she had committed and what the potential consequences were. She cried some more. He told her how they could work together to coerce the new occupants to comply, and leave. She shook and buried her head in her hands. He backed off and said nothing until she stopped crying. He asked her to sit down so he could calmly reason with her. She started crying again. He asked her to call her friends and tell them to move out. She picked up the phone and called 911. She said there was an intruder in the house. The property manager exited immediately. He had learned the hard way that a tenant in possession of a property could deny the landlord and property manager access, forcing them to get an injunction in court before returning. The police knew the drill. They always told the landlord to leave and seek civil remedies. He went back to his office and took his "Landlord-Tenant Law for Idiots" book off the shelf.

75. The Open Curtains

The tenant died of cardiac arrest. Her body was removed from her the rental townhouse. Her family and heirs planned the disposition of her personal property and made funeral arrangements. They alerted the property manager the next day. All parties agreed to terminate the lease and assess no rents or other charges not already paid by the tenant. The heirs asked for two weeks to remove all of her personal possessions.

The property manager entered the house and inspected it before he gave keys to the heirs, so he would have an assessment of the house's condition and a record of her possessions, before the family disturbed the scene. He walked through the house, writing a detailed inventory on his clipboard. He looked at the pictures on the walls of the deceased's lifelong friends and family. He saw her cheap jewelry and reading glasses on the bureau. He saw her diplomas and awards, her glass cases of figurines, and he read the titles on her collection of well-worn paperbacks. He saw her one-year chip and Big Book. It was her life history. After two and a half hours in her home, he felt he knew her well.

When he was finished, he looked at her full name on the lease. He called her name out loud and said, "Goodbye and Godspeed," out of a sense of obligation and respect, and in case she was listening. He didn't believe in ghosts, and he wasn't sure about angels, but he was open-minded. He closed all the drapes so curious neighbors could not peek in. He locked the front door. He walked to his car across the street. He looked back at the house one more time. In one of the three windows in the master bedroom upstairs he saw one set of drapes still left open. He must have missed that one.

76. Suit and Tie

After the tenant moved out, the owners returned to live in their home. They met the property manager for a walk-through, to say thanks and goodbye. After they talked about cleaning the gutters and replacing the old appliances, the property manager asked their opinion of his firm's services while they were away. They said they were glad they chose the best management firm from the start.

Before their original decision, several years before, to market the house for rent, they had interviewed three property management firms. The first asked them to come to his cramped office for an interview. The second came to their house wearing a polo shirt and khakis. His firm's representative had arrived in a navy suit and tie. He had a laptop on which he showed them the prices of competing rentals on the market. He had spread sheets showing how much they should expect to pay for repairs and marketing each year.

It was a no-brainer. They hired his firm instantly. They really didn't need the laptop or the sales pitch. They knew they would hire him as soon as he arrived at their home in a suit and tie.

77. NSF

The tenant's rent payment bounced. The bank notified the property manager. The property manager called the tenant to notify him of his error.

"Good morning. The bank has notified us there are insufficient funds in your account."

"Insufficient funds? For what?"

"For your rent. When can we expect payment?"

"It's automatic. Direct deposit."

"Well they notified us there are insufficient funds in your account to make the payment."

"But it's automatic. So what's wrong?"

"Your rent bounced."

"It can't bounce. It's not like a check. It's automatic."

"Direct payments bounce if there is not enough money in your account."

"That's ridiculous."

"Direct deposit works just like a check, just paperless."

"It's online. It happens automatically."

"Can you check with your bank? Can you ask them what happened?"

"Why don't you call your bank?"

"Our bank notified us, and it notified your bank. We notify you. Your account with your bank needs to be reconciled."

"Well, you can call the banks all you want, but I know I have money in my account."

"Your bank refused to pay our bank because they didn't have the money."

"Can you prove it? I don't have to listen to this."

"I can't prove it. I want your help to figure it out before we go to collections, court, or the credit reporting agencies."

"Are you threatening me?"

"No, I'm asking for your help. If we made a mistake I'll apologize. If you made a mistake, we'll help you fix it. If the bank made a mistake, they will rectify it. We're all in this together."

"You're a jerk."

"I know. That's not the point."

78. I'm Not a Miracle Worker

"You haven't fixed my wall yet."

"What is your address?"

"1234 Lancaster."

"Oh, the drywall crack."

"I moved in a month ago and you haven't fixed the crack."

"Well, I saw the crack when the house was empty. It's just a normal settlement crack."

"It's not normal to me. It's a big crack."

"I have pictures from the move-in. It's a hairline crack."

"It's a long crack."

"It's normal settling. It's really just cosmetic."

"Bugs can get in through the crack."

"No, it's just a crack in the tape or the skim coat. The drywall is sound."

"You have to fix it. It's a hazard."

"The rest of the house is in great shape though."

"Yes, it's like new, that's why I rented it. But you have to fix that crack."

"Can I come to your house today and look at the crack? To see if it's getting worse?"

"I work all day."

"How about tomorrow?"

"I work all week."

"How about I go in with my key and look at it while you're at work."

"No. I want to be there."

"Didn't the handyman try to meet you too?"

"Yes, but he wanted to come in during work hours on a weekday."

"That's when he works."

"I told him it would have to be on the weekend."

"And?"

"And he said no."

"So we've taken your calls, offered to come by or send a contractor, and you've said No."

"I'm the customer."

"Okay. Tell me when you want me to look at the crack."

"I'm available Sunday morning."

"Oh, I'm sorry but we don't make appointments on Sunday."

"You have to fix that crack."

"I'm not a miracle worker. I just take your phone calls. Then I call the handyman. Then he calls you to make an appointment. Then you say No. Then you call me again. Then I call the handyman again. Round and round and round it goes. Please call me again, anytime you want to talk about that crack."

79. Gas Odor

"There's a gas smell in my house."

"Did you call the gas company?"

"No, I'm calling you."

"If there's a gas leak you should to call the fire department immediately."

"Why can't you call them?"

"Okay, I'll call them. They will come right away."

"I have to go to work."

"In a gas emergency they will go in immediately."

"Can't you just fix it?"

"The gas company can come out immediately and search for the leak."

"I'm at work."

"Do you want me to let them in?"

"I want to be there."

"Where is the smell coming from?"

"The garage."

"The gas meter is out back. The gas line goes straight down to the basement."

"I smell it in the garage."

"What does it smell like?"

"It smells like gasoline."

"Is your mower in the garage?"

"Yes."

"Do you have one of those red gas cans in the garage?"

"Yes."

"Natural gas doesn't smell like gasoline, it smells like bad eggs."

"How do you know?"

"I've smelled a lot of things in a lot of houses. Part of my job."

"Okay. You can come and sniff around. Check it out."

"I'll come over now. If it's natural gas, it's urgent."

"Okay, you can smell the garage, but no smelling in the house."

80. The Bidet

The tenant called the property manager and reported a leaking toilet. A plumber was called immediately and sent to the house. The plumber fixed the leak and reported to the property manager that the tenant had apparently attempted to attach a water line from the toilet's water supply line to a bidet attachment. The bidet kit parts were seen in the bathroom. The tenant denied attempting any amateur plumbing.

The property manager called the tenant and told him he would have to pay for the repair because he had caused the damage by trying to install a bidet. The tenant said he had not done anything. The property manager said the plumber had documented the problem, which was a lease violation. The tenant refused to pay the bill.

The tenant continued paying rent on time but would not pay the plumbing bill. At the end of the lease term the tenant requested a lease extension of one more year. The property manager said he had been a good tenant, except for the bidet problem he caused. The tenant denied it again. The property manager said he could not renew the lease unless the tenant paid the plumbing bill. The tenant said no. The property manager sent the tenant written notice to vacate at the end of the lease.

The tenant came into the property manager's office and offered to pay the plumbing bill if he could simultaneously sign a lease renewal. The property manager agreed, if the tenant would admit to causing the problem in the first place. The tenant refused. The property manager said that if the tenant would admit he had caused the leak, and then lied about it, they had a deal.

The tenant said no and insisted the plumber was the liar.

The property manager said the tenant could take it or leave it. Confess and pay up, or move out. The tenant waffled. The property manager demanded:

1. A written confession from the tenant.
2. A re-inspection of the toilet by the plumber.
3. Immediate reimbursement for the plumbing bill.
4. A signed lease extension with a reasonable rent increase.
5. An increase in inspections from annual to semi-annual.

The tenant agreed to all terms, on one condition: Next time the property manager would have to call a different plumber.

81. The Leak at the End of the Week

On Friday, at a quarter to five, just fifteen minutes before closing, the property manager received a call from the tenant. The tenant said the toilet was leaking. There was water puddling on the floor behind the toilet.

The property manager said, "On evenings and weekends, plumbers charge emergency rates. Can you put a pan under the leak and wait until Monday?"

"No," said the tenant. "I won't be able to sleep worrying about the leak."

The property manager asked, "Can you just turn off the water supply valve behind the toilet?"

"No. I don't know how."

"When did you first notice the leak?"

The tenant said, "Monday."

"Why did you wait all week to report it?"

"I work all the time."

The property manager said, "I can't authorize emergency weekend work for a repair you neglected all week, unless you pay the emergency charge."

"No way."

"Just put a pan under it and a plumber will come out Monday morning."

"I can't Monday. I'm busy."

The property manager said, "I work Monday to Friday. The plumber works Monday to Friday. Everyone works Monday to Friday. Emergency plumbers on weekends charge a lot. I'll give the plumber a key on Monday."

"What about my right to privacy?"

"You want privacy. I want privacy. The plumber wants the weekend off. You waited four days to report the leak. Put a pan under it."

The tenant said, "I don't have a pan."

82. Returning from Afghanistan

The property manager hired a veteran to perform property inspections. The vet had just returned from active duty in Afghanistan and didn't know what kind of job he wanted yet. Just any job would do at first.

The vet was sent to several houses to do move-in and move-out inspections. Most of the problems he documented were dirty carpets and dirty bathrooms.

After one of his move-out inspections he emailed the photos and inspection forms to the property manager. The photos were primarily of toilets. Dirty toilets, broken toilets, leaky toilets.

One day the vet appeared to be in a bad mood. The property manager asked him if he was enjoying his job. He said no, he had just returned from fighting for his country. He had witnessed heroic acts and endured great tragedy. All the time he knew he was serving a higher purpose. Now he was taking pictures of toilets. It wasn't right.

The property manager thanked him for his service and encouraged him to continue his job search, or return to his unit, or whatever he needed. Whether he stayed in inspections or moved on, the property manager would support him.

The vet quit the inspection job and got a job in a restaurant. Later he got a job with a limo company. He was still restless, searching for something meaningful. He was disappointed with the lack of respect civilian customers showed him, and each other. But at least he wasn't taking pictures of toilets anymore, and that gave him hope. He called the property manager and told him how purposeless and monotonous all his subsequent jobs seemed, but at least they were better than property management had been. The property manager took the afternoon off to think about that for a while.

83. The Rock Band

The tenants were in a rock band. They practiced in the living room. They had loud parties with lots of guests, beer cans in the yard, dozens of cars on the street. All of the neighbors were families with children. They went to bed early and went to church early on Sunday mornings. The hated the rockers. They called the property manager. He went to the house and met the tenants. The tenants had unique hair and unusual clothes. The house smelled funny, like beer and weed, and looked like a frat house.

The property manager told the tenants what the neighbors' complaints were. The tenants said things like "Oh" and "Okay" and "What?" The property manager asked if they could try to quiet down, straighten up, and fit in. They said "Dude" and "Maybe" and "What?"

The property manager walked the neighborhood, knocking on doors. He told the neighbors that the tenants had not technically broken the lease. If the tenants broke local noise ordinances, then he could to something. If neighbors called the police and the tenants were cited, a police report would document a breach of lease. With that, the property manager could take meaningful steps against the tenants. The neighbors said they didn't want to call the police, for fear of retribution.

One neighbor asked the property manager if he would put up with loud rockers on his own street. The property manager yes, he could and did. He said he had lived like that himself, twenty-five years ago. He had the long hair and the giant speakers. He offended neighbors and bent laws. Then he grew up and settled down in a nice, quiet family neighborhood. Recently there were rowdy rocking parties next door to him, too. He put up with it. So he had been on both sides. He told the rockers' neighbors that if they would call the police, get him a police report, a citation or violation, anything like that, then he would run those damn rockers out of town. And he sounded like he meant it.

84. A Sick Child

When the property inspector did his annual inspection, the tenant told him not to go in the small bedroom, there was a sick child in there. When the property manager came by to look at some repair issues, the tenant said don't go in the small bedroom, there's a sick child in there. At the move-out inspection the tenant said please don't go in the small bedroom, there's a sick child in there. After the tenant moved out the property manager went in to the small bedroom. The tenants had redecorated it. They had covered the walls with large flat flagstones, glued to the walls and mortared at the joints. All of the walls would have to be replaced, right down to the studs. It would cost a fortune.

The property manager called the tenant and asked her if her child was still sick. She said no; maybe it was the house making her sick. He asked her if she had redecorated the small bedroom with stone walls. She said she could not recall, no, nothing came to mind. She asked when she could get her security deposit back.

85. Original Condition

A prospective client called the property management office.

"I'd like to inquire about your services. I have a house I'd like to market as a rental."

The property manager replied, "Let's start with your questions and concerns."

"Okay, first, when I come back in I expect my house to be in its original condition."

"Well, renting your house out will cause some wear and tear."

"I expect it to be returned to its original condition."

"Damage done by tenants can be deducted from their deposit, but you should expect normal wear and tear."

"What's the difference?"

"A traffic pattern on carpet is wear and tear. A stain or torn carpet is damage."

"I have new carpets."

"Light scuff marks on walls, and small nail holes for pictures, are normal wear and tear. Ink, crayon marks, sizeable dents and holes are damage."

"The walls were just painted."

"You can expect normal fading and dulling of hard surfaces like wood or vinyl floors."

"But who will pay for all that?"

"The tenant is only responsible for damage due to neglect or misuse. Normal wear and tear is something you, the landlord, need to prepare to accept."

"But I want my house to stay just the way it is."

"Have you thought of draining the pipes, shutting the blinds, locking it up and leaving it empty while you're gone?"

"That's crazy. I need the rent money."

"Do you think you can you live with normal wear and tear, normal expenses?"

"Who says what's 'normal'?"

"It's my job to tell you what's normal. So you don't get upset later."

"I'm upset now. I want my house back in its original condition."

"If you rented out your car it wouldn't come back in its original condition."

"What does that have to do with it?"

"If you hired me to babysit your son for a couple years he wouldn't stay in original condition. Things change. Time passes."

"Where are you going with this?"

"Your house is like a family member, your prized possession, your biggest investment. I get that. You just can't leave it with strangers for years and expect it not to change"

"How do you know?"

"I've rented thousands of houses. Seen hundreds of broken hearts. Gone through millions of gallons of paint. Acres of carpet."

"But I'm the client."

"Not yet. You said you're just inquiring about our services."

86. No Electricity

The tenant's lights went out just after midnight. She called the property manager's after-hours emergency number. Her call was taken by the unfortunate property management staffer who had emergency-call duty that night.

"My electricity went out."

"Did you check the breakers?"

"What's breakers?"

"The breaker box. The fuse box. It's probably in the basement."

"It's dark down there. Send me an electrician."

"You should check the breakers first. Did you look at your neighbors' houses? Is the whole street out or just yours?"

"I don't know. I just want my power back on. You need to do something."

"If I call an electrician and the power is off on the whole street, you will have to pay the electrician, at emergency rates. If I call an electrician and it's just your breaker box, you'll also have to pay the electrician."

"Call an electrician."

"Okay, I'll call an electrician, but if the electrician tells me it's your fault for not checking the breakers or the neighborhood, we're billing you."

"Send the electrician. It's getting cold."

The property manager made the call. Two hours later he got a call back from the electrician.

"Hello, I'm Sam with Electricon. I'm at the rental. The tenant is right here. I just got here, walked in, and the power came back on. The whole street was out, now it's back on.

There's a power company truck right in front of the house here. Yellow lights flashing."

"Okay, thank you. How much is your service call?"

"Weekend, evening, emergency rate is two hundred fifty just for showing up."

"Can you ask the tenant to pay it?"

"She said she's not paying anything. She said she didn't even call me. She said you called us."

"Okay. Send me the bill and I'll try to collect from her."

"Will do."

"And please tell the tenant it's her fault. Write that on the invoice. Write Stupidity Charge on it or something. False Alarm due to Laziness. Put the blame on her, on the ticket, okay?"

"She's standing right here. You want to tell her?"

"Hell no. It's three in the morning. Just get out of there and send me the bill."

"I charge extra for placing blame."

"It's worth it."

87. Diplomatic Immunity

The tenant failed to pay the last two months rent at the end of the lease term. The property manager called him.

"You haven't paid the last two rents."

"It's not my fault. My government was supposed to pay."

"We may have to sue."

"I have diplomatic immunity."

The property manager said, "I think that's for crimes, not debts."

"I have diplomatic immunity."

"You're not in the diplomatic corps. You're a military attaché."

"I have diplomatic immunity," said the tenant.

"The ambassador and his family and staff have immunity. You don't."

"I'm under the diplomatic umbrella."

The property manager said, "You're just another guy on our soil."

"You can't touch me," the tenant insisted.

The property manager contacted an attorney, who said a claim of immunity would have to be challenged in court, so the property manager would have the burden of proof. That meant a lot of time and money would be wasted, just to start a lawsuit.

The property manager, undaunted, looked up the embassy website and called every phone number on it. He emailed every email address on it. He got the street address of the embassy and mailed letters to the tenant, care of the embassy. He wrote letters to all of the names on the website, including the ambassador himself. Then he waited.

Two weeks later he got a call from a mid-level bureaucrat at the embassy. He warned the property manager to back off. It was wrong to try to embarrass diplomatic guests of the United States.

The property manager said, "I might walk up and down in front of the embassy carrying signs. I might tell every property manager in the state to avoid renting houses to anyone from your embassy."

"You can't do that. The U.S. State Department protects us."

"They don't protect you from my free speech. We don't jail dissidents here. I will reach the ambassador, eventually."

The embassy spokesperson said, "I'll talk to someone. I'll find out who writes the rent checks. Maybe there was a mix-up."

"Thank you. It is an honor speaking with a person of such high station. A guy who can get things done."

88. How Does This Work?

The new tenant was a diplomat from a foreign nation. Houses were built differently in his country. Everything was different. At the move-in inspection the tenant asked the property manager how to operate the washer and dryer. He had never seen appliances quite like them. He asked how to operate the microwave. He asked how to use the garage door opener. He even asked how to open the windows. The window latches were different in his country. Plus, he had always had servants to do things for him.

The move-in walk-through took more than four hours. Explaining the digital thermostat alone took fifteen minutes. When they were finished, the tenant was very grateful. He was considered brilliant in his home country, but felt so helpless here. The property manager said he was glad to help. The diplomat said that his wife was flying in the next weekend. She had never wanted to come here. She would question everything. She would kill him if things didn't go smoothly. The property manager called his office and cancelled the rest of his appointments for the day. He told the tenant he would like to go over everything again.

89. Squirrels in the Attic

"Property management. Good morning."

"Hello, I live in 123 Baker Street. I have squirrels in my attic."

"Oh. Are you sure they're squirrels?"

"I assume. I'm not going up there to find out."

"Are they a nuisance?"

"They'll tear up the insulation and chew holes in the plywood."

"I'll call the pest guy."

"What will he do to them?"

"Trap them, take them away, and block their entrances."

"Humane traps?"

"Okay. Sure. Humane. Probably."

"Where will he take them?"

"Out to the country somewhere I guess."

"But he won't kill them?"

"No. I don't think so."

"Can you ask him?"

"No. They know what they're doing."

"The squirrels?"

"The pest guys."

"If they turn out to be rats you can go ahead and kill them."

"Thanks. But I think the pest guys have a code of silence."

"What do you mean?"

"Pest guys are like hit men for homeowners. It's best not to ask questions."

"You're weird."

"I've been called worse. But I have some experience. I once had a skunk nesting under my front porch. It stunk up the whole house. I called the pest guy. He put a big metal cage trap, a humane trap, beside my porch. The first morning I came out and found a possum in the trap. The next morning it was a raccoon. The third day it was my neighbor's cat Romeo."

"Did they ever catch the skunk?"

"No. I couldn't believe it."

"What did you do?"

"I went on the internet and looked for home-made solutions."

"And?"

"First I put a radio under the porch playing country music twenty-four hours a day. When that didn't work I put mothballs under the porch. Finally I actually ordered fox urine on the internet and dripped it all around the porch, like the territorial mark of a predator."

"And?"

"Nothing. The skunk moved out after her kids grew up. Then I poured a concrete wall around the base of the porch."

"How do you know you didn't seal the skunk inside and starved it to death?"

"See? That's why there's a code of silence."

90. Dead Squirrels in the Attic

During a move-in inspection the property manager found a dead squirrel in the attic. He called a pest control firm. The pest control contractor inspected and told him there was a nest and some dead baby squirrels too. There were squirrel feces. It was a hazmat situation that required immediate cleanup, trapping, sealing the area, and blocking all potential entrances. The pest control contractor quoted the local health ordinance that applied. It would cost over two thousand dollars. The property manager authorized the work immediately. He had a tenant moving in within the week and could not afford to have the house condemned or found unfit for habitation.

The pest people did their thing. The property manager inspected the attic afterward. It was clean as a kitchen. He wondered: What if they just swept everything up and left? What if there was no such thing as a dead squirrel hazmat situation? He called them and asked for more details. They sent him a confusing page of specs from the EPA. He didn't know for sure, but he suspected it was the exterminator's code of silence thing again.

91. The Squirrel in the Range Hood

A tenant called to report screaming and scratching sounds in the range hood. The property manager sent a handyman immediately. The handyman said it was probably a squirrel that came down the roof vent stack and couldn't get out. The handyman would not touch the job. The tenant asked if the squirrel might die in there. The handyman said if it died it would stink in a couple days. They would know.

The property manager called a pest company next. The pest guy went to the house the next day. There was no scratching and no screaming. Maybe it was gone. Maybe it escaped. Maybe it was dead. The pest guy told the tenant to call him if the house started to stink up in a day or two.

The tenant called the property manager and said he was not comfortable with the possibility of a dead squirrel right there over the stove. He didn't think it fair that he should have to wait for it to decompose and stink up the house. The property manager grabbed his tool box and went to the house and detached the range hood from the cabinets and the wall. He looked inside the duct work. No squirrel, no nuts, no nest, no hair, no nothing. He used a flashlight and a mirror to show the tenant the empty range hood vent and ductwork, and assured him the squirrel must have escaped. He offered to have the duct professionally cleaned all the way out to the exterior vent.

The property manager went back to his office and called the pest control guy. He asked why the pest guy hadn't removed the range hood and looked inside. The pest guy said he didn't think a squirrel could get in there in the first place. He thought the tenant was lying about the screaming. Squirrels don't scream, they squeak and chatter. Plus it was five o'clock on a Friday and he had plans.

The property manager asked if there was a code of silence. The pest guy said No. No such thing. Never heard of it.

92. The Ground Hog

The tenant called to complain about a ground hog in the back yard. It had dug a hole under the deck and was occasionally seen scurrying across the yard, from the deck to the woods. What could be done about it?

The property manager called the county Animal Control office. They told him that groundhogs were wild-life, not pests. If it was rabid, or bit someone, or damaged the house, they could come out and kill it and dispose of it, but not trap or rescue. They could not alter migration or nesting habits without upsetting natural habitat. They could either kill it or leave it be.

The property manager called the tenant, who said, "No, don't kill it. We don't want that." It was kind of cute after all. And they had learned that groundhogs were harmless. So they dropped their complaint. Their kids had named it Chubby. They put dog biscuits out for it at dusk.

The property manager called Animal Control again and asked what would happen if the groundhog bit someone. The animal control rep wouldn't say. He referred him to their website. Each case was different. They would do whatever they had to. The code.

93. Ants Everywhere

A tenant called and complained there were ants everywhere. A pest control company was called. They found no ants in the house, but treated for ants anyway. The tenant called the property manager again and again, complaining that there were ants everywhere.

The property manager made an appointment and met the tenant at the house to see for himself. They looked around the kitchen, but found no ants. They searched the basement, but there were no ants. They looked in all the bathrooms and bedrooms. No ants. Lastly, they checked the master bedroom. The tenant insisted there were ants between the baseboard and the carpet. The property manager got on his hands and knees and shined his flashlight in every nook and cranny. Nothing. The tenant said the ants were in the walk-in closet. The property manager crawled around in the closet with his light and camera but there were no ants.

The property manager told the tenant there were no ants. The tenant said she saw ants all the time. She asked if he could come back the next day and look again. He shook his head.

When the property manager got back to his office he checked his voice mail. The tenant had left a message shortly after he left the house. The ants were back. They were everywhere.

The property manager looked up the symbolism of ants in dreams and literature. He researched ant hallucinations during drug and alcohol withdrawal. He told the other property managers the ant story. They laughed and told tales of past complaints about basements full of crickets and garages infested with spiders.

When the landlord got the pest control bill on his monthly statement he called the property manager and asked if the ants were gone. The property manager said that no ants had been found or observed. The landlord was relieved. He had seen ants everywhere when he lived there but could never get rid of them.

94. As Is 2

A prospective tenant called the property manager. He had gotten the phone number from the sign in front of the house. He wanted to rent the house as soon as possible.

"Would you like me to show you the house this afternoon?" asked the property manager.

"No. I need to rent it now. I'm out of time. I'll sign anything."

"That's so risky. The house needs cleaning and painting. It needs some repairs."

The prospective tenant said, "I'll take it As Is. I'll fix it up. I'm a contractor."

The property manager warned him. "The owner would love it if you take it As Is and move in now. She doesn't want to spend any money on fix-up. But I know you will not be happy if you move in now. You will ask for cleaning or painting later. You will."

"I'll sign anything. My wife kicked me out. All my stuff is in a van."

The property manager reluctantly agreed. The prospective tenant filled out an application and provided security deposit and rent checks, all in one day. He signed a lease the next day. An "As Is" addendum was added to the lease. The property manager met him at the house for the move-in. They walked through the house and documented the condition.

The tenant said, "This place is filthy."

The property manager said, "You wanted it As Is."

"But it stinks. There's a pet smell."

"You didn't want to see it first."

"The walls are all ghetto."

"You agreed it was As Is. I warned you."

"But I didn't expect it to be this bad. There's old food in the fridge. What's that stain on the carpet? Blood? Urine? I didn't expect it to be this bad."

"You haven't moved your stuff in. I haven't given you the key. Do you want to back out of the deal? You may have to forfeit your deposit."

"Are you trying to rip me off?"

"You said As Is."

"That was then."

"I asked you to please let me show you the house."

"But look at this place."

"As Is means As is."

"Not to me."

"As is. As is. As is. We even defined 'As is' in your lease addendum."

"I can't move in here."

"Let's leave. Go find another house. I'll discuss the deposit status with my attorney."

"I want my money back. Today."

"I'll defer to the lease and the law. I'll call you."

"I will kick your ass."

"I'm fifty-five. You're like, twenty-five. It wouldn't be a fair fight."

95. Twenty-One Cars

A famous professional basketball player rented a house from the property manager. The athlete's agents and assistants made all the arrangements, from application, to lease, to move-in. The property manager was never to meet the star or contact him. His handlers did everything. The rent was paid on time, the house was well kept, and the occupants were, by all accounts, responsible tenants.

At the end of the two-year lease the tenant moved out. The house was vacated. But the basketball star and his entourage had left behind twenty-one cars, motorcycles, trucks, and SUVs in the long circular driveway. The property manager waited a few days before making the call.

"Hello, I'm the property manager in charge of the rental property your associate rented on Country Road in Estateville."

"What's up?" asked the star's representative.

"Thanks for asking. The house is vacant and in good shape. We appreciate that. But there are twenty-one vehicles still on the property."

The star's rep said, "Oh. What do you want me to do about it?"

"When can you remove the vehicles? A new tenant moves in soon."

"I don't know anything about it. What do you want me to do?"

"Remove the cars? Please?" asked the property manager.

"We've moved to L.A. We don't have any people in your area anymore," said the rep.

The property manager said, "We need the full use of the property, including the driveway. The security deposit won't cover the cost of hauling all those cars away. We need your help."

The star's rep asked, "Can you deliver them? I can get you an address to send them to."

"I'm sorry but that's not our job."

"It's not my job either."

"The lease states that personal property left behind may become the possession of the landlord after proper notice and thirty days storage."

"What are you saying?"

"I'm saying you get the cars or my client gets them. It's legal. I checked."

"You know who you're dealing with, don't you?"

"Yes, yes, I used to be a fan. Now I'm just a guy asking you a favor. I'm just a guy who has your bosses' cars and doesn't want them. Do you think I can talk to him?"

"You don't know who you're dealing with, do you?"

"Yes, some guy who left a bunch of cars in someone else's yard. It usually happens in bad neighborhoods, with abandoned cars and junkers."

"Show respect now."

"Finders keepers?"

"Bullshit. We'll sue your ass off."

"Good. Send us the papers. The towing company needs something in writing."

96. A Pile of Junk

The tenant moved out, leaving a pile of junk on the street in front of the house. Broken chairs, a dirty mattress, boxes full of books and magazines, garbage, kitty litter, lamps and bookshelves. A neighbor took the lamps. Rain soaked the rest. Neighbors complained to the property manager.

The property manager called the former tenant and asked him to remove the junk. The tenant said it was not junk, it was his stuff, leave it there, and he would pick it up. The property manager asked when? The tenant said he didn't know.

The property manager hired a contractor who hauled the junk away. A new tenant moved in. Three weeks later the old tenant called and said he had driven by the house. His stuff was gone. Where was it?

The former tenant asked, "Where's my stuff?"

"What stuff?"

"The stuff I left by the curb."

The property manager lied. "I don't know. I thought you picked it up."

"No. Who took it? I want to go through it. There was some good stuff in there."

"Maybe somebody stole it. Maybe you should call the police. Maybe the neighbors took it. Maybe the town took it. Maybe the health department. Maybe it was attracting rats. Do you want me to make some calls and find out?"

"You'd do that?" asked the tenant.

"Sure. Glad to help. I'm your guy."

"Thanks."

"Bye."

The property manager happily did nothing.

97. The Train Out Back

A homeowner advertised his home for rent. The description in the advertising and listing said "Three bedroom, two bath contemporary home, close to schools and shopping. Great for commuters. Right on commuter rail."

Prospective tenants called the property manager and were shown the house. They loved it. They filled out rental applications. The homeowner accepted.

The tenants moved in. On their first evening in the house they sat out on the back deck in the fading afternoon light and drank wine to celebrate their new home.

Just then the clattering racket of a commuter train broke their peace and quiet. The train ran behind their house, just behind the tree-line. They hadn't seen it when they were shown the house. The homeowners hadn't mentioned it. The property manager hadn't mentioned it. They called the property manager.

"Good afternoon, Property Management Services."

"Hey, it's me, the guy who just moved into the house on Main Street."

"Ah, hello, how is the move-in going?"

"The move-in was done. Then a train screamed through our back yard. What the hell?"

"You're kidding. I didn't know. The owner never told me."

"Sure. It's false advertising or something. You screwed us."

"I'm sorry, I didn't know. The neighborhood was so quiet whenever I was there."

"Should I get a lawyer or are you going to make it right?"

"Wait a minute. Let me look up the advertising, the listing and property description. Wait, wait, here it is. Oh, it says it's right on the commuter rail."

98. Water Main Break

The main water line under the front yard broke at a rental property. Water gushed up out of the ground. A plumber diagnosed the issue and turned off the water main at the street. The water company came and confirmed that the leak was in the water line owned by the property owner and not in the municipality's equipment. All the tenants knew was that they had no water.

The property manager immediately got two estimates from large plumbing firms that had the equipment to dig up the front yard and replace the main water line. The estimates were for three to four thousand dollars.

The landlord said the prices were too high. He demanded a third estimate. The property manager got another estimate. It was still too high for the landlord. The landlord said he would get his own estimates.

The tenant went without water for days. He called the property manager every day to complain. The property manager explained the costs, and time involved, and the landlord's devious delays for more estimates.

A week passed. The property manager called the landlord every day. He explained that water was a requirement for habitability by state law. The house did not meet the state standards and could conceivably be condemned. The tenant had to move to a hotel just to shower and shave.

The landlord called a friend who was in construction and tried to get a sweetheart deal. He tried to negotiate with different plumbers.

The tenant called the town and the county. He talked to the water company, the zoning department, and the health department. He went online and asked for free legal advice. He got a zoning inspector to come to the property. He got the house condemned. He stopped paying rent and moved out.

The property manager called the landlord and told him the house was condemned and the tenant was gone. No more rent payments would be forthcoming under the lease. The landlord said he didn't understand. He was doing everything he could. Could he sue the tenant? Would the security deposit be enough to pay for the new water line?

The property manager contacted an attorney, released the security deposit to the tenant immediately, and terminated the management contract with the homeowner. The owner sold the house through a property broker who specialized in quick sales for distressed properties for twenty thousand dollars under market value.

99. I Was There

The property manager made an appointment to meet the tenant at his rental for an annual inspection. When the property manager arrived, he rang the bell and knocked on the door. Receiving no answer, he knocked and rang the doorbell again. There was no car in the driveway. He walked around the house. He knocked on the back door. No answer. He sat in his car for fifteen minutes, waiting. He returned to his office and called the tenant.

"Hello. We had an appointment. Did you forget?"

"No. I was there."

"I was there a couple minutes early. I knocked and rang the bell for a while."

"I was there. Where were you?"

"Your car wasn't there. I knocked on all your doors."

"I was there. You must have had the wrong time."

"I made the appointment for noon. I confirmed it on the phone and by email with you."

"I was there."

"I was there from eleven fifty-five to twelve fifteen. When were you there?"

"Noon."

"Well, I tell you what. I'll come back tomorrow at noon and if you're not there, I'll go on in with my key."

"No. I have to be there. Tomorrow is no good."

"Then when are you available?"

"After work. About seven."

"I don't work that late."

"I have to work too, you know."

"Okay. Tell you what. I'll be there at seven this evening, if you admit you stood me up."

"No. I was there."

"Admit you lied and I will meet you any time."

"I didn't lie."

"Confess, or I'll enter the house with my key, without you."

"No. I was there."

"Come on. Admit it. All will be forgiven. Just admit you're lying."

"I was there."

100. I'll Ask the Owner

"Can I wallpaper the dining room?"

"I'll ask the owner."

"It would look good."

"I'll have to ask the owner."

"It would be a big improvement."

"Yes it would, I'll ask the owner."

"Will you pay for the materials?"

"I'll have to ask the owner about that."

"That room has no blinds. We'd like you to get us some blinds."

"The owner might consider that."

"What about the yard?"

"What about it?"

"We'd like to do some landscaping."

"The owner would have to approve."

"A flower bed under the bay window would be nice."

"I'll ask the owner."

"Could you reimburse us for mulch and plants?"

"That would be up to the owner."

"Can't you make any decisions without the owner's approval?"

"Sure. If it doesn't cost anything. For example, I can let you can clean the gutters."

"Thanks a lot."

"You're lease expires in a couple months. Do you want to stay another year?"

"I'll ask my husband."

"The rent might go up a little."

"You'd have to talk to my husband."

101. You Made My Fiancé Cry

An occupant of a rental called the property manager.

"You made my fiancé cry."

"With whom am I speaking?"

"Like you don't know. Winterwood Court. You were here yesterday."

"Oh, yes, so you're the husband?"

"Boyfriend. Fiancé I mean."

"I met Carla at the house yesterday. I thought it went well."

"You made her cry."

"I'm sorry, but she didn't cry when I was there. She was in good spirits."

"Well, when I came home she was crying."

"Why. What did I do?"

"You told her I couldn't move in with her."

"No. I told her you would have to apply to join the lease."

"But I already live here."

"I know. So it's a formality. You apply, we make sure you didn't trash your last house or declare bankruptcy, then we add you to the lease."

"Why do you need me to apply? She's already in the house, paying rent."

"We like to weed out people who've been evicted before, or serial killers."

"I'm trying to be serious."

"Okay. Let's be serious. If you apply and you look good on paper, you go on the lease. If you don't apply, we give your fiancé notice she is in breach of lease, we make her cry again."

"You're an asshole."

"Yes, I know. I'll send you some forms. Think it over. Call me."

102. The Security Deposit Isn't Rent

It was the last month of the tenant's lease. The rent was late. The property manager called the tenant to collect.

"Good morning. How are you?"

"Fine, who's this?"

"Property Management Services. Our records show we have not received your rent."

"It's my last month. I paid first and last month rent when I moved in."

"No, you paid a security deposit and first month rent."

"I'm pretty sure it was first and last."

"That's a common misperception, but the listing, lease and application, everything you signed, said it was a deposit. The lease says you may not use the deposit as rent."

"Well that's not how I remember it. Plus I just paid a deposit on my next house, so I don't have it."

"You agreed to pay rent every month for twelve months. That's all I'm saying."

"I'm pretty sure I paid first and last month rent."

"I have sent you a late notice, with a late fee included. If you don't pay the last month rent we will have to pursue the debt through the normal procedures described in the lease."

"You can't exactly evict me. I'm moving out."

"I know. It's too late to evict you. But we can send the debt to collections agencies, credit bureaus, or courts. I call them the 3Cs. Not that we want to. We just want the rent."

"Are you threatening me?"

"Oh, no, I don't mean to threaten. I'm just telling you what you agreed to."

"Just take the rent out of my deposit."

"The deposit is for property damage, if any, found at the move-out inspection. Anything beyond normal wear and tear."

"The house is perfect. There's no damage."

"What about that big hole you put in the stairway wall when you were carrying that filing cabinet in?"

"How did you know about that? Are you spying on me?"

"I was there when you moved in, remember? I had just finished the move-in inspection. I held the storm door open when you brought it in. We talked about where it should go. You said you were going to use the small bedroom as your office or den. We were both drinking coffee from Starbucks. You apologized for putting a hole in the drywall. You were a little embarrassed. I told you that you could repair it during the lease term, otherwise it would become a deposit issue."

"You're being difficult. Why can't you be like a normal person?"

"I used to be like a normal person. Now I'm a property manager. I feel like a nagging mother all the time. Nag, nag, nag. Pay the rent or else. Tenants hate me. It sucks."

"You're so weird."

103. No Smoking

The property manager called the tenant after an annual inspection. The tenant answered "Hey, what's up?"

"We did an inspection last week. The inspector said you've been smoking in the condo"

"So?"

"It's a non-smoking condo. It's a no-smoking lease."

"I don't smoke."

"The inspector smelled cigarette smoke."

"Maybe the neighbors smoke."

"The inspector saw two ashtrays, one in the living room, one in the master."

"Ashtrays are legal."

"There were cigarette butts in them."

"But no one was smoking. I wasn't even there."

"There was a pack of Marlboro Lights on the kitchen counter."

"Again. No one was smoking. No one was home."

"The sheers near the living room ashtray are turning brown from the smoke."

"Do you have pictures?"

"Twenty five digital pictures."

"I didn't give you permission to photograph my stuff."

"You did when you signed the lease."

"Who reads the lease? It's like ten pages."

"Twelve."

"I don't smoke."

"The paint on the ceilings in the two rooms is starting to yellow."

"I can't believe this."

"Your furnace filter is filthy. It stinks of tobacco smoke."

"You guys are crazy."

"I'm asking you to stop smoking inside. Please smoke outside. And try to clean the smoke and smoke smell up before move-out so we don't have to keep your deposit."

"Is this your job? Telling people how to live in their own homes?'

"It is. It is my job. It's not as glamorous as it sounds."

104. No Smoking 2

The tenant's neighbors complained to the property manager. The tenants chain-smoked. The smell came through the walls of the condo into the neighboring units. It went up through the ceiling to the unit upstairs. The property manager called the tenant.

"Hello. We are receiving complaints about cigarette smoke from your neighbors."

"How can they smell through the walls?"

"The walls and ceilings are porous. Wood and drywall. Paint and fiberglass and stuff."

"Well I like to smoke. I'm not going to stop for them."

"It's a no-smoking lease."

"I didn't read the lease. I didn't have time. I was moving. I was very busy."

"Can't you just smoke outside?"

"It's too cold outside. Maybe I can smoke outside in the spring."

"Can you move out? Wouldn't you like to live somewhere smoking is allowed?"

"My lease lasts another year. I'm not moving."

"It lasts until May. Four months from now."

"I don't want to move."

"I'll send you a formal written lease termination. In May, you have to move. I wish it were sooner. I'm getting so much grief from your neighbors."

"What about my rights?"

"Free speech and religion and all that? Smoking is not a right."

"What about my right to privacy?"

"You have a right to privacy in your rented home. But not to damage it."

"The lease says it's my home for a year."

"I thought you said you didn't read the lease."

105. The Naked Tenant

The property manager went to the tenant's rental house to check out the new carpet. He had spoken with the tenant and made an appointment in advance. She expected to be at work and the house would be empty. She said he could enter with his key.

When he arrived he saw her car was gone, so he was sure she was at work. Just in case, he rang the doorbell twice, then waited a minute, and knocked on the door. After another minute he opened the front door with his key and walked into the foyer. He announced himself loudly, just in case. "HELLO. PROPERTY MANAGEMENT SERVICES." The house was silent.

He walked through the entire house and noted that the carpet was installed professionally, and confirmed that it was the beige color he had ordered. After inspecting the rest of the house, he walked into the master bedroom to find a naked young woman in bed, sound asleep.

He tiptoed backwards out of the bedroom, crept quietly down the stairs, out the front door. He locked the door and then rang the doorbell twice, waited a minute, knocked on the door, waited, knocked again very loudly, and waited. After several minutes, the door opened and the groggy young woman stood in the doorway, wearing a robe. She asked him what he wanted. He said he was from Property Management Services. He had an appointment. Could he come in?

She apologized and said she forgot. She overslept. She had skipped work. She had partied all night. She looked in the driveway. She said, "Where's my car?"

106. The Naked Tenant 2

The property manager scheduled an inspection at a rental property. The tenants were police officers. The property manager knocked on the door, rang the bell, and entered. He announced himself as he entered.

"HELLO. PROPERTY MANAGEMENT SERVICES. ANYONE HOME?" There was no answer. He walked through the top two floors and then went to the basement. As he walked into the basement bedroom a large naked man jumped up from the bed and appeared to be reaching for the nightstand, possibly for a gun.

The property manager said, "PROPERTY MANAGEMENT SERVICES! I HAVE AN APPOINTMENT!"

The tenant/police officer put away his gun and yelled, "WHAT ARE YOU DOING? I ALMOST SHOT YOU! YOU CAN'T JUST WALK INTO A MAN'S HOME!!"

The property manager said, "I made an appointment with you, or your roommate. We verified the time and date in an email. I knocked, and rang the bell, and yelled, announcing myself, when I came in."

"Oh. Well, even if you made an appointment, it still would have been a justified shooting. This is my home."

The property manager said, "If you shot me, they'd put you on administrative leave for a week."

"Now, that's funny," said the naked tenant.

"Maybe without pay."

"You don't quit, do you?"

"If I lived, I would have kept your deposit."

"Hey, give me a second to me put some clothes on."

"Please."

107. The Satin Slip

The tenant called the property manager and said there was a draft in her master bedroom. She had closed the windows and storm windows. All the heat registers were open. She was always cold. It might make her sick. She claimed it was wasting her heat and probably costing more for electricity.

The property manager went to the house, at her request. When the tenant answered the doorbell she was wearing a satin slip. She invited him in and led him to the master bedroom. She told him to stand next to the window where he could feel the draft.

"Do you feel it? The cold air?" she asked.

"Not yet," said the property manager.

"Right there. Move to your left a little," she said.

"No, nothing yet," he said.

She said, "Here." She moved to the window and stood right beside him. "Right here."

He said, "I don't feel it. But I'm dressed warmly. You're not."

"Take your jacket off."

He said, "Do you ever wear sweaters?"

She said, "What do you mean?"

"Have you tried putting on a bathrobe or a house coat?"

"Not really. I'm very casual at home."

He asked her "What about slippers? Or socks. I wear socks around the house in the winter."

She said, "You're missing the point. I'm cold. Look at my goose bumps. Look at my arms and legs. Goose bumps."

He said, "It's a little hot in here. I'm going back downstairs."

In the foyer she asked, "You really don't feel it? Aren't you cold?"

He said, "No, I'm very warm. Turn the thermostat up and let me know how it goes."

She said, "How about some coffee?"

He returned to his office and told his co-workers the satin slip story. They thought he was exaggerating. He brought it up at the weekly staff meeting. It was agreed that from then on, if a tenant was not fully dressed, they would not enter the house. They would excuse themselves politely and reschedule the appointment. A female property manager was assigned to handle the satin slip account from then on. The property manager started a new file for future reference. It contained a list of risky situations he had found himself in. It was titled: Naked tenants, satin slips, inappropriate remarks, and uncomfortable situations.

108. The Shower Leak

The tenant reported a water leak on the dining room ceiling. A plumber was sent. He found that the leak was directly under the upstairs shower. The plumber and the tenant looked at the shower. The caulk and grout were sound. The diverter and the overflow gasket were normal. The plumber found no problem, except one: There was no shower curtain. The water from the shower was spraying on the floor and leaking through the joints between the vinyl floor squares. The tenant wasn't buying it. She said he had never had a shower curtain in her life. She didn't believe the plumber. The plumber offered to install a shower curtain. If that didn't solve the problem, the plumber would give the property manager an estimate for a glass shower enclosure. The dining room ceiling would be repaired later. The tenant said no, she didn't like shower curtains. She said she had seen too many *Psycho* shower scenes in movies. The plumber explained further. The floor was not waterproof. Nothing is waterproof. Water creeps through seams and cracks in everything. The tenant became angry. She said it wasn't her fault. She said she would prove the plumber wrong. She would take a shower to prove her point. The tenant turned on the shower and began to disrobe. The plumber immediately left without a word and called the property manager. The property manager added that tenant to his naked, inappropriate, uncomfortable list. Then he searched the internet for a female plumber in the metro area.

109. Inspecting the Wrong House

The property manager went to the tenant's house. The occupant answered the door. The property manager announced that he was there for the annual inspection. The occupant invited him in. They walked through the house together. They checked the furnace filter and tested the smoke detectors. They looked at potential repair issues and discussed the proper use the household systems. They checked the setting on the digital thermostat. All the fixtures and appliances were in good working order.

The inspector thanked the occupant. As he was leaving he gave the occupant a copy of the report and his business card. The occupant looked at the card and asked:

"Who is Property Management Services?"

The inspector said, "That's us. We rent the house to you."

The occupant said, "What do you mean rent? I own the house."

The inspector said, "I don't think so. We only inspect our own rentals."

The occupant said, "I've owned this house for twenty years."

The inspector looked at his paperwork. "This is 124 Lafayette Court, right?"

"No, it's 421 Lafayette," said the occupant.

"You're not Mr. Anderson, our tenant?" asked the inspector.

"No, I'm Jacob Wilson, the owner, like I said," said the occupant.

"I can't believe it. I got the wrong house. Oh, no, I am so sorry."

The occupant said, "That's okay. The house needed an inspection anyway."

The inspector asked, "Why did you let me in if you don't know who we are?"

The occupant said, "I thought you were from the government."

110. Painting the Wrong House

The exterior paint was peeling on one of the property manager's rentals. He got estimates, the landlord chose one, and he sent the painters to paint the home. He gave the painters the incorrect address: 13 Brinks Court. It was supposed to be 15 Brinks Court. A crew of eight painters painted the house in one day. When the owners of the painted house came home, the painters were packing up. They talked to the painters. They got the property manager's number, and called. The stunned property manager agreed to repaint the house. The neighbor said he liked the paint job just fine, but wanted twenty-two hundred dollars, the cost of painting, in case he changed his mind. The property manager said he would prefer to pay a contractor to do the work required, to make things right. He did not want to pay a monetary settlement of any kind. They went back and forth. They agreed to a cash settlement of fifteen hundred dollars and a signed release of liability. Both felt fortunate.

The Wrong Yard

Another time, the property manager hired a lawn service for a rental property, beginning in May. The lawn contractor accidentally mowed the wrong address, the neighbor's yard, bi-weekly. The neighbor did not complain until August. He agreed to accept the free mowing, and disregarded the trespassing.

The Wrong Tree

Yet another time, a tree fell in a storm. The tenant complained and the property manager had the dead tree removed. It turned out to be the neighbor's tree, which had fallen across the fence into the tenant's yard. The property manager agreed to the neighbor's demand that he fix the fence, and buy a new tree. The neighbor said the tree company had trespassed. He wanted compensation. The property manager told him trespassing was a crime. He could call the police. Have the tree guy arrested. But he wasn't getting any money. Just a tree and fence.

The Wrong Door

The property manager placed lockboxes on the doorknobs of four houses and put up For Rent signs in four yards in one day. In his haste, he got one of the addresses wrong. The owner of the mistaken house called the number on the For Rent sign, and demanded he remove the lockbox and sign immediately. When the property manager arrived, the owner was standing in the front yard with a scowl on his face and his arms crossed over his chest. The property manager pulled the sign up and removed the lockbox as fast as he could. The owner asked him if he had gotten any offers.

111. The Divorced Tenant

During the lease term the tenants got divorced. The husband moved out. His name was removed from the lease by a mutually executed addendum. The lease was put in her maiden name. Later in the lease term, she remarried. She contacted the property manager, her new husband applied, was screened and qualified, and the lease was modified again. Her new husband's name and her new name were added to the lease. At the move-out inspection at the end of the lease term the property manager and female tenant discussed the changes in her life.

"You've had two name changes this year."

She said, "Thank God. My first husband was such a loser. I really married up the second time around."

He said, "Half of my friends are divorced. It's so common these days."

She said, "It's no wonder. There are so many choices."

"Choices?"

She said, "So many people in the world. You can always find a better one."

He said, "I hadn't thought of it that way."

"How about you and your wife? Are things good there?"

"Yes, yes."

She said, "You know what I mean though. You see all the other women out there. You can always trade up."

He said, "Maybe I could, but we own a house. It's a lot harder to change names on a mortgage than on a lease."

112. Why Don't You Just Move Out?

The tenant demanded upgrades and repairs before moving in. He demanded more repairs after moving in. He demanded repairs every month. He demanded new carpet, new paint, and new appliances. The tenant demanded parking permits be delivered to him. He demanded someone get him pool passes. He demanded the neighbors not mow their yards on Sunday. He demanded free mowing, free leaf raking, free shoveling of snow on his walkway, free cable TV. He demanded reimbursement whenever his power bills went up. He demanded reimbursement for high water bills.

Finally, the property manager was fed up, and said, "IF YOU HATE THE PLACE SO MUCH, WHY DON'T YOU JUST MOVE OUT?"

The tenant moved out the next weekend, unilaterally breaking the lease. The property manager didn't know if his spoken words gave the tenant a way out of the lease or not. He contacted an attorney, who told him that under state law, verbal agreements do not mitigate written contracts. But, said the attorney, the property manager would have a tough time in court and would look foolish. He recommended the property manager confess his mistake and face the music.

The property manager told the landlord the tenant had broken the lease. The landlord demanded to know why, and how. The property manager confessed it was partly his fault. He had verbally given the tenant an out. The tenant didn't have the right, but he had a point. The landlord demanded the property manager pay for his losses: lost rent, marketing costs, painting and cleaning, everything.

The property manager's firm paid for everything and took a loss. His boss gave the property manager hell. A new tenant was found and moved in. Everything was back on track. The landlord terminated the management contract and found another property management firm.

The property manager got a call from a lender. The tenant who had skipped out had chosen a house to buy, and applied for a home loan. Part of the qualifying process required the lender get a landlord reference. The lender wanted the property manager's opinion.

113. The Leaves Next Door

The tenant called the property manager in the fall. The neighbor had raked up leaves, and dumped them over the fence, into the tenant's yard. When the tenant complained, the neighbor said they were the tenant's leaves, then he began dumping the leaves on the tenant's front walk and rear deck. The tenant was afraid the neighbor was dangerous, or insane, or both. Could the property manager please talk to him?

The property manager knocked on the neighbor's door and politely asked the neighbor about the leaf problem.

The property manager said, "Good afternoon. I manage the rental next door."

"Good. I've been meaning to talk to you about the leaf problem."

"Yes. The tenants tell me you are putting your leaves in their yard?"

The neighbor said, "No, not my leaves. Every fall it's the same thing. The leaves fall from your clients' trees into my yard. I have to rake them up. I shouldn't have to. They're not my leaves."

"Oh. Let me see if I understand. You are responsible for the leaves from your trees and they are responsible for the leaves from their trees. But no one is responsible the leaves in their own yard, just for the leaves that originate from their own trees?"

"You make it sound crazy, but yes."

"So the other neighbor's yard, on the other side of your house, do you remove your trees' leaves from their yard?"

"My tree leaves don't go into their yard. The wind is different on that side."

"I see you have three oak trees and your neighbors on both sides have poplars. You and I could walk around and determine whose leaves are whose, by the shapes of the leaves."

"Don't you dare go in my yard."

"I just want to help. You have a right to your leaves and your neighbors have a right to theirs. The property lines don't matter anymore if we assign possession by leaf type and tree species. I'm on your side. We need to get to the bottom of this."

"I don't need you meddling in this."

"Oh, look. There. Oak leaves on the neighbor's driveway. Must be yours. You want me to get them for you?"

114. A Million Coat Hangers

A tenant who had recently moved out called the property manager.

"Where is the rest of my security deposit?"

"Let's see. We deducted thirty-five dollars for removal of coat hangers."

"Coat hangers? You're joking."

"No. You left behind a lot of coat hangers."

"Coat hangers. Big deal."

"The closets were full of coat hangers."

"So what. A few coat hangers."

"Like a million coat hangers."

"One million?"

"No. Sorry. It's right here. Two hundred and fifty coat hangers. Give or take."

"They're not mine."

"They weren't there when you moved in."

"How do you know? Can you prove it?"

"We take a hundred pictures at move-in and move-out."

"They could be pictures of any closets in any house."

"And we take a lot of notes."

"Where are these notes?"

"In files, in emails attachments, in the cloud. I can send you everything."

"They're not my coat hangers. I never saw any coat hangers."

"One coat hanger had a dry cleaning receipt attached. Your phone number was on it."

"OKAY. One coat hanger. I'll take responsibility for that one coat hanger."

"Disposing of one coat hanger costs the same as removing two hundred and fifty."

"Says who?"

"Thirty five dollars is the lowest minimum charge. The trip charge. The service call."

"You could have hired a kid to do it for ten bucks."

"I wouldn't hire a kid. Child labor laws, licenses, lawsuits, blah blah blah."

"I could have thrown out those coat hangers for free."

"That's what I'm saying."

115. Creaking Floors

"Property Management Services. How may I help you?"

"I need a repairman."

"What's wrong?"

"When my husband goes to the bathroom at night, the floors creak. It wakes me up."

"That's normal. Floors do squeak."

"But it's so loud. There must be something you can do."

"My floors are the same way. I just live with it."

"I'm paying over two thousand dollars per month in rent. I expect you to take care of it."

"In my house I pulled up the carpets and screwed the subfloor plywood back down tight to the floor joists. It still squeaks. Some houses are like that."

"I just can't sleep."

"I Googled it. A lot of houses have this issue."

"Could he fall through the floor?"

"No, but isn't your husband a really big guy?"

"What does that have to do with it?"

"I'm just saying."

"What's your name?"

"Can I come over and listen to the squeaky floors myself?"

"What's your job title?"

"Can I talk to your husband?"

"I want to talk to your supervisor."

116. My Mother is an Attorney

The property manager often had to deny tenant's requests for the return of their security deposits. Other times he denied requests for repairs, or for permission to add roommates or pets to the lease. Saying no, on behalf of the landlord, was a big part of his job. Saying no was sometimes followed by a tenant's threat to file a lawsuit. Often, the tenants who threatened to sue had no attorney, and no intention of hiring one.

Property manager: "No, I'm sorry but we cannot terminate the lease early."

Tenant: "If you don't, I'll sue you."

Property manager: "Who's your attorney?"

Tenant: "My mother's an attorney."

Property manager: "No, pets are not allowed in the property."

Tenant: "You don't know who you're talking to. My brother-in-law is an attorney."

Property manager: "The landlord refused your request to build a tree-house."

Tenant: "I could sue you. My wife is a paralegal."

Property manager: "No, sorry, you can't keep a horse in the back yard."
Tenant: "You'll be talking to my Jag officer."

Property manager: "You'll have to get rid of the above-ground pool. It's an HOA violation."
Tenant: "I'll sue you."
Property manager: "Who's your attorney?"
Tenant: "Bob Goodlaff."
Property manager: "He's a divorce attorney."

Tenant: "You'll be hearing from the Smithlock and Anderbook law firm."
Property manager: "Oh. I've seen their ads on TV. They aren't licensed in this state."

Tenant: "You don't know who I am. I'm an attorney."
Property manager: "I know. It's on your rental application. You're a patent attorney."

Tenant: "I have the best attorney in Spring City."
Property manager: "Spring City is five hours away. Your attorney will bill you for driving time. It will cost you three thousand dollars per court date."
Tenant: "I'll sue you for attorney's fees, too."

Tenant: "I've hired an attorney. You'll be hearing from Rob Prufrock."
Property manager: "Oh. He's a real landlord-tenant attorney. He's good. We don't want to go to court against him. Let's settle this out of court."

117. Stuck Windows

The tenant called the property manager after she moved in. She couldn't open the windows. The painter had painted them shut. They were stuck. She had tried everything.

The property manager called the painter. The painter said there would be an extra charge. The landlord refused to pay the extra charge.

The tenant called the town zoning office. She called the county fire marshal. She claimed the stuck windows provided no exit in case of fire. She convinced them to send an inspector. The inspector agreed with her. It was a code requirement that windows open for proper egress, especially in bedrooms. There were stories about families being trapped in their homes and dying in fires in the news regularly.

The code compliance officer gave the property manager and landlord written notice of a code violation. The landlord had thirty days to fix the problem. The landlord dragged his feet. Weeks passed. The property manager got an estimate for seven hundred dollars to un-stick the windows and clear the tracks of paint and obstruction. The landlord asked for two more estimates. It was too late. Thirty days were almost up.

The property manager made an appointment with the tenant to meet at the house and look at the windows himself. The tenant showed him the windows. She tried with all her strength to open them. She pushed upward on the lower sash and pulled down on the upper sash. They didn't budge. Paint was visible on the metal tracks in the frame. She tried until she was red in the face and panting.

The property manager tried the opposite approach. It was an old trick. He learned it after he painted his own house. He pushed the sashes in the opposite direction, as if he was trying to close them. It gave him much more leverage, because it allowed him greater arm extension. It also worked better, because there was usually less paint build-up at the end of the sash and track travel. The windows made a loud crack sound as they slid into the top header and bottom sill. Then they slid up and down normally.

The property manager un-stuck the rest of the windows swiftly. The tenant asked him why he hadn't done it earlier. Why had he waited so long? He said he wasn't paid to do repairs. He wasn't a licensed contractor. He had no contractor insurance. What if he had broken the glass? What if he had cut himself? The tenant didn't get it. He left.

The property manager called the landlord, who demanded to know why he hadn't unstuck the windows sooner. The property manager said that if he were a contractor he would have charged eighty-five dollars for the first hour and thirty-five dollars for each hour after that. He would include driving time and billing time. He would include offsets for license, bond and workman's comp. And gas. It would have cost over three hundred dollars. He asked the landlord if he would have paid that much. The landlord said, "No way."

118. Good Cop, Bad Cop

Two property managers went to the tenant's house to confront her about the neighbors' complaints. Too many parties, too many cars, too many people, and too many police calls. On the ride over, the property managers agreed that they did not have clear and provable lease violations. They did not witness the transgressions. They would not accuse the tenant based on second-hand reports. The neighbors had called the police but there had been no citations, no police reports, just verbal warnings. No paper trail.

They decided to play good cop, bad cop. The bad cop would make vague legal threats. The good cop would interrupt and try to work things out. The bad cop would be holding a file full of papers and threaten legal notices, subpoenas, and eviction. The good cop would say maybe the neighbors were too touchy. He would ask for her side of the story. They wanted her to admit to disturbing the neighborhood and apologize for their trouble. They hoped she would say she would change her ways. They wanted her to panic a little and promise to be a good little tenant from now on.

When they arrived there were no extra cars, no signs of extra people. The house and yard were perfect. The neighborhood was perfect.

They knocked. She answered the door. They asked if they could come in. She said no. She closed the door and locked it.

The good cop and bad cop went back to their office and wrote up notices of lease violations that would never make it to court. They mailed them by certified mail to the tenant. They sent letters to the neighbors asking them to please call the police again, and next time, please ask the police to make a written report. The property manager called the police and asked if they had a party policy. Did they measure decibel levels with some kind of sound meter when they were called out by noise complaints? Did they play good cop / bad cop? The police were amused.

One day an off-duty police officer came into their office looking for a house to rent. The property manager used the opportunity to ask him what the policy and procedure was for noisy party complaints. The officer said the police always try to convince people to talk to their neighbors and work things out amicably. He said police officers hate trying to settle petty personal disagreements. They would rather be chasing bank robbers. They would rather be shot at by drug lords.

119. The Neighbors Barged In

A young married couple rented a townhouse from the property manager. They had good income, credit, employment, and references. The landlord had readily accepted their application, but was still curious about "what kind of people" they were. Unbeknownst to the property manager, the landlord asked the neighbors to check up on the tenants. The neighbors went to the tenants' door and knocked. When the tenant opened the door, the neighbors walked right in without being invited. They said "Welcome to the Neighborhood" then asked nosy questions and snooped around. The next day the tenants called the property manager.

"The neighbors barged into our home."

"What?"

The tenant repeated, "The neighbors barged in and asked a lot of questions."

"What on earth for?"

"They were checking on us. Interrogating us for the landlord."

"Oh, god," said the property manager. "If that's true they were way out of line."

"We're pretty sure it's true. We would like an explanation and an apology."

"Ouch. I'll have to be careful how I bring it up. I don't want to accuse the owner."

"And tell the owner we won't be renewing our lease next year."

"Okay. I'll bring it up, but let's not assume the worst just yet."

The tenant said, "The next time any neighbors come around, we'll be ready."

"Yikes. That's no way to live. Do you want me to talk to the neighbors?"

"Do whatever you want. We know our rights."

The property manager called the landlord and asked if she was aware of the neighbor's intrusion.

"Oh, yes, we asked our neighbors to check up on them, just to be safe."

The property manager said, "Well, they feel like they're being spied on. It's not good. They will stay for the lease term, but no longer. They say they're out next year."

"We can always replace them."

"But they were perfect on paper. And I assume they were perfect in person?"

"Yes. Our neighbors loved them."

"Well, next year you might not get such good tenants, and you will have some vacancy time, fix-up costs, and some marketing costs. Keeping a good tenant an extra year can save you thousands."

"Listen to me. It's my house. I have to look out for my own best interest. You work for me, don't you?"

"Yes, you're right. Our contract with you says so, unless you go rogue."

"That's what I thought."

The property manager concluded, "I will take the blame, and apologize to the tenants. I won't talk to the neighbors, unless they barge in again. The tenants said they would call the police next time. I will just keep records of complaints, times, dates, calls, reports, statements made, and try to stay out of it as best I can. We'll make the best of it."

The owner replied, "What about hidden cameras? Can we install those?"

120. The Sex Dungeon

A house, formerly managed by the property manager, was in the news. Its new owner was arrested for human trafficking and transporting a minor across state lines. The police found a sex dungeon in the basement. The news reporters researched it and looked at the property tax records to see who the owner was. They accidentally published the name of the wrong owner, the former owner, a former client of the property manager, from ten years prior. The former homeowner, shocked to see his name associated with a house and crime he was not connected to, called the police and the newspapers, trying to clear his name, and then he called the property manager.

"What the hell is going on?"

"Oh, you read about the sex dungeon?"

"Read about it? I'm in it. They think I'm the pervert."

The property manager explained how the tax records list the names of all previous owners of the property. The reporters didn't know that, and used the wrong name.

The owner said, "Well, what should I do about it?"

"I don't know. You have to contact the reporters. You should publicize your innocence."

"Well, can't you help me? Aren't you in the property business? Aren't you a part of this whole mess?"

The property manager said, "No. Absolutely not. I'm not associated with you or the property anymore. I have nothing to do with the police report or news report. Like you, I don't want my name in this. I'm out. I wish I could help."

"Well can you recommend a course of action? Surely you must have come across this kind of thing before."

"Sex dungeons? No. Never. I know nothing about it. I'm a Presbyterian."

"Well, what is a sex dungeon anyway? What's in there?"

"I don't know. I've been happily married for twenty years. I don't know anything about sex. I mean sex dungeons."

121. Wearing Only a Towel

The property manager agreed to meet the new tenants at their house to assess the damage from a bathroom leak. The tenant wanted a new toilet and tub. The plumber recommended a new flapper and some caulk.

The husband answered the door and greeted the property manager. They walked upstairs to the bathroom in question. They opened the bathroom door to find the wife standing in front of the mirror wearing only a towel.

She said, "OOOHHH. I'M SORRY, I'M SORRY. CLOSE THE DOOR."

The property manager said, "OH, NO, I'M SORRY. I DIDN'T SEE ANYTHING. I'LL LEAVE."

The husband said, "You're not leaving until you look at that bathroom. Forget my wife. Every time we have company or contractors in the house, she's in a towel. Every time."

She said, "We never go out. I have no good clothes. What am I supposed to do? Wear a burka?"

The property manager turned and left. He called a plumber.

"Just caulk the tub and replace the flapper. Try to schedule the repairs with the husband, not the wife."

The plumber said, "Oh, one of those horny housebound housewife things?"

"God yes," said the property manager. "You get a lot of those?"

"Mister, you ain't seen nothin'."

"I didn't know what to do. I panicked and left."

The plumber said, "I either say I'm happily married or I'm gay."

"Does that work?"

"It all depends on that towel."

122. Wearing Only a Towel 2

The tenant agreed the property manager could inspect the house while he was at work. The property manager entered with his key. He inspected the main floor and the basement, then he went upstairs to the bedrooms. As he walked down the hall toward the master, the hall bathroom door opened and a woman, the tenant's wife, walked out into the hall wearing only a towel. She saw the property manager and screamed, jumping an inch or two off the floor. The property manager jumped and yelled too. She ran back into the bathroom and slammed the door. He ran downstairs and out the front door yelling "I'M SORRY, SORRY, SORRY, SORRY." He got in his car and called the husband. He told him about the jumping and screaming. The husband said, "Oh, I thought I told her you were coming. Sorry." The property manager said, "Don't sorry me. Call her and explain. Now, please. Before she calls the police or something."

The husband called his wife. The property manager called his office. The police were not called. After a few minutes the wife came out of the house in jeans and a sweatshirt and approached the property manager's car. He opened his car window.

She said, "I'm sorry about the mix-up. My husband is an idiot."

He said, "No, I'm sorry, so sorry. I didn't see anything. I was just scared. You popped out of nowhere and I, I'm sorry."

She asked, "Do you want to come in and inspect the house now? I think we can put it behind us. We're adults."

He said, "Alright. You're very kind. I already inspected the first two floors so it won't take long."

She said, "I wish I knew you were coming. The house is a mess."

He said, "That doesn't matter now. My report will say everything was perfect. You and your husband are perfect tenants. I'll tell the landlord everything is perfect."

She said, "But no mention of me being half naked and all?"

"No, no, no, no, no. Don't even say the word naked. I'm still shaking."

"Hey. I work out and all. It wasn't that bad, was it?"

He laughed nervously but he couldn't look at her. She giggled and walked up the sidewalk toward the house. "Come on. Grow up. Get in here and finish your inspection."

The property manager followed her, ten feet behind, staring at his clipboard.

123. It Slows Down in the Fall

The property manager was hired in the spring. During June the workload doubled. In July there were so many move-ins and move-outs he couldn't keep up. In August the office was total chaos. Managers were running in and out, filing reports and making appointments, working ten hours a day. The new property manager was feeling overwhelmed.

A veteran property manager in the office told the new guy "It slows down in the fall."

The new guy said, "I hope so."

The veteran said, "Everyone moves in the summer so they can get their kids in school by September. The market is hot, prices are prime, and we move rentals like hot cakes. In the fall we put our feet up and catch our breath."

"Thank God" said the rookie.

They were relieved when September came, but there was still a backlog of reports and repairs. They looked forward to October, but October was busy with a marketing drive for new clients. Come November and December they were busy with late rents and collections, because tenants had holiday expenses, and were trying to juggle their credit card bills. In January there was an ice storm and they were overloaded with frozen pipes, leaks, falling trees, wet ceilings and downed gutters.

The new guy asked, "Hey, didn't you say work slows down in the fall?"

The veteran laughed. "We say that in the summer. It gives us hope."

"Did it slow down for you?"

"Well," said the veteran, "I'm working forty hours a week instead of fifty, so yes."

The rookie said, "Oh, I guess I am working fewer weekends and evenings."

"See? It is slower. It's just the same stress level. That never changes."

The rookie said, "I'm thinking about taking a vacation, for that stress thing."

The veteran said, "Okay, but when you come back, you'll have a thousand emails and voicemails. You'll never catch up. You'll worry about that your whole vacation."

"You know, you've taught me a lot of valuable things about property management, and I consider you a friend, but you're a total asshole."

"Oh, yeah, I forgot to tell you. In your second year here you become a total asshole."

124. I Bought a House

The tenant called the property manager and said, "I just bought a house. How do I get out of the lease?"

"Well, you don't. It's a one-year contract."

"But how do I break the lease?"

"You can only break it with a mutual written lease termination agreement with the landlord."

"How do I do that?"

"You can mail or email me a written request with your terms and conditions. I will forward it to the landlord and he will reply in writing, saying 'no thank you'."

"Why wouldn't he want me to buy a house?"

"It's not that. You agreed to pay twelve months rent. He wants to stick with that."

"So I can't move out?"

"You can move. The house is not a prison. But you have to continue to pay rent."

"Why should I pay rent if don't live there?"

"When you buy a new car, do you just leave your old car by the side of the road and stop making payments?"

"Don't be ridiculous."

"I'm just saying you can't terminate a contract unilaterally."

"What if I just move and stop paying rent?"

"We'll file a warrant in debt and get a judgement in court. Just like you would if someone defaulted on a contract with you."

"I don't think you can do that."

"We do that. When we do, there are dozens of property managers, and landlords, and tenants, in a courtroom. The tenants fall like dominoes. A judgement goes on your credit report and makes it harder to buy a house, or a car, or anything."

"Are you threatening me?"

"No, I'm describing our policies and procedures in cases of defaults on leases."

"I don't think you can do that. I'll talk to an attorney."

"Oh, thank God. I was afraid we were going to have to argue all day. Please let me know what your attorney says. Just give him your lease and tell him you want to move and walk away from your house and contract. Your attorney will understand."

"What do you want from me? I just bought a house. American dream and all that."

"Congratulations. But I want you to stay where you are and pay rent. Where is your new house?"

"I'm still looking."

125. A Million Dildos

The property manager inspected a house when the tenant was at work, after giving her proper and reasonable written notice of entry, and getting her acknowledgement by phone. He found the house clean and neat, but a lot of personal property was stuffed into overflowing closets, as if she had quickly cleaned up for the inspection.

When he was inspecting her bedroom he tripped over something protruding from under the bed. It was a rubbery duplicate of a male sex organ. It was significantly larger than real life, as far as he knew.

Against his better judgement, he kneeled and peeked under the bed. There were battery-operated massage devices, strap-on things, chokers and chains. He made no note of the fact, and considered it none of his business. Nevertheless, it stayed on his mind as he drove back to the office.

Back in his cubicle, he gathered his male co-workers around and told them.

"You should have seen. I was inspecting Maple Street and found a million dildos."

"Maple? I know that woman. I moved her in, I think."

"I met her when she signed the lease in the conference room. She didn't look like she needed a million dildos."

"What does a woman who needs dildos look like?"

"Lonely?"

"Come on. They're no different than men."

"Oh, you have a million dildos?"

"No. I mean we have magazines and things."

"I thought we were talking about a woman and her dildos. I don't want to think about you and your magazines."

"Hey, what if that dildo was moved when you tripped on it, and she notices it out of place?"

"SHIT."

"What if she calls here and complains to the boss?"

"She could sue you for sexual harassment."

"Or violating her privacy."

"Or disturbing the piece."

126. In the Closet with a Knife

The tenant stopped paying rent for two months. The property manager filed for Unlawful Detainer, won possession and back rent in court, got a writ of possession, and met the sheriff and a locksmith at the house. All in compliance with the lease and the law, with due process, and on the order of the court.

When he arrived there was no sign of the tenant's car. He assumed the tenant had fled. The locksmith was waiting in his van for permission from the sheriff to change the locks. The sheriff stood at the front door wearing a bulletproof vest, a holstered Beretta, extra magazines, handcuffs, and a belt full of things like tasers and pepper spray. The property manager approached.

The property manager said, "Good morning. I appreciate your assistance. Is the tenant here?"

The sheriff replied, "Don't know. Here's the plan. The locksmith will unlock the door. I will enter and clear the house. Once it's clear I will escort you in. Then I'll tell the locksmith to start rekeying or replacing locks."

"Clear the house? What does that mean?"

"Make sure the tenant is gone and you are in no danger."

"What kind of danger do you usually encounter?"

"Once, a guy jumped out of a closet with a knife. Another time there was a shotgun tied to a chair in the foyer with a string from the trigger to the door knob."

"No! You do this every day?"

"We do fifty a day in this county. Ever since the real estate bubble broke. You know, evictions, foreclosures, bankruptcies."

"What's the worst thing you've seen?"

"One guy hung himself in the living room before he could be evicted."

"Wow. I thought my job was hard."

"This isn't hard. Hard is going into drug houses and finding crack mothers and babies. Hard is sitting by the highway all day with a radar gun and not catching anybody. This is a piece of cake. Almost all the deadbeat tenants skip town before we get here."

"I appreciate everything you do. It's good to know you're on our side."

"I'm not on your side. You shouldn't rent to deadbeats. You should screen your tenants better. And when everything turns to shit, you should talk to them, and help them find something they can afford. You're just clogging up the courts."

"Oh. Sorry. Anyway, thanks for the knife-jumping, shotgun-booby-trap stories."

"Glad to be of service, sir."

127. Cleaning Supplies

The landlord moved out and the tenant moved in. The house was empty, except for cleaning supplies under the kitchen sink, on shelves over the washer-dryer, and in the utility room.

The new tenant said, "What's all this crap doing here?"

The property manager said, "The owner left it. I guess he thought you could use it."

"Do I look like I can't afford my own Windex?"

"No. People leave stuff like that behind for some reason."

"It's an insult. Half a thing of Tide? Who wants that?"

"It happens all the time. I don't know why."

"What's that? A broom and a dust pan? I have a broom and a dustpan."

"Sorry. I'll remove this stuff myself right now."

"I want you to report this to the owner."

"But I'm solving the problem right now."

"It's the principle."

"What principle?"

"The pissed-off principle."

"How do you like the house overall?"

"I love the house. What's your point?"

"I like to look on the bright side."

"You're just defending the owner."

"I believe people are basically good."

"What?"

"The sun will come up tomorrow."

"God almighty. Get this stuff out of my house."

"Okay. I can use some of this stuff. Look. A dustbuster. Cool."

"Hey. Leave that. I could use that."

128. That's My Storage Space

When the tenant moved into a vacant house he filled the closets and storage areas first. There was a large closet in the basement that was locked with a deadbolt. A note on the door said, "Do not use. Storage for homeowner only."

The tenant called the property manager.

"Hey, what's the deal with the locked closet?"

"Oh, the owner left her stuff in there."

"But that's my closet."

"She just wanted to leave some things in there. She didn't think you'd mind."

"But isn't that my closet? Aren't I paying for twenty three hundred square feet? Not twenty-two fifty."

"You have a point there. Do you have any flexibility or should I have the closet emptied?"

"Empty the closet. Or reduce my rent."

"You mean reduce rent proportionally to the space denied?"

"No I mean reduce it by a hundred dollars."

"What formula are you using?"

"I'm using the formula that it's my house now, every square foot, and I demand satisfaction."

"I can come to your house now and remove everything from the closet."

"You're just trying to appease me."

"Yes. Yes sir. That's exactly right."

"That's not good enough."

"What else do you want?"

"An apology."

"Written or spoken?"

"Both."

"I'll type one up and come over right now and apologize verbally too."

"Is that all?"

"Do you want me to grovel?"

"Are you making fun of me?"

"Trying to keep it light."

"Very unprofessional."
"See you in thirty minutes."

129. The Crack

At the annual inspection the property manager noted a crack in the drywall. It was a hairline crack over a door frame. It was a normal settlement crack. As a house settles, the stiff drywall and brittle patching compounds crack, and need occasional taping and spackling. It's normal routine maintenance.

The rookie property manager was not familiar with construction. Instead of writing "settlement crack" in his report he wrote "foundation crack." A foundation crack is a crack in the block or concrete floor, walls or foundation, often the poured concrete basement walls. It would have been very serious. The inexperienced property manager didn't know the difference.

The inspection report was sent to the landlord overseas. The landlord looked up the definition of "foundation crack." He panicked, thinking his house was falling apart, and flew home to see the crack. He called his insurer and arranged to meet a structural engineer at the house.

Two property managers met the landlord at the house. The rookie who had inspected the house showed the crack over the bedroom door to the landlord. The veteran property manager explained it was not a serious foundation crack, it was just a drywall crack, a common occurrence. It was basically cosmetic. The landlord agreed. He had thoroughly researched household cracks after the inspection report. He was relieved it was not a crisis, but upset he had been misinformed.

The young property manager who did the inspection said, "Oh. Sorry for the mix-up." The older property manager said, "It won't happen again." The landlord said, "Do you know how much my airfare was?"

130. The Paint Color Chart

A landlord was returning to her home after renting it out for five years. She asked the property manager to have the interior painted white. The property manager hired a painter, and it was done for eighteen hundred dollars.

The landlord came home and walked through her home. It was freshly painted off-white. She called the property manager and complained that she had said white, not off-white. The property manager said interiors are generally painted off-white. The landlord said she wanted white. The property manager said white was usually used in industrial and sterile applications like kitchens, operating rooms, and garages. The landlord insisted she said white. She had it in writing. White.

After much disagreement, the landlord sued the property manager for eighteen hundred dollars plus attorney's fees and court costs.

In court, the plaintiff made her claim, showing her correspondence requesting white paint. The defendant rebutted, saying that white paint was not in style for traditional home interiors. He said he had the painter as his witness, with a color chart, waiting out in the anteroom. The painter was called to the stand. He said he had painted a thousand houses, always in oyster white or bone white. No one ever used white in traditional or colonial homes, just in the occasional modern or contemporary home. He had worked with dozens of interior decorators and looked at millions of paint charts, carpet samples and fabric swatches. He offered as evidence some interior color charts from major paint stores and manufacturers.

The judge said that color was a subjective matter. He and his wife had discussed decorating colors for years and never seen eye to eye. He knew the difference between white off-white. He had used an interior decorator. He warned the attorneys to settle their frivolous case, or he would render a judgment both would dislike.

The attorneys, landlords, property manager, and painter gathered in the anteroom. They tried to discuss color but the painter was the only one who knew a shade from a tint. He knew what color the White House and the Louvre were painted. He knew his trade and related trades. The attorneys asked their clients to drop it and just pay attorney's fees. The landlord refused. The painter offered to repaint the interior white for the cost of materials. The landlord said no, she no longer wanted her house to be white anymore. She just wanted eighteen hundred dollars.

Out of court settlement failed. The case was heard. The judge split the difference. The property manager would refund half the cost of painting, or nine hundred dollars. The landlord would not pocket the money, but would have the work done and provide the property manager an invoice when the repainting was done. The painter would be reimbursed by both parties for the cost of one day's lost labor for his day in court. The judge scanned the galley and said that if there were any more vague and vindictive cases on the docket, they should settle out of court now, or be dismissed with prejudice. The docket would be cleared by three, come hell or high water.

131. How Does the Thermostat Work?

A difficult tenant rented a house in the summer. Her English was fair but she was unfamiliar with American houses. The AC was off and the house was hot. The tenant had never seen an American digital thermostat. She asked the property manager how it worked. He turned on the AC, walking her through the process, gave her the manual, and showed her the website address where there were also instructions and specifications.

Six months later, at the mid-term inspection in mid-winter, the heat was off and the house was cold. The tenant still had not figured out the thermostat. He gave her a tutorial again and showed her the online manual.

At the move-out the next summer the house was hot and the AC off. The tenant complained the heat and air-conditioning never worked. She had never figured out the thermostat. Could she have all of her rent money back?

132. The Jewelry Box

The property manager showed a rental property to two prospective tenants. The house was occupied, and the existing tenant was aware of the appointment and knew the property manager would enter using the key in the lockbox, while the tenants were at work. While being shown the house, the husband suddenly veered off to the basement while the wife went upstairs to the bedroom level. The property manager had been taught to keep groups of prospective tenants together at all times and observe them so that the occupants' belongings would not be disturbed by nosy applicants. When his clients split up, the property manager started to follow the husband, then thought better of it and hurried upstairs to the master bedroom. The wife was standing in front of the bureau. On top of it was an open jewelry box. The property manager did not believe anything amiss. He asked her to accompany him downstairs and catch up with her husband. The couple suddenly lost interest. They said it was not the house for them. The property manager asked if he could show them more houses. They said no thanks. They had seen enough for one day.

When he returned to his office he talked to his employer. Had he ever heard of potential renters stealing anything? Or couples working together to deceive realtors? His boss said he had not heard of anything like that since they changed from old-fashioned keyed lockboxes to electronic lockboxes. Once, many years ago, there was an unconfirmed story about a customer stealing some cash from a drawer during a house showing, but the occupant declined to press charges because he was not sure how much cash there was, so there probably wasn't much. Nonetheless, it brought to a halt all marketing and showing of that house until after the move-out.

Rumors about realtors, property managers or their customers occasionally surface, but modern electronic lockboxes record the time and date of every entry, and the name and license of each realtor who enters, so most accusations have been shown to be "misunderstandings." In this case, the property manager was certain he had nearly been conned. After that he always herded his customers together in a cluster, all in one room at a time. If one person left the group and disappeared, he declared the showing over and marched them all out of the house.

133. Dead Animal in the Wall

A tenant complained about a smell in the house. It was getting worse. The property manager visited and they agreed it was worst near the outside wall of the dining room. They searched, found nothing in the heat ducts or under the carpet.

The property manager had recently heard a pitch from a home inspector who had an infrared device that could detect cold spots and hot spots behind the drywall. It helped to locate missing insulation, leaking ducts, holes in sidings, sometimes even wet spots. The infrared imaging was like heat-vision. Like superman's x-ray vision or some CSI gadget.

The technology was relatively new but not expensive to use. The contractor gave him an introductory bargain price for his first house, so he could demonstrate it and drum up business.

The contractor walked through the house with the tenant and property manager, scanning walls and reading normal variations where insulation was thicker or thinner. When they scanned the dining room wall in question, there was a hotspot near the floor. He asked permission to cut a hole in the drywall and look inside. The property manager and tenant agreed.

He cut open the wall. The smell got much worse. In the hole there was the rotting carcass of a mouse that had died in the wall. Decomposition releases heat which shows up on infrared.

The problem was identified, but not quite solved. The property manager asked the contractor if he would remove the varmint. No, that wasn't his job. Would he mitigate the smell, or disinfect or deodorize? No, not his area. The property manager made an appointment to return the next day with rubber gloves, plastic trash bags, a shop-vac, Lysol, bleach, rags, and anything else he could think of.

The property manager told other property managers the story. No one had ever heard of such a thing. He asked if they had ever dealt with bad smells like that. Yes they had, but eventually the smells go away. Eventually bacteria, ants, bugs or worms or God knows what, eats everything up and the smell is gone. Of course, sometimes the tenant has fled by then, too. The property manager started a smell file called Odors: Causes and Remedies. In his office they dubbed him the King of Stink.

134. Police at the Door

The property manager entered a vacant house that was for rent. There was a for rent sign in the yard and a lockbox on the door. He didn't know the Neighborhood Watch was watching.

A watchful neighbor called the police after the property manager entered. After his walk-through, as he was about to leave, a police officer tried to push the front door open. The property manager was right inside the door and pushed back, thinking it might be an intruder. The police pushed again. The property manager pushed back harder.

The officer warned, "Glendale Police! Open Up!"

The property manager replied, "Jak Vaille! Property Management Services!"

He opened the door. The police officer entered with one hand on his holster.

The officer said, "A neighbor called us. They thought you were suspicious."

"I am," said the property manager. He showed his business card.

The officer looked around at the empty house and said, "Don't push back next time."

"Next time?" asked the property manager.

The officer left. The property manager walked out the front door and waved to all the neighboring houses and smiled. Maybe someone was watching. He wanted them to recognize him next time.

135. The Alarm System

The property manager made an appointment to inspect a rental. The tenant said she would not be home. He entered with his key. The alarm system went off, emitting a piercing sound. The tenant had forgotten to turn it off for the inspection. The property manager could flee, or try to disarm the alarm with the keypad. He found the control panel in the kitchen and punched 0000 into the keypad, then 1234. No luck. Then he called the tenant at work to ask for the code but he couldn't hear her over the alarm. The alarm alerted the police, who arrived while the property manager was still in the kitchen trying to disconnect the security panel from the wall.

The police entered through the front door, which the property manager had left unlocked. Two officers crept up behind him in the kitchen and yelled "Police!" over the alarm noise. He turned around to see two uniformed officers with their hands on their holsters. He shouted back "Property Manager!" and showed his hands. They walked him outside and asked him a few questions. The police, satisfied he was not an intruder, drove away. The property manager remained standing on the front walk, with the alarm still going off, as all the neighbors came out and watched him with their hands on their hips and scowls on their faces.

The tenant left work and came home. She apologized to the property manager in the driveway and went in to kitchen. She entered 1111 in the keypad. The alarm stopped. The neighbors disappeared. The property manager called his office. He told them about the hands on the holsters, his blood pressure, his pounding headache from the alarm, and said he was going home to lie down for the rest of the day.

136. Home Invasion

A family rented a house from the property manager. At the move-in inspection they asked if they could add door locks or a security system. The property manager asked the owner, who agreed.

Two weeks later the tenant reported an attempted break-in. Nothing was broken or stolen. The tenants read in the papers about a string of home invasions in the area. Without permission, they built a wall at the top of the stairs on the bedroom level, with a solid door and two deadbolts. The top floor was a panic room. Any home invaders would have to stay downstairs.

The property manager did a winter inspection and was shocked to see the wall and door separating the levels. He explained that interior doors and locks would impede escape in a fire. Interior locks should not be keyed or bolted. It was fire code. The tenants explained their fear of home invasions, especially after first incident.

The property manager asked what the police had said about the supposed break-in attempt, because nothing had been broken or taken. The tenants admitted they had not called the police. He asked them what the neighbors had seen? They never talked to the neighbors. How did they know there was an invasion? They said they heard the front door open in the middle of the night and heard voices and footsteps. The property manager asked if he could look around. Everything was normal, except their teenage son's room. It had a padlock on the door and a black sign that said Pit of Despair.

The property manager asked where the teenager was. They didn't know. He had quit school. He came and went at all hours. He was in with a bad crowd. He had his own key.

The property manager suggested it had been their son, not an intruder. He told them to remove the security wall and door and return the property to its original condition. He told them to talk to their son about it.

The tenants asked the property manager if he could help them find an apartment or something for their son.

137. Memory

A landlord returned from abroad after renting her house out for five years. She met the property manager at the house and inspected for damage.

"Look at the dining room curtain rod. It's bent. Is that a security deposit issue?"

"My notes say that was bent before you left."

"What about the living room wall paint? It's scuffed up."

"It was scuffed up before you left. The tenant didn't seem to mind."

"There are nicks in the counter. Did the tenant do that?"

"Those were there before, according to my inspection reports."

"The carpet is torn in the corner there."

"That was like that before, too."

"I don't remember all these things being like that before."

"You lived here with it fully furnished. You only saw it empty for a few hours before you left. When it's empty you see all these little things."

"Well, what is the tenant supposed to pay for?"

"They just pay rent. Their deposit is for damage above and beyond normal wear and tear."

"Don't I get any of it? I always thought the house would be fixed up when I got back."

"That's up to you. Once you start fixing it up, you'll enjoy the process. It won't feel like it's your home again until you're hands-on."

"I just want it back the way it was."

"Let me send you the pictures I took of the house when you moved out."

"I thought it was perfect."

"It wasn't. Not perfect at all."

"Are you sure?"

"See that dent in the front door?"

"Yes. Did the tenant do that?"

"No. Your son did that carrying out his bar bells."

"Are you sure?"

"Yes. You and I were in the kitchen. You yelled at him."

"Oh. I forgot about that."

"You had a million things to do. I was here to get the house keys from you. Remember you forgot to get the change of address form from the post office? Remember when the movers dropped the end table?"

"Oh. Yes. I remember that. That was the worst day ever."

"Moving is very stressful."

"You must have a good memory."

"I have a terrible memory in my house. But in your house I take notes."

"What are you writing in your notes now?"

"I just noticed your dining room chandelier is missing. See those loose wires?"

"Oh, I didn't notice."

138. Wood Floors

The landlord moved out. He had just installed brand new wood floors.

"I love these floors. Please make sure the tenant takes good care of them."

"I will. There might be some wear or fade though."

"Don't say that. My heart will break."

The house was rented. The property manager warned the tenant to respect the floors. The tenants took off their shoes and wore only socks whenever they were in the house.

The landlord came back two years later to review the house and look around.

"Oh, my wood floors. They're not new anymore. What have you done to them?"

"That's just some fading from sunlight. See, it's only in the south-facing rooms. Your wood floors have held up great."

"Can you tell the next tenants to keep the curtains closed to keep the sun out?"

"No, but the floors still look great to me."

The landlord rented the house again. The property manager begged the next tenant to be careful on the floors. The landlord loved those floors ridiculously.

Three years later the tenant moved out and the landlord returned to house. There was a foot-long scratch on the wood floor where the mover had dragged a chair leg. When the landlord saw it, the property manager apologized and promised it would be fixed.

The property manager said, "We'll fix it. It'll be like new. Sorry, sorry, sorry."

The landlord said, "No problem. We might refinish the floors, remodel, and sell the house. Who knows? Not a problem."

139. The Cardboard Box

The tenants were moving out. When the property manager arrived there was a moving truck in the driveway. Friends and family were packing and taping boxes. The house was almost empty. There was a cardboard box on the lawn by the walk.

The property manager asked, "May I look around the house now?"

"Sure," said the dad.

"Help yourself," said mom.

As he walked up the walk to the house he heard "Hey Mister. Look. We're in the box" from a little boy and girl inside the big cardboard box.

The property manager inspected the house, took notes, and took pictures. He looked at the main level for ten minutes or so, then the basement level for five minutes, then went up to the bedroom level. After he looked at the bedrooms, there was one room left. He opened the hall bathroom door. The little boy from the cardboard box had gone upstairs to bathe. The door knob hit him in the head. He started crying and screaming. He was naked.

The property manager said, "SORRY" and scrambled downstairs.

He passed the dad in the foyer and said, "SORRY."

Dad said, "WHAT DID YOU DO?"

He passed the mom on the front steps and said, "SORRY."

Mom said, "GET OUT OF OUR HOUSE."

As he walked past the cardboard box, the little girl inside said, "You in twubble."

140. The Invisible Taxi

A tenant moved into a townhouse community that had strict HOA rules. No work trucks, no work vans, no cars or trucks with signage or advertising on them. No vehicles with ladder racks, no taxi cabs, and no pizza delivery signs on cars. The HOA strove to look like a family community, to maintain an appearance that would keep property values up.

The tenant moved in and parked his taxi in front of the house. He received a violation notice on his windshield warning it would be towed. He called the property manager.

"They're going to tow my taxi."

"The HOA doesn't allow business vehicles."

"Why didn't you tell me?"

"The listing said there were HOA rules. You agreed to comply in your lease."

"Why didn't you tell me?"

"I asked you to come to my office before you signed the lease."

"I didn't have time."

"On your application you left the vehicle section blank."

"My taxi is going to be towed."

"Did you call the number on the notice? Did you ask how you can comply?"

"No."

"Have you looked for blank magnetic signage covers?"

"What's that?"

"A blank magnetic sign panel that covers up the taxi signs."

"I don't get it."

"You buy a magnetic sign panel that matches your car paint. It covers the letters and your car looks like a regular car.

Like an invisible taxi. Then you take the magnets off when you're working."

"Where do I get those?"

"Did you ask your taxi company?"

"No."

"Do you talk to other taxi drivers about their parking problems?"

"No. Why didn't you tell me about it?"

"At the airport you can only park in the designated area, right?"

"Yes, that's different."

"At the hotels they only have one area for taxis."

"Okay, okay."

"You're in a highly regulated industry."

"But why didn't you tell me?"

"Why didn't you tell me you were a cab driver?"

"It was on my application."

"Nope. You put 'Limo Driver' on your application."

"That's what I call it. I do taxi and limo service."

"Why didn't you tell me?"

"How much do the magnets cost?"

"Less than the cost of towing and impoundment."

141. Boat in the Garage

A tenant moved into a neighborhood that had many HOA regulations about vehicles and parking. They had rules against RVs, motor homes, trailers, boats and work trucks. The tenant had never lived in a community with rules. He parked his boat on the street.

The property manager called him. "The community association sent us a violation notice. It says you have a boat parked on the street."

"Yes, I do."

"Sorry, but that's not allowed by the HOA."

"What's an HOA?"

"An association of all the owners of houses in your neighborhood. They have rules."

"Why didn't you tell me? I have a boat."

"Your lease says no vehicle storage. Including boat trailers."

"That's insane. Everyone I know has a boat."

"You have to move the boat. Will it fit in the garage?"

"How should I know?"

"Do you have a tape measure?"

"Okay, it's just a little outboard. I'll put it in the garage."

A month later the property manager got another violation notice. The boat was still visible. The property manager arranged to meet the tenant at the house.

"Oh, I get it," said the property manager. "The front of the boat trailer is sticking out. The garage door won't close. The trailer's a foot too long."

"I shoved the boat in as far as I could."

"It's still a foot too long."

"What can I do?"

"Why don't you take the motor off?"

"Oh. Good idea."

142. The Double Murder

A condo was rented to two young women. They had entry-level jobs and sold drugs on the side to make ends meet. One of their drug customers came to their door one day without calling ahead and demanded drugs. They were fresh out. He demanded drugs. He needed something immediately to calm him down. They said, no, they had nothing for him.

The drug customer forced his way into the condo and searched for drugs. They demanded he leave. He bludgeoned them to death.

The police cleared the house. The medical examiner said the cause of death was blunt force trauma. The police searched the house and found a check written to one of the victims. The owner of the checking account had priors. They went to the address on the check and arrested the killer.

The property manager hired a carpet company to remove the bloody carpet. The carpet guy walked out when he saw the blood. The property manager hired a painter. The painter left when he saw blood on the walls. The property manager offered a contractor a hundred dollars an hour to remove the carpet, clean the sub-floor and walls of blood, and use bleach and primer to neutralize all visual evidence of the crime. The contractor said he would do it for two hundred dollars an hour, no estimate, no limit. The property manager and the landlord had to say yes. The condo was made to look new.

Realtors showed the house, but they felt obliged to disclose the murders. There was too much news coverage to cover it up. The condo wouldn't rent. The property manager lowered the price. He lowered the price again. After a year the condo was rented to two construction laborers. They had heard all the news. They thought it was cool. They gave tours of the house for twenty dollars a head. They made five hundred dollars on Halloween.

143. Smoke Smell

A condo was rented. The occupants in the condo below were chain-smokers. The smell permeated the neighboring condos. The new tenants couldn't stand the smell. They had children. They were worried about their health. They moved out. The property manager returned their deposit and let them move without penalty or obligation.

The condo was put back on the rental market. The smell was too much for any tenant to stand. No one wanted to live there. The property manager talked to the tenant below.

"Your smoking is ruining the condo upstairs."

"Oh, no. Sorry."

"Can you smoke outside? Can you help me out?"

"Sorry. We can't smoke at work. We can't smoke in restaurants and bars. We can't smoke anywhere any more. We're definitely going to smoke in our own home. We can't help you."

The property manager hired contractors to seal cracks and vents in the condo. It didn't solve the problem. He hired home inspectors. They told him there were too many ways for smoke to penetrate: dead space, plumbing stacks, electric conduit openings, floor and wall joints and seams, bathroom vent stacks, countless openings between condos.

The property manager called the condo association. They had no pertinent regulations in place yet. He consulted an attorney, who couldn't find court precedents. He searched state court records online for related lawsuits, but found none. He visited dozens of websites with relevant news articles. He could find no legal remedy. He could sue the smokers, or he could sue the builder, but there were no relevant laws or precedents to back him up.

The property manager contacted the owner of the unit below and told him his tenants were offending all of the neighbors. He convinced him not to extend their lease, for the sake of his own property damage as well, when it expired. Ten months later the smokers moved out. The owners of both condos, upstairs and down, renovated and sold their condos, at a loss. The property manager closed the account and filed the folder in his "Smell" file. The Smell File included smell cases involving:

1. Cigarette Smoke.
2. Marijuana Smoke.
3. Kitchen fire smoke.
4. Chimney soot and creosote.
5. Rotten Food.
6. Dead Mice.
7. Garbage.
8. Litter Boxes.
9. Pets.
10. Wet basements.
11. Mold.
12. Dirty ductwork
13. Clogged filters
14. Gas.
15. Children.
16. College students.

144. Gas Smell

The tenant reported a gas smell. The property manager asked if it was coming from the gas meter. No. Was it coming from the basement? No. Was it coming from the garage? No. Did it smell like gasoline? No. Did it smell like natural gas? No. Did it smell like propane? No. Did it smell like swamp gas? No. Did it smell like sulfur? No. Did it smell like rotten eggs? No.

The property manager asked, "Well, what does it smell like?"

"Like gas. Like farts."

"Where do you smell it?"

"In the bathroom."

"Is it all the time?"

"No."

"When does it occur?"

"After someone uses the bathroom."

"How long does it last?"

"Up to a half hour."

"Have you talked to your roommates about it?"

"Not yet. I wanted to talk to you first."

145. The House with No Address

Someone saw a For Rent sign in front of a house. He parked in front of the house and called the property management's phone number on the sign.

"How much is the rent on this house?"

"Which house?"

"The one with the For Rent sign."

"We have a lot of houses with signs in the yard. What is the address?"

"I don't know. I just saw the house and pulled over."

"What street are you on?"

"I don't know. I didn't look."

"Can you go to the end of the street and look at the sign?"

"It's a little white house. White fence."

"What town are you in?"

"Don't you know how much the rent is?"

"I don't know what house it is."

"How many houses can there be?"

"We currently have over thirty houses on the market with signs in the yard."

"How much are they?"

"Anywhere from a twelve hundred to thirty-five hundred a month."

"This is probably the twelve hundred one. It's little."

"What is the street number? I can search our inventory by the number on the house."

"I don't know."

"Is there a number on the mailbox?"

"I don't know. I'm driving now. I'm way down the street now."

"Well, keep my phone number. I can show you lots of houses."

"I'm not looking for a house. I'm just out for a drive. Just curious."

"Oh. Then let me recommend our competition. Raven Rentals. 702-555-6789. They have a lot more houses on the market than we do. Call them."

"Should I mention you referred me?"

"No. Don't use my name. I just want to give them the business."

146. Well-Dressed Painters

The property manager hired a painting company that gave him the lowest of three bids to paint the interior of a client's house. Two painters came to his office in dark suits and ties to pick up the keys. The property manager was curious. Contractors are generally dressed in work clothes. He had never met one in a suit.

Two days later he drove to the house to see how the painting was progressing. He entered and found the painters working in their boxers. Their suits were hung on hangers in the foyer closet. They had a system.

147. The Painter Who Wouldn't Leave

A painter was hired to paint the interior of a large house. He worked alone. It was a big house so it would take him two weeks. His price was low, so he got the job.

After two weeks, the property manager went to the house. The front door was locked. The painter came to the door and said the property manager should stay out because of the fumes. He said he was a perfectionist and it would take a while longer.

A week later the property manager went to the house again. The painter was still there but asked the property manager to stay out because there was wet paint everywhere. It was too messy; he should come back later. He said he would take a little longer, maybe a week.

A week later the property manager went to the house at night. The painter's van was in the driveway. The house lights were on. He peeked in the window. The painter was cooking dinner. He had a bed and TV in the living room. His kids were sleeping in a tent in the rec room. The property manager rang the doorbell. The painter answered. He said he wasn't quite finished. He needed more time. It would be the best paint job ever. He asked if he could get paid now. He needed money to buy paint.

148. Long Distance Phone Call

The property manager couldn't collect rent from some foreign exchange students in one of his rentals. He emailed and left messages at the sponsoring embassy. They called him back.

"Hello. Embassy desk calling."

"Oh, thanks for calling. You got my email."

"Yes. How can we help you?"

"My email detailed a debt owed by your transfer students."

"We pay the student's expenses directly to them."

"They paid rent for the first two months. Now, nothing."

"The students receive three thousand per month for housing."

"That's plenty. Their rent is more like two thousand."

"You should contact them about payment."

"I have, many times. They don't respond. They're never home. Please help."

"You should take it up with foreign education sponsor, not us."

"My only recourse now is to evict them."

"Is that legal?"

"Yes. It happens all the time."

"We don't have eviction in Qatar."

"Can you direct me to the sponsoring organization?"

"Can you come to our office?"

"Where is your office?"

"Doha."

"Aren't you calling from the embassy in D.C.?"

"I'm in Dohar. Do you have our address?"

"No. I'm in the U.S., thousands of miles away."

"Oh. I see."

"What I propose is this: Pay up or I tell every property manager and landlord in the state that your students don't pay rent and you don't care."

"You shouldn't do that."

"And I'll write letters to the embassy, and to the ambassador."

"That's not necessary."

"I'll protest outside embassy with signs that say your citizens don't pay their debts."

"You can't do that."

"I'll contact the State Department Public Affairs desk."

"You're overreacting."

"I know. The landlord, the owner of the house has asked me to get the money any way I can. I'm out of ideas. Out of patience. I'm going rogue."

"Will you hold please? I'll transfer your call to the diplomatic office."

"What office am I speaking to now?"

"I'm just a translator."

"You speak perfect English."

"Yes. Please hold. I'll connect you with someone who doesn't."

149. The Light Switches Don't Work

The tenant moved in and immediately called the property manager.

"The light switches don't work."

"Did you check the breaker box?"

"Yes. All the electricity is good, but the wall switches in the bedrooms don't work."

"Did you try replacing the light bulbs in those rooms?"

"There are no light bulbs. There are no fixtures. Just a switch that doesn't work."

"Oh. Some older houses have ceiling lamps in the bedrooms. Not yours."

"My last house did. This house has none."

"In newer houses the wall switch turns on one of the outlets in the room. So you walk in to the bedroom, hit the switch, and the outlet by the bed turns on, and bingo, your bedside lamp turns on."

"But I like ceiling lamps."

"Your house doesn't have them."

"But the switches do nothing."

"They turn on your lamps, the ones you brought with you, the ones you turn on to read in bed. You know. They turn on the outlets. You get it?"

"I don't read in bed."

"But the switches work."

"No they don't."

"Yes they do."

"No. They. Don't."

"Are you alone in the house now?"

"No. My wife is in the kitchen."

"Does she read in bed?"

"God yes. Drives me crazy."

"May I talk to her, please?"

150. A Roomful of Women

The property manager visited the rental property to look at the windows. The tenant said they leaked cold air. They walked through the house and found a number of windows that needed weather-stripping. The tenant told the property manager he could not go in the last bedroom.

"Please, you don't go in there."

"Why not?"

"Women are in there."

"How many women do you have?"

"Wife. Daughter. Mother. Sister."

"Why are you hiding them?"

"I am protecting them from being seen by outsiders. By men not of my family. It is my culture."

"Oh, I get it. I respect that. But I should look at those windows in there."

"Please no. You have seen enough now."

"But the window repairman will have to go in there."

"They can't see my women."

"Can you hide the women in the closet?"

"I don't know."

"Can you cover your women with blankets or tarps?"

"I don't know. This is not my rules."

"Can you move them to another room for a few minutes?"

"This is the women's room. This room is."

"You called me. Your windows leak air. It's drafty in here. What should we do?"

"Compensation."

"Money?"

"Ah, you understand."

"Can't do that. We can fix your women's windows or not. No money."

"In my country, air is not cold, women have no windows. Women not to be seen."

"I can't wait to tell my wife. She's gonna flip."

151. Jump into the Foyer

The rent was late. The tenant did not answer her phone. Emails were not returned. Notice of impending entry was posted on her door. The property manager arrived on the appointed day and knocked on the door. An older man answered.

"Good morning. Is Lara here?"

"She is not here."

"Who are you?"

"Her father."

"Mind if I look around?"

"Please don't. I'm still cleaning."

"Where is she?"

"She is moving."

"The place looks empty. May I look around?"

"No, please."

"See this notice on the door? I put it there. I have the legal and contractual right to enter. You are not the tenant, she is. You're not even on the lease. You have no legal or contractual right of possession. I'm coming in."

The old man began to close the door in the property manager's face. When it was halfway closed the property manager turned his body sideways and jumped through the narrowing doorway opening, landing on his feet in the foyer behind the old man. The old man turned to face him. The property manager turned away and walked into the living room.

"Thank you for letting me in. Please call your daughter for me. She never answers my calls."

"She has a new phone number."

"Oh. Give her a call. I'll look around."

"I'll call the police."

"Please do. I have all the paperwork here that gives me the right to be here. You got nothin'."

"Who are you?"

"I'm the guy who put the notice on the door. Try to keep up."

152. Case Dismissed

A tenant sued the landlord and property management firm because she couldn't use her bathroom. It had a leak that was taking weeks to fix. She wanted a free month's rent. When it got to court, the case was at the end of the docket so the parties had to wait hours for it to come. When her case was called the tenant and property manager stood before the judge. The clerk of the court spoke up and said the tenant had not paid the filing fees before the court date. The case could not be heard. The judge dismissed the case. The tenant angrily made her accusations and demands anyway. The judge threatened contempt. The tenant's boyfriend gently but persistently pulled her out of the courtroom by her arm. The property manager's attorney took him to lunch across the street. The attorney billed him for two hours because case took so long to get to. The attorney's bill was six hundred dollars. The bill for bathroom repairs was six hundred dollars. Lunch was free, in a manner of speaking.

153. Suits Versus Sneakers

The tenant sued the property manager. The property manager and his attorney arrived in landlord-tenant court in dark suits and sat in the front row. The attorneys and property managers for other cases were also in the front row, in suits and ties. Witnesses called by the property managers were close behind, in suits as well. Behind them, clustered toward the rear of the gallery, were people in jeans and sneakers. They were the tenants. They put their feet up and were warned by the bailiff. They spoke while cases were being heard and were scolded by the bailiff. When their cases were heard they did not present their cases in the language or protocol of the court. They spoke out of turn. They raised their voices in indignation. About sixty cases were heard that day. The people in suits won every case that day. The people in sneakers and jeans lost. They were mystified.

154. Bladder Problem

The tenant sued the property management firm and the landlord to contest a deduction from his security deposit. The judge called the case. At the last minute in court, the plaintiff's attorney said his client could not make to court due to a bladder problem.

The judge said, "I'm granting a continuance of one week from today."

The defendant's attorney said, "Your honor, we are ready for trial. The plaintiff's attorney is here and can represent the plaintiff. We'd like to go to trial today."

The judge said, "I'm going to give the plaintiff a second bite of the apple." Second bite of the apple was an old phrase that meant everyone gets a second chance.

The attorney said, "Your honor, we have three witnesses here today: the property manager, an inspector, and a contractor, who all saw the house on the move-out date. They took time off of work to be here today."

The judge asked, "I'm giving the other party the benefit of the doubt. A second chance is customary. Is next Friday okay?"

"Yes, your honor."

The next Friday the plaintiff arrived and the case was called. The judge asked the tenant to present his claim.

"Your honor, the management company withheld one hundred and eighty-five dollars from my deposit for a cracked toilet tank top. I didn't crack it."

The judge asked the defendant's attorney if he disputed the claim.

"Yes, your honor. The tenant reported during the lease term that his four-year old cracked the tank. We have the email he sent to the management firm's repairs department. We would like to counter-sue the tenant for one hundred eighty-five dollars in property damage, one hundred in court costs and filing costs, and eight hundred dollars in reasonable attorney's fees for two court dates."

The judge said to the plaintiff, "Your claim will proceed to trial. The countersuit will be heard."

The plaintiff said, "I only asked for one hundred and eighty-five dollars. I don't want to take it any further."

The judge said, "You started it. You sued them. They may countersue. I suggest you consult a urologist and have your bladder ready for trial next time."

155. GFCI

A new tenant called the property manager. One of her lights went out and would not work, even with a new bulb.

The property manager asked, "Did you check the breakers?"

"What are breakers?"

"They're electrical switches, like fuses. Usually in the basement or utility room."

"I don't know. I never heard of that."

"Are you on a wireless phone like a cell, or a landline?"

"Wireless."

"Okay. I'm going to walk you through this."

With the tenant on the phone, he instructed her as she walked to the basement and checked the breaker box. All the breaker switches were on.

"Okay. You need to check your GFCIs."

"I don't know. What's that?"

"Little buttons on electrical outlets, usually near sinks, usually black or red, in kitchens and bathrooms."

He walked her through the house, checking the outlets and pushing the reset buttons. When she pressed the GFCI reset in the master bath, the light came back on. Problem solved.

"There. We solved the problem without wasting money on an electrician, and you learned something."

"What did I learn?"

"To push your own buttons."

"Thank you. Thank you for your time."

"It was only a half hour. Glad to help."

"Oh. I forgot. The house is too cold."

"Did you check the thermostat?"

"Where's that?"

"You haven't checked your thermostat?"

"My husband always took care of those things, God rest his soul."

156. She Wouldn't Negotiate

A tenant moved to the U.S. He wanted to rent a condo. An agent in the property manager's office showed him three condos that were available. He chose a one bedroom advertised for twelve hundred dollars month. He applied, offering eleven hundred dollars per month, which was one hundred dollars below list. The landlord turned down his offer. The applicant met the agent in her conference room. He tried to bargain with her. Eleven hundred. She said no. Eleven twenty-five. The offer was declined. Eleven fifty. No. She said it was twelve hundred firm. The landlord had told the agent not to negotiate. The applicant broke down and accepted the full price.

The next day the applicant called the property manager, and demanded to talk to the agent's supervisor.

The applicant said, "Your agent would not negotiate with me."

"What do you mean?"

"I offered eleven hundred. She said no. She would not compromise."

"Well, the landlord who owns the house wouldn't budge."

"But the agent, she would not negotiate."

"Let me look into this. I'll call you back."

The property manager spoke to the agent.

She said, "He kept low-balling. The price was already rock-bottom."

"He said you wouldn't negotiate."

"He said he wanted to talk to a man. He didn't want to negotiate with a woman."

"Why not?"

"He said in his culture women do not make deals. Only men."

"Oh. I get it. Say no more."

The property manager called the applicant.

"I spoke with the agent. It turns out she did negotiate with you."

"She lies."

"She said the price was good, you offered less, she said no, you tried to compromise, and she said no."

"See? She did not negotiate."

"She did. She negotiated with you. She won. You lost. She negotiated better."

157. The Landlord Negotiated

An agent showed a house. The owner was home during the showing. The renter's agent client did not like the wall colors. She asked the owners, in the home, if they would repaint. They said yes. The property manager was not present, just the renter's agent.

The agent presented an offer to the property manager, with a contingency for painting.

The property manager told the agent, "The house was already painted."

"But my client doesn't like the colors."

"The contingency is denied. There are several other people applying for this house. It will easily rent with existing colors."

"But the owners were home when we showed the house. They said they would paint."

"You negotiated directly with my clients?"

"Yes."

"I represent the owner in this deal. You should go through me."

"It was a simple request."

"May I bypass you and negotiate directly with your clients?"

"No."

"Do you understand the rules of agency and representation in real estate?"

"Of course."

"Does your firm allow agents to bypass homeowners' representatives?"

"What are you saying?"

"You negotiated with my client behind my back. We don't do that. Everything goes through agents or else agents aren't necessary. You took the ethics class, no?"

"Hey, what I did is not a big deal."

"Your offer is denied."

"Are you saying the kitchen will stay that ugly yellow?"

158. Praise the Lord

A potential tenant applied to rent a house. His application was weak. Poor credit, marginal income. But the house had been on the market for six weeks, and the owner was desperate. She accepted the offer.

The new tenant thanked the property manager. "Thanks for making this happen. We were turned down for two houses before. Praise the Lord."

The tenant was late paying the second month's rent. The third month was even later. The property manager called the tenant. "You're late again. What's going on? The landlord is hurting. They need the money."

"We'll be coming into some money soon. We'll catch up, you wait and see. Praise the Lord."

The tenant was late paying every subsequent rent. The landlord could not imagine evicting anyone. The property manager went to the house and sat down with the tenant.

"What's going on? Did you lose your job? Are you in trouble?"

"No, Thank the Lord, we expect good things to come. We have been praying on it. We will be renewed and you will be replenished."

"I believe in God too. Do you have any way of getting money without God's help?"

"Nothing comes without God's help."

"No. I mean do you have any money in the bank? Do you have any friends or family that can help you? Do you have anything you can sell or pawn? We have one rule: Pay rent or leave."

"What we have given will be returned tenfold. Praise the Lord."

"Okay, okay, I get it. Praise the Lord. I will return one day soon in the form of a sheriff and set you free."

159. The Microwave

When the tenants' lease was up, they moved out, and the landlord returned to the home. Walking through the house with the property manager, the owner asked, "Where did my microwave go?"

The property manager replied, "There was no built-in microwave."

"No. It was on the counter."

"I don't remember it. But that's personal property, not a fixture. We don't manage personal property."

"Why not? It's mine."

"Well, if you left a car in the driveway the tenant could have it towed away. They own possession of the driveway. If you left a table in the dining room you couldn't require they store your table in their house."

"But it's my house."

"Now it is. For two years it was their house. You couldn't even enter it without proper notice. Possession is absolute."

"That's crazy. I want my microwave back."

Just then the landlord's wife walked into the kitchen and overheard him complaining about the missing microwave.

She said, "We didn't leave a microwave here."

"Yes we did. On the counter."

"I junked it. It didn't work. It was very old. I told you I want a new one."

"Are you sure?"

"No microwave, honey."

"What about the recliner I left in the garage?"

"Purple Heart wouldn't take it. Goodwill just laughed."

"You put it in storage?"

"Landfill."

160. The Power Meter

The tenant called the property manager to complain about high electric bills. The refrigerator was noisy. He said it must not be energy efficient. He wanted a new refrigerator or compensation for his power bills. The property manager went to the hardware store and bought a "power meter," a small black handheld device. He didn't know if it measured volts or watts or amps. He didn't know anything about electricity.

He took the power meter to the tenant's house. He plugged it into the outlet behind the refrigerator and plugged the refrigerator into the meter. The digital display came on and showed some slowly changing digits.

"Oh, look, the digits are changing slowly. Good, the amperage is below normal."

"What?" asked the tenant.

"If the voltage was driving excess amps, the wattage would be high and the digits on the display would be spinning like a top. Look how slow they change."

"Oh. That's good?"

"Yes. Let me just stick a rag between the coils on the back of the refrigerator and presto, no more rattling fridge!"

"Well then why are my electric bills so high?"

"Do you use space heaters or box fans?"

"Sure, in season."

"There you go. The motors in those things are full of coiled copper wire motor things. You got amps out the ying-yang."

"Well, that's a load off my mind. Thanks for coming over."

"No prob. Any time."

The property manager went back to his office and showed the power meter to his co-workers. They asked him how it works. He said he had no idea.

161. Black Light

The tenant complained of a musty smell in her house. Maybe a dog smell. Maybe in the carpet. She wanted carpet cleaning or a new carpet, maybe duct cleaning. Maybe something was rotting. Maybe the house was contaminated.

The property manager had seen a TV show where crime scene investigators used black light or infrared or something to see latent blood spatter, sex residue, and other organic matter. Not understanding science, he bought a black light from the Halloween section of a party store. He took it to the house.

The tenant closed all the window shades so the house was dark. The property manager plugged in the black light and turned it on. Suddenly the inside of the house showed big glowing spots and marks on the walls. There were glowing sparkles and streaks on the floors. The bathrooms were spattered with constellations of white glowing specks. It looked like there had been a massacre, or an orgy, or an explosion of god-knows-what.

The tenant said she was moving out. The property manager went back to his office and did some research. Online, he learned that anything organic glows under black light, as does cotton, lint, toothpaste, fabric softener, and many other substances. Maybe he watched too much TV.

The property manager tried to calm down the panicky tenant in her house of horrors. He told his coworkers to never use a black light. Never even mention it. He warned other property management firms. He hoped the black light show he had put on in her house was really an illusion, and not a serial sex killer thing.

162. Smudges

The property manager and the landlord walked through the house, after the tenant left.

The landlord asked, "What are those smudges on the door frame?"

The property manager said, "fingerprints" and wiped them off with his shirtsleeve.

The landlord asked, "What is that dirty discoloration on my countertop?"

The property manager said, "Dust," and brushed it off with his hand.

The landlord asked, "What about those black marks on my baseboards?"

The property manager said, "Shoe scuffs," and scrubbed them off with a rag.

The landlord asked, "Who broke that window?"

The property manager said, "A bird," and pointed to some feathers on the outside windowsill.

The landlord asked, "Whose side are you on? Mine, or the tenant's?"

The property manager said, "The house was already dirty when the tenants moved in. They never complained about anything for three years. Everyone in my office liked them. Your neighbors loved them. I'd like to refund their deposit to them in full. I'm so happy with the condition they left your house in. No offense."

163. Three Satellite Dishes

The move-out inspection found no damages to the house. The owner drove up and got out of his car. He looked at his house.

"What are those three satellite dishes doing on my roof?"

The inspector said, "Oh, I didn't look up there."

They walked inside. There were hooks in the kitchen ceiling over the island where the tenant had installed a pot rack. "What are those hooks doing up there?" asked the owner.

"Oh, I forgot to look up."

The owner pointed out that the skylight in the bathroom was left open and rain had gotten in.

"I guess I forgot to look up," said the inspector.

The owner stomped through the house with the inspector slouching behind.

When they were done, the owner asked for a corrected inspection report and demanded compensation from the tenant's deposit. The inspector nodded in agreement and drove away. On his way back to the office, he ran a red light because he didn't look up.

164. The Carport Just Fell

A tenant reported to the property manager that the carport had collapsed.

The property manager asked, "Do you know why?"

"No idea."

"Did a tree fall on it?"

"Nope."

"A tree branch?"

"No. It just fell."

"Was it during that snow storm?"

"I don't know. The snow may have melted by then."

"But it was after the snow storm?"

"After, yes. But caused by? I don't know."

The property manager called the Landlord. The landlord filed an insurance claim. He gave the date of the incident and the supposed cause, the weight of the snow. The insurance company checked the weather records and found the date of collapse did not coincide with snow or storms. They called and interviewed the tenant. They inspected the lumber and fallen debris from the carport. They denied the claim, saying the cause was rotten wood, termites, years of neglect. There was peeling paint and rotten wood on much of the trim and siding on the house. The owner had failed to maintain the property in a normal manner.

The landlord called the property manager.

"Why didn't you tell me about the termites?"

"We have only managed your house a short while."

"Why didn't you tell me about the rotten wood?"

"We did when we first met you and saw the house."

"Who is responsible for this?"

"You. It's your house. You hired us to manage it and we told you to fix it up."

"How do I terminate our contract?"

"Just say the word. In writing."

"I'll find another property management firm."

"There are a lot of good firms out there. The good ones will tell you to fix it up. You might want to find a discount property manager who won't hassle you, or keep records, or take photographs, or make recommendations, or keep the value of your property up. I can recommend a few of those firms if you like."

165. Frozen Pipes

The tenant reported a leak. The property manager sent a plumber. The plumber found frozen pipes in the kitchen sink, dishwasher, clothes washer, and bathroom. The tenants had left the doors and windows open in fifteen-degree weather. The plumber told the tenants they shouldn't leave the doors open in fifteen-degree weather. The tenants asked why. Pipes didn't freeze in their home country. They had never known fifteen-degree weather. Why close the doors and window? Why do pipes leak? They agreed to close the doors and windows.

The property manager told the tenants they would have to pay for repairs. They asked why? The tenants complained to their sponsors in their embassy. The education office that transferred the students to the U.S. agreed with the property manager, and agreed to pay the plumbing charges.

A month later another pipe burst. The tenants were out of town. The thermostat was turned off. A neighbor reported water coming out of the house and freezing on the sidewalk.

166. Take My Picture

The property manager inspected the rental while the tenant was home.

She greeted him and offered him coffee.

She invited him to sit in the living room and chat.

The property manager said he was just there to take notes and take pictures.

She said, "No pictures please."

He said, "It's just protocol. Routine."

She insisted, "No pictures. I haven't picked things up. The house is a mess."

The property manager said, "Just a few pictures. It's my job."

She laid down on the couch, put her feet up, and said, "Okay. Take my picture."

The property manager nervously walked away, taking one picture of each room.

She followed him. He sweated. She laughed. He left.

He made a note in the file. It said, "Caution. Friendly tenant."

167. Dead Bug in the Sink

The property manager sent the new guy out to show a rental. He instructed him to arrive early and spray some air freshener, open windows, tidy up. He explained sometimes an empty house would be stuffy, or have a stale smell, or have an ugly surprise that could turn off a client. Like a dead bug in the sink.

The new guy arrived early. There were newspapers in the driveway. He threw them out. The toilets had not been flushed and the water was gray with mineral sediment. He flushed them.

When the potential tenants arrived, he showed them the house. When they got to the kitchen he saw a dead bug in the sink. A big spider cricket. He squashed it quickly with his bare hand and rinsed it down the drain. But it was too late, they had seen him. They asked him what kind of bug it was.

"Cockroach? Silverfish? Stinkbug?" they asked.

"No," he lied. "Just a ladybug. Everyone loves ladybugs."

168. You're Not on the Lease

"Hello. I'm calling to report a broken garbage disposal."

"What's wrong with it?"

"I said it's broken."

"Have you tried pressing the reset button?"

"What's that?"

"On the bottom there's a red button. It pops like a circuit breaker. You pop it back in."

"I've never done that. I'd get dirty."

"Did you try turning the blades?"

"What?"

"Disposers come with hex wrenches. Use it to turn the blades and un-jam it."

"I'm not very handy."

"Let me get your info. What's the name and address?"

"Sam Johnson. 1515 Main Street."

"Hmm. There's no Sam Johnson at that address. Just Mary Smith."

"That's my girlfriend."

"Can you ask Mary to call in the repair request?"

"Why? Broken is broken."

"You aren't on the lease. I can't spend money to fix things for some strange man I never heard of."

"Are you kidding? Listen, I live here. Ask Mary."

"I'll ask her. I'll ask who you are, how long you've been living there, and I'll ask about the garbage disposal that you won't be bothered to press a button on."

"Wait wait. Why can't I make a simple repair request?"

"I bet Mary would press that button."

"Why won't you just send a repair man?"

"I bet Mary would grab that hex wrench and un-stick that motor."

"You don't even know her."

"I met her when she moved in. She seemed responsible."

"Well, she does change the furnace filter."

"She's level-headed."

"She did change the smoke detector batteries."

"She's good at everything. Except picking friends."

169. He's Going to Burn for This

A tenant called the property manager's office. The receptionist said he was not in the office at that time. The tenant told the receptionist that the property manager had misrepresented the condition of the house, blaming the tenant for petty damages. The tenant was unhappy. He might sue. He would file a complaint. He said, "He's going to burn for this." When the property manager returned, the receptionist told him he was "going to burn for this."

The property manager asked the receptionist to write down the time and date on a memo, including the tenant's name and address and phone number, and include the offending statement: "He's going to burn for this."

The property manager called the police non-emergency line. Would they take a report for such a statement? Was it too petty? Did it qualify as a threat?

It was a slow day at the police station. They sent an officer to the management office. The officer made a written report that would only be made public if there were further threats or actions. The property manager was given the officer's business card with a report number on it.

The tenant never made another threat. The original threat probably wasn't a threat at all. Probably just a figure of speech. But the property manager kept that card and hoped he would get a chance to use it one day.

170. The Toilet Broke by Itself

A tenant called the property manager. The toilet tank broke. The tenant said it had just cracked by itself for no reason. A plumber was dispatched. The plumber said it might have been a "double-decker."

The property manager called the landlord and said he needed a new toilet.

"What happened to my toilet?"

"The tank cracked."

"But why?"

"The tenant said it just cracked by itself."

"Is that possible?"

"The plumber said it might have been a "double-decker.""

"What's a double-decker?"

"It's a prank. You take the lid off the tank, take down your pants, sit on the tank, and instead of going in the toilet bowl, you go in the tank. Then when someone flushes it, surprise, stuff comes into the bowl instead of leaving the bowl."

"My god. Who would do that?"

"Young men I think. College grads. Drunk guys. You know."

"I thought you screened these tenants. I thought you did background."

"They have good credit, good jobs, good money. That's what we look for. There's no database for this kind of thing."

"What are you going to do?"

"Bill them. Warn them. Threaten them. That's all I can think of."

"Can you call their parents?"

171. The Shower Curtain Rod Fell for No Reason

The tenant called the property manager about a repair.

"Our shower curtain rod fell down."

"Oh. What happened?"

"It just fell."

"Were you in the shower?"

"No. I wasn't home."

"Is it a spring tension bar?"

"No, it was screwed into the wall."

"Were the screws loose?"

"No. They were ripped right out of the wall."

"You weren't home?"

"I was at work."

"Was anyone home?"

"My parents, my girlfriend and our two kids."

"What did they say?"

"Why would they say anything?"

"Did they see it or hear it?"

"It just fell by itself. No one pulled it down."

"Did you ask the kids?"

"No. They don't know anything."

"It takes a lot to pull those shower curtain rods down."

"Nobody broke it. We didn't do anything wrong."

"Can I come look at it?"

"No. Why?"

"The owner will want an explanation. Maybe I can figure out what happened."

"There's nothing to see. We already threw out the rod and curtain and put up a new one."

"Great. Problem solved."

"But we want you to pay for the new shower curtain and bar."

"Oh. You're not asking for a repair. You want money."

"Of course. It just fell by itself."

172. The Mirror Just Broke

During the move-out inspection the property manager saw that the bathroom mirror was broken.

He told the tenant, "That mirror is broken."

The tenant said, "That was like that."

"No. It was like new."

"How do you know?"

"I have a picture of the bathroom when you moved in."

"It must have broken all by itself."

"That must have scared the hell out of you."

"Not really. Things break."

"If you look at the mirror, you see a point of impact where something hit it."

"I don't see that."

"And look, the other cracks spider-web outward from the point of impact."

"You have a good imagination."

"Look, the impact point is exactly at your shoulder level, like you hit it."

"Don't you accuse me."

"Come clean. If you confess now I won't charge you for it."

"It broke by itself."

"I meant to tell you, some of the money in your security deposit is gone."

"Very funny."

"It just happened."

"How?"

"It just disappeared."

"How?"

"All by itself."

173. Midnight Emergency Call

A tenant called the property manager's emergency hotline at midnight. The service call was forwarded to the property manager's cell phone.

"Hello. What's your emergency?"

"I have a leak."

"Where is the leak?"

"In the sink."

"Is it damaging the floor or anything?"

"No. It's dripping in the sink."

"The faucet drips into the sink?"

"Yes."

"So it's dripping in the sink and the water is going safely down the drain?"

"Yes."

"It's not really an emergency. Can you call our office in the morning?"

"But it's keeping me awake."

"Did you try closing the bathroom door?"

"I leave it open so I can find the bathroom in the dark."

"Did you try putting a washcloth under the drip to silence it?"

"I didn't think of that."

"How long has it been dripping?"

"A couple weeks."

"You should have called sooner."

"I'm very busy."

"I can't call a plumber and pay emergency rates. Call us tomorrow."

"Oh. I forgot to tell you."

"What."

"The storm door squeaks."

174. Greedy Capitalist Bastards

The prospective tenant asked, "How much is the rent?"

The property manager said, "Eighteen hundred."

"Are there any other costs?"

"If the rent is late there's a five percent late fee."

"That's high. Anything else?"

"If you break something in the house it could come out of your deposit."

"I don't like the sound of that."

"We require a pet deposit."

"You sure have a lot of rules."

"You have to get tenant insurance."

"I don't think so."

"You have to pay for utilities."

"No one told me that."

"There's a charge for bounced checks or insufficient funds."

"Are you enjoying this?"

"You will be charged for any parking violations."

"I'll decide that."

"If you don't mow the yard they can fine you."

"Who is they?"

"It's all in the lease."

"Who would sign a lease like that?"

"Sorry. It's just business."

"Who do you think you are?"

"We're greedy capitalist bastards."

"You got that right."

"We believe in making a profit. I know it sounds weird."

"I'm not signing your lease."

"Whew."

175. Mass Mailing

The property manager's assistant drew up several leases, a couple lease addendums, and some written late rent notices, all for different properties. In a rush, she inadvertently put them all in one envelope and sent them to one tenant, Mr. Smith on Grant Street.

Mr. Smith called the property manager and told him about the mistake. He offered to mail everything back. The property manager said yes, thanks.

The property manager told his assistant about the mistake. She was mortified. She apologized profusely. The property manager said it was not a big deal. He had made similar mistakes. Mistakes were allowed.

A week later the property manager prepared twenty forms to twenty different tenants allowing them to get their pool passes. He gave them to his assistant for mailing. He told her to address them all to Mr. Smith on Grant Street. It was a joke. She walked out and didn't return until the next day. He addressed the envelopes himself.

176. It's Not My Fault

The property manager met the tenant at the house to look at a bathroom sink.

The tenant showed him. "This is what I wanted you to see. The sink just broke."

"The porcelain is cracked. That takes a lot of force."

"It's not my fault."

"The towel bar is missing."

"It fell off. It wasn't our fault."

"There's no shower curtain."

"There never was."

"The mirror has a crack."

"That's definitely not our fault."

"Do you use this bathroom every day?"

"No. I use the master. My sons use this bathroom."

"Did you ask them about these broken things?"

"No. They're just kids. It's not their fault."

"Can I ask them?"

"No."

"Are they home?"

"They're out in the back yard. Leave them out of this."

As the property manager left, he peeked over the fence into the back yard. There were two youngsters smashing a TV with baseball bats.

177. The Ceiling Fan Fell on My Son

The tenant called the property manager.

"The ceiling fan fell on my son."

"OH, NO! Is he okay?"

"He's okay but I'm furious."

"I can come see it right now."

"Okay. I'll wait for you."

He drove to the house.

She showed him the ceiling fan in the family room.

He said, "It's still on the ceiling. I thought you said it fell."

"It's going to. Look at it."

There was a gap between the fan base and the ceiling.

The property manager said, "I can adjust that. There's a little screw on the shaft."

"It's going to fall. My son plays in here."

"I thought you said it fell on your son."

"I said that because I want action."

"I am so happy he's okay. I'll send a repair person to adjust it and put your mind at ease."

"It's too dangerous. We can't use this room. It's not safe."

"If you have a step stool and a screwdriver I can take the fan down now."

"But then we won't have a fan."

"Exactly."

"We're paying for a fan."

"You told me it fell on your son."

"I want a discount on the rent."

"No. The fan is fine. I'll leave the fan as it is. Let me know when it falls on your son again."

"I'll sue you."

"Get in line."

178. Too Many Logs on the Fire

The tenant reported that there was a chimney fire in one of his rentals. The property manager met the fire marshal at the house.

"Thanks for putting out the fire so quickly. It looks like just smoke damage."

"There's more damage than that. We're still cutting open the fireplace wall."

"What caused the fire?"

The fire marshal explained. "The tenant stacked a lot of those artificial logs in the fireplace. He stacked them two feet high. They burn too fast and everything got too hot. The fire came out of the firebox and burned the mantel and the wall above it. It's all really cooked."

"Will your report show who's at fault?"

"Absolutely."

"Does insurance cover this kind of thing?"

"Does your tenant have insurance?"

"He's required to in the lease. I'll ask."

The property manager told the tenant what the fire marshal said. He asked him what insurance company he had his tenant insurance with.

"I don't have insurance."

"It's required in the lease."

"I didn't read the whole lease."

"It'll come out of your pocket then."

"It wasn't my fault."

"The fire marshal said it was your fault."

"I wasn't even home."

"Who built the fire?"

"My mother. She watches the kids when I'm at work."

"May I talk to her?"

"It won't help. She has dementia or something. She won't remember anything."

"May I talk to your kids?"

"They don't know anything. They're just kids."

"Do you have a place to stay?"

"What do you mean?"

"You should stay in a hotel, or with friends."

"Why?"

"The house may not be safe until after the fire department and repairmen finish."

"We can't leave."

"You have to. The house will be condemned if necessary."

"We have no place to go."

"A competent adult should have been here."

"It's not our fault."

"Here. You can have this copy of the fire marshal's report. Look at the line that says what the cause was. See where it says what your mother did wrong."

"You can't kick me out of my house."

"No. Those guys are doing that. Those big guys with the helmets and axes."

"Will I get a discount on the rent?"

179. The Toilet in the Back Yard

The owner moved out. The tenant moved in. The tenant complained the same day.

"Hey, there's a toilet in the back yard."

"I saw that. I thought the owner was going to throw it away."

"So you can get rid of it?"

"Sure. In the mean time, don't use it."

"Very funny."

The property manager called the owner.

"You left a toilet in the yard. I have a guy who can haul it away. Cheap."

"It's a planter."

"Are you serious?"

"Yes. I got the idea from a magazine."

"Well, the tenant and I agree it should go. Okay?"

"I think it's kind of fun. Off-beat. It's kitschy."

"What does kitschy mean?"

"Sort of tacky and trendy at the same time."

"Please let me get rid of it."

"I'm kind of attached to it."

"What about the neighbors?"

"Screw the neighbors."

"I can have it moved into your tool shed. Cheap."

"Can you take the plant out of it and put it in the garden?"

"The plant's dead."

"Are you sure? It might be dormant."

"I have a gardener who can check it out. Cheap."

180. Photo ID in the Toilet

A tenant had four active kids, no job, and no spouse. Her children were rough on the house. Annual inspections showed screens pushed out and cabinet doors broken off. The tenant could not keep up. The property manager was sympathetic.

A plumber was called after the tenant reported a clogged kitchen sink. The plumber found the disposal jammed with crayons. The tenant had to pay the bill.

Later in the lease term a plumber was called for a clogged toilet. He found a sock clogged deep in the toilet drain pipe. The tenant was charged for the repair, and paid.

A third time a plumber was called. The master toilet was clogged. The tenant said it was not her fault. Her kids were not allowed in the master bathroom. She would not pay any more plumbing bills.

The plumber found it too jammed to unclog with a plunger. He could not snake it out either. He had to unbolt the toilet from the floor. Inside the pipe he found the blockage. It was a gym membership card with the tenant's name on it, wedged in tight.

The plumber explained the cause of the blockage to the tenant. He showed her the gym card. He gave her a three-dollar plunger and a ten-dollar snake from the hardware store. He gave her his direct number. She never called the property manager about plumbing again.

181. Refrigerator Magnets

The tenants stopped paying rent. They did not respond to phone calls, emails, regular mail, or notices posted on the front door. After posting a notice of his intention to enter, the property manager waited twenty-four hours and went in.

Inside the house, the property manager found that the house had eight beds. There were only three persons on the lease. The property manager looked at the pile of mail on the kitchen counter. There were five different names on bills and letters. None of those names were on the lease. He saw school schedules, homework, and crayon art on the refrigerator. None of the children were listed on the application as minor occupants, as required.

The property manager talked to neighbors, who were glad to have a chance to complain about the tenants. The neighbors said the family on the lease had moved out. An unauthorized family had moved in. If rent was being paid it was being paid to the original tenant, not to the owner. He gave his business card to the neighbors and asked them to report anything they saw.

The property manager wanted to treat the sub-letters as trespassers and kick them out immediately, but he knew the police, courts, and attorneys would not allow it. Eviction was a long, drawn out, civil process.

Before he left the house, he wrote on the kitchen counter with a dry-erase marker: "Please move out. You have no right to be here." He arranged the alphabet magnets on the refrigerator to spell out: "GET OUT." He had a copy of the lease with him. He posted it on the bulletin board in the kitchen with a push-pin. He left feeling angry and cheated.

He continued to try to contact the tenants, without luck. Two weeks later he received a call from one of the neighbors. The unauthorized tenants had moved out. He went to the house, erased the words on the counter, made sure the magnets were gone, and changed the locks. Then he put the house back on the rental market. As soon as the For Rent sign went up in the yard, he got calls from the neighbors. They wanted to meet any future tenants before move-in. They wanted to talk to the owner of the house, their old neighbor. They wanted keys.

182. Furniture Thieves

The tenant was moving out. A neighbor of the tenant called the property manager. She had called the police and reported furniture being stolen from the house. The police had arrived and found out it was a simple move-out. The tenants were moving their own furniture. The neighbor, being thorough, had called the property manager and the authorities. The property manager called the tenants to warn them they were being watched. Yes they were moving. Yes it was them moving furniture. Yes the police had questioned them. He called the nosy neighbor back and said it was just a move-out. She said she was home all day. She was watching the TV news. They kept saying "See Something-Say Something." It was two days after the Boston marathon bombing. He thanked her and said he would keep an eye on the neighborhood. He would tell her if he saw anything suspicious. He would call the police so she wouldn't have to. She should just call him and leave the police and the neighbors out of it.

183. Smoking on the Deck

During an annual inspection the inspector smelled cigarette smoke. Smoking was prohibited by the lease. Smoking could cause thousands of dollars in damage to paint, carpet, and other porous surfaces. He asked the tenant about it.

"I smell smoke. Do you smoke?"

"No."

"Do your roommates smoke?"

"I don't know. What's the big deal?"

"Smoking is prohibited in the lease."

"Oh. I didn't read that."

"Your roommates can smoke outside. Just not inside."

"Can they smoke on the deck?"

"Sure. Let's look at the deck."

They walked on the deck. There were patio chairs and a table near the deck door. There was an ashtray full of butts and ashes. The table was three feet from the door.

"I think I see the problem here. Maybe they're smoking right here and leaving the door open."

"But you said they could smoke outside."

"Not with the door open."

"The screen door closes by itself. So it's not open."

"Smoke goes through the screen."

"This conversation is not going anywhere."

"No. I have to protect the property and you have to protect your smoking rights."

"That's what I'm talking about. Smoker's rights."

"I was joking. There's no smoking rights."

"What about privacy rights? What about that?"

"Your lease ends soon. You should look for a house with privacy and smoking allowed. Have you started looking for a new house yet?"

"No. Why? We like it here."

184. Home Invasion

A tenant called the property manager.

"We had a home invasion. We need to move out."

"What did the police say?"

"We didn't call them. We don't want a revenge attack."

"You can't just move out."

"What if we're in danger?"

"Then you have to call the police. Please."

"We just want to leave."

"You can leave. Your house is not a prison. But you have to keep paying rent."

"You're not listening. We had a home invasion."

"Was anyone hurt?"

"We weren't home."

"What was stolen?"

"Nothing. Thank God."

"Was the door smashed in?"

"No."

"How do you know there was a home invasion?"

"We saw it on TV. It happened twice in the area."

"But you, your house, what happened?"

"We think they came in looking for us."

"Do you have any evidence? I really can't do anything without evidence and police."

"Well, we've been getting those hang-up phone calls."

"I get those."

"And the neighbors don't like us."

"My neighbors hate me."

"We need to move out. And stop paying rent too."

"I have to say no. No."

"No? Just no?"

"No. No. No."

"Please."

"No, no, no, no. Stop me any time."

"You're an idiot."

"Don't change the subject."

185. Handy Tenant

At the move-in inspection the kitchen faucet was dripping. The property manager said, "I can get a plumber for that." The tenant said, "Don't bother. I can fix it. It's probably just a washer." Then they found a broken door jamb. "I'll get a carpenter," said the property manager. "Don't bother. I'll nail it and caulk it. No problem," said the tenant.

A month later the tenant sent the property manager a bill for five hundred dollars for one rubber washer, two wood screws, and two-hours labor.

186. The IT Guy

An IT guy applied to rent a house. He was self-employed and acted as a consultant or contractor so it was difficult to confirm his income and employment.

The property manager asked the IT guy, "What's your annual income?"

"I make like two hundred, two fifty. Thousand."

"Can you verify that?"

"I don't have a boss so I don't exactly have pay stubs."

"Do you have a W-2, or 1040, or anything."

"I'm moving. All that stuff is in boxes. You know?"

"Do you have a permit to operate a business out of your home?"

"I'm from another state dude."

"Do you have a business card?"

"That's your generation's thing."

"I couldn't find your website."

"It's down. I'm making a new one."

"Professional references?"

"My clients like their privacy."

"I need something. Give me something."

"I make a ton. I drive a hybrid."

"I Googled your name and got nothing."

"I use a separate business name."

"I'm thinking you're not in IT. I'm thinking car sales."

"Whoa. Dude. You're good."

187. What Day is Trash Pick-Up?

The tenant called the property manager.

"What day is trash pick-up?"

"Not sure. Did you ask the HOA?"

"What's HOA mean?"

"Did you ask your neighbors?"

"I just moved in. I don't know them."

"Have you looked down the street to see when others put their trash out?"

"I never thought of that."

The tenant looked down the street all week. He put out the trash the same day his neighbors did. Problem solved. The tenant called the property manager again the next week.

"What day do they pick up recycling?"

188. The Tenant Altered the Lease

A potential tenant applied to rent a house, was accepted, and signed a lease. The lease looked slightly reformatted when the property manager got it back. He read it over. The tenant had made changes. He called the tenant.

"Hello. What's the deal with this lease?"

"We signed it."

"You changed it."

"Well you made the lease, so we thought we could add to it."

"Giving you the lease was an offer. Signing it would have been an acceptance. Changing it is a counter-offer. A voidable counter-offer. Not disclosing the change is just plain weird. It's like fraud."

"But you made up the whole lease. Why can't we participate?"

"You can. You can negotiate. Before you sign it."

"I don't get it."

"Now we don't have a lease at all. We're not signing it, it's not fully executed."

"We still want the house. We still get to move in, right?"

"I'm canceling the move-in. I'm recommending the owner void the contract."

"All we did was change a few lines here and there."

"What if I change it? What if I double the rent and then sign it? You okay with that?"

"You can't do that."

"No, I can't. Excellent point."

189. I Didn't Say That

A potential renter applied for a house, but could not document any ability to pay. He had no employment. He was living on a trust fund. He was moving out of his parent's house. He could not demonstrate any qualifications or offer any references. His application was denied. He called the property manager.

"I really want that house. Won't you reconsider?"

"I'd love to, but you're a ghost on paper. You just don't qualify."

"But I have lots of money. I can pay cash."

"We need you to show you can pay every month. Not just pay us some cash up front."

"I can pay for the whole year. I can pay thirty thousand cash in advance. I'm a safe bet."

"Let me call the owner and get back to you."

He called the owner and described the cash offer.

The owner said, "That's great. Sign him up."

"There are risks."

"Like what?"

"He has no track record. He's been with mommy and daddy his whole life."

"Get a big deposit. He can afford it."

"Also, he has no credit. No cards, no loans."

"Isn't that good?"

"He has no record of paying his debts."

"But he's paying up front."

"What if he turns your house into a frat house, or a zoo? If he has paid all the rent in advance it will be hard to evict him. He could countersue for the return of the balance of the rent."

"It's more complicated than I thought. But I accept. I need that money. I'm behind on my mortgage. My son got accepted at Stanford."

The property manager called the trust-fund baby back.

"The owner accepts your offer. You pay the entire rent advance and we have a deal."

"I didn't say that. I didn't say I would pay the whole thing cash in advance."

"I thought you did."

"No. I said I CAN pay cash in advance. I didn't say I WILL. I was just making a point."

"Good point. You got me. I'll tell the owner you said no. Bye."

"Wait wait, don't hang up. My dad's a senator. Does that help?"

"Is he a good reference? Can you put me in touch with him? Will he cosign?"

"No. He kicked me out. I'm not talking to him. I'm just making a point."

190. I Have to Move in Today

A man in a van pulled up to the management office. The driver entered the office.

"I saw that house you have for rent on First Street. I need to move in ASAP."

"Let me get you a rental application. You can fill it out in our conference room. We'll get you an answer by Friday."

"No. I need to move in today."

"That's just not possible."

"My van is in your parking lot. Everything I own is in it. I have nowhere to go."

"We couldn't possibly move you in now."

"Why not? My money is good."

"Somebody still lives there. They move out at the end of the month."

"What else do you have? I'll take any house I can move into now."

"There's a hotel two miles away."

"I'm serious."

"Sorry. We can't do it that quick."

"I'm not leaving this office until you help me find a place."

"You can't sleep here. We close in an hour."

He just sat there. The office workers ignored him. At closing time he was still there. The property manager called the police. The police escorted him out of the building. He slept in his van in the parking lot. When they opened in the morning he walked right in and sat back down in the waiting area. The property manager put a rental application and a pen in front of him. He brought him a glass of water. Then he called a towing company.

191. I Locked Myself Out

The tenant called. He had locked himself out. He demanded someone bring him a key.

"We don't do that," said the property manager.

"Why not?"

"It costs us money to send someone out."

"But I'm locked out."

"You can call a locksmith."

"That costs money."

The property manager said, "This is going to cost one of us money."

"It should be you," said the tenant.

"No. You."

"No. You."

The tenant said, "Stop. Let's talk about this like adults."

"No. I'm enjoying this. Your turn."

192. Interrogation over Dinner

When the owners moved out, they asked their neighbors to keep an eye on their tenants. The neighbors agreed. After they moved in, the neighbors invited them over for dinner. The tenant called the property manager the next day.

"Hi. Are you my property manager?"

"Yes. How was the move-in?"

"Great. But we met the neighbors."

"Good. How are they?"

"They invited us over for dinner."

"Great."

"Not great. It was polite at first, but it was clearly an interrogation. It was a set-up. They asked us way too many questions. It was obvious."

"Oh, no. I've heard of this kind of thing before."

"We already let you do screening and background. This was too much."

"I'm sorry. If the owner told me they were going to do this I would've stopped them."

"We're not talking to the neighbors again."

"This is bad."

"We're going to stay for the one year we committed to. Then we're out."

"You have to do what you have to do."

"We want you to tell the owner we have considered contacting an attorney."

"Okay. Let me know if there's anything I can do. I feel awful."

The property manager called the owner.

The owner said, "Hey. My neighbors love the new tenants."

The property manager said, "The tenants hate the neighbors."

"But they said dinner went well."

"The tenants hate you too."

"What are you going to do? Can you fix this?"

"Let them cool off. Pay to have the locks changed."

"But then my keys won't work."

"It's a good faith gesture."

"I don't know about that."

"How about an apology."

"Is it really that bad?"

"No. They didn't call the police. They didn't get an attorney. Win win."

193. The Landlord Trespasses

The tenant called the property manager.

"The weirdest thing happened. While we were at work someone came into our house and fixed some things."

"That is weird. Did you call a repairman?"

"No. Did you?"

"No. Was it a break-in?"

"No. They must have had a key."

"Did you call the police?"

"Not yet."

"What did they fix?"

"They put new hinges on the loose cabinet door, and they put weather stripping on the back door frame."

"I'll call you back in five minutes."

The property manager called the owner immediately.

"The tenants reported an intruder. Did you go in?"

"Yes. It's my house. I did some work there."

"You can't go in without notice."

"It's my house."

"It's trespassing. They might call the police."

"I think I can go in my own house."

"No. You effectively sold your right of possession for a year. Now you're a trespasser."

"Don't get so excited. I went to a year of law school. I was a cop too. I got this."

The property manager called the tenant. He lied and said the owner didn't know what happened. Maybe it was a handyman who was hired before the house was rented.

"I'm so sorry this happened. What a mystery."

"We won't call the police this time. But make sure it doesn't happen again."

A week later the tenant called the property manager again.

"We just came home from work. There's a man mulching the gardens. He says he owns the house. What should we do?"

"I can't offer you any advice that is not in the best interest of my client, but if I were in your shoes I would call the police. I'm not saying you should. I'm speaking hypothetically. Don't tell that mulching man it was my idea."

194. Our Cheapest House

A couple asked the property manager to show them some rentals. They said they didn't have much money. He showed them the worst first.

"This is our cheapest house."

"The walls are dingy. Are you going to paint it?"

"The owner has no intentions of painting at this time."

"The carpets are threadbare. Is he going to replace them?"

"The owner has no intentions of carpeting at this time."

"What about new mini-blinds?"

"The owner has no intention of replacing anything at this time."

"You sound like a robot."

"Cyborg."

195. The Airport

A tenant called the property manager to complain.

"This house you rented us is right under the airport flight path."

"Oh. I didn't know that."

"Jets are driving me crazy."

"I had no idea."

"Why didn't you tell me?"

"Nobody told me either."

"Somebody had to know. You should have told us."

"I don't know what to say. We are required to disclose all known material defects, but airports are not on our radar. No pun intended."

"I think its false advertising."

"We don't advertise airports."

"I mean it's false advertising *not* to mention airports in your ads."

"Interesting."

"Who would want to live here?"

"The owner. He's a pilot."

"So you knew."

"Oops."

196. I Nailed the Windows Shut

The property manager went to visit a tenant. She was an artist whose paintings came from a youth lived in the early to mid-twentieth century. Her works were Cezanne-ish, O'Keefe-ish, through Hopper-ish. She had shown her work in Europe after the war and in New York after the next war. Now her only showings were in her rented house, for neighbors, friends, and for one lucky property manager to see.

He walked among the easels in her living and dining rooms. The air was thick with the fumes of drying oils. He tried to open a window but it was stuck. He tried another. It was also stuck.

He said, "You need some air in here, but I can't open the windows."

"I nailed them shut."

"Oh, that's not a good idea. You need air. You need an escape route in case of fire."

"If there's a fire I'm not leaving. Look around. I can't leave them."

"But firemen would drag you out screaming."

"I nailed them shut to keep bugs out."

"Bugs will find a way in."

"I've nailed my windows shut my whole life."

"It doesn't make sense. I need to get a handyman to fix this."

"Please no. I need to keep people out, too."

"You mean burglars?"

"No. You're too young to remember. There was a time when they came looking for people like me."

"Oh, you mean Them."

"Yes."

"They're gone. I promise. We won that war."

"What about your handyman?"

"He's a good guy. I know him."

"How do I know he's not one of Them?"

197. Two Hundred Thousand Dollars

A tenant called. "You need to fix up my house. I pay nineteen hundred a year. I think you can afford some paint and carpet once in a while."

"You had new carpet and paint when you moved in. What happened?"

"Life happened. I've been here ten years. I've paid you over two hundred thousand dollars in rent. Tell the owner it's time to open his wallet, for once."

"He died. His wife gets a small pension. She can't even afford to paint her own house."

"Well, I have standards. I'd like to have friends over but I'm embarrassed to."

"Do you want to paint it yourself?"

"I can do that?"

"I think the owner would like that."

"Can I carpet it?"

"As long as you use neutral colors, you can decorate. No wild wallpaper or purple paint."

"I'll talk to my husband. I can buy the paint and he can do all the work."

"Teamwork."

"Do I get a discount on the rent?"

"In a way. I'll stop raising the rent every two years."

198. Racism

The property manager called a rental applicant to deny her application.

"I'm sorry, but the landlord turned down your application."

"Why? I really want to rent that house."

"The other applicant had better income and credit."

"But I have good credit."

"Good, yes, but the other applicant had excellent credit."

"Was the other applicant white?"

"I have no idea."

"You turned me down because I'm black."

"I don't know your race. I don't know the other applicant's race, either."

"How could you not know I was black?"

"You didn't tell me. It's not on your application."

"You met me when you showed me the house."

"Your agent showed you the house. She's not with our firm."

"She must have told you."

"We follow all the fair housing guidelines. We decide based on employment, credit, and references."

"I'm going to report you."

"Report me? But what did I do?"

"You're a racist."

"What color am I?"

"White?"

199. The Plumber Tried to Kiss Me

A tenant reported her toilet was running. A plumber was sent. After the appointment she called the property manager.

"Your plumber tried to kiss me."

"Oh, no. I'll call him right away."

"You should fire him."

"He's independent."

"Well, don't ever send him to my house again." The property manager sent a different plumber next time. The plumber fixed it and called him.

"The tenant tried to kiss me."

"What? That's weird. She said the other plumber tried to kiss her. Are you sure?"

"She didn't really touch me. She just put her face up to mine."

"Oh, great. I'll call her."

He called her and asked if the toilet was okay.

"Yes, it stopped running. Thank you."

"Was the plumber okay?"

"Yes. Very professional."

A month later the toilet started running again. Instead of calling a plumber, the property manager went to see it. He had fixed his own toilets before. Maybe he could diagnose the problem. The tenant showed him the bathroom. He opened the toilet tank top and fiddled with the flapper. It was not a perfect fit for the drain.

"I think I see the problem. These flappers vary. Maybe I can get another and try it. They only cost five bucks."

The tenant stood a foot away from him when she talked. Too close.

"When can you fix it?"

He backed up two feet. His own personal space was three feet, one arm length. He had read about people with personal space issues in a magazine. She moved forward and talked with her face just fifteen inches from his. She was a "Close Talker." There was an episode on Seinfeld about it. Some people just stand too close. They don't know they're doing it.

"I'll go buy a flapper and come back tomorrow."

"Okay."

"When the plumber tried to kiss you, were you right here in the bathroom?"

"Yes. Right here."

He could feel her breath on his face. He smelled coffee on her breath.

"Was the plumber right here by the toilet?"

"Yes."

"And were you right there by the sink, blocking his exit?"

"Where is this going?"

"You're standing too close to me. I can't get to the door without brushing by you."

"So I'm a people person."

"I think the plumber thought you were being aggressive."

"No way. I would never kiss a plumber."

"Either would I. But you have to back up or I can't get out of here."

"My boyfriend gets jealous when I talk to other guys. Do you think this is why?"

"One more step back. A little more. That's it."

200. The Elevator

A tenant moved out of a high-rise condo building. He got his couch stuck halfway in the elevator. The elevator doors were damaged upon repeated attempts to load it.

After he moved he called the property manager.

"Can I have my security deposit back now?"

"Not yet. The building management is charging for elevator damage."

"I didn't damage anything."

"The door mechanism broke while you were using it."

"How do you know I used the elevator?"

"It's like ten floors. You didn't carry your stuff down the stairs."

"And I didn't break anything."

"The freight elevator can only take so much."

"I didn't use the freight elevator. I used the regular elevator."

"You can't use the regular elevator for furniture. It's not allowed."

"Oh. That's why all those other people were mad at me."

"The regular elevator doors don't lock open for loading."

"Oh. That's why they kept closing and banging around."

"It may be expensive. I'm keeping your deposit. You broke the elevator."

"Prove it."

"Cameras. There are cameras."

201. Sign Language

A tenant lived in a townhouse association. He was a contractor. Occasionally he dumped leftover construction debris in the dumpster. The dumpster was clearly marked. Only household trash was allowed. Nothing from outside. Nothing commercial. One day he was dumping broken drywall and two-by-fours into the dumpster. The association president saw him and approached.

"HEY! NO DUMPING. CAN'T YOU READ?"

The tenant looked at the president and pretended to do sign language. Pretended he was deaf. The president knew he was faking it, but thought the guy might be a psycho. He backed away and said nothing more. He called the property manager. The property manager called the tenant. The tenant denied it ever happened. He said, "Prove it."

202. House Numbers

One of the property manager's clients spruced up the front of his house. He planted some flowers, painted the mailbox, and moved the house numbers. The numbers had been installed horizontally above the door. He removed them and hung them vertically on the side of the door frame. It was easier to see from the street. He received a violation notice. All the houses in the neighborhood had to be the same. The numbers must be horizontal above the door. The homeowner refused. He received a final notice that there would be fines, per the association bylaws. He moved the numbers back and complied. A month later he painted his mailbox purple and waited for the next notice. After the notice, before the fines, he complied and painted it white again. He planned to commit little violations, over and over, then comply just before the fine deadlines. Just to piss off the association. His neighbors noticed, and were amused. They didn't liked the HOA either. One painted his front door pink. Another put a statue of Mary in his front yard. The association just kept sending notices.

203. Dick Little

The management company's receptionist received a call. It was for the property manager.

"Hey, it's an agent on the phone. He's asking about Sycamore Street."

"Who is it? Which agent?"

"He's with Rogers Realty."

"What's his name?"

"Dick Little."

"Must be a prank call."

Another property manager spoke up.

"No. He's real. His client applied to rent Sycamore Street yesterday."

"I can't talk to him with a straight face."

"He can't see your face on the phone."

"You take it then."

"You take it. Sycamore Street is your account."

"Take a message. I can't talk to every Dick who calls."

The receptionist picked up the phone. "Sorry to keep you on hold, Mr. Little. He's right here. Just a second."

204. First Come, First Served

A potential tenant wanted to rent a house.

"I saw the house on Windover Street. I'd like to rent it."

"Okay. Send me your application."

"Then do I get the house?"

"No. We process your background and present it to the landlord."

"Then I get it?"

"No. They decide. If they accept you, then you get the house."

"Who else would get the house? Is anyone in front of me in line?"

"No. Yours will be the first application."

"Then don't I get the house? Isn't it first come, first served?"

"No. It's most qualified."

"But nobody else has applied. So I'm the most qualified."

"We have to learn about you first."

"Like what? I have money and I need a house. What else do you want to know?"

"Income, credit, employment, rental history, landlord references."

"And then I get the house?"

"We're very picky. The owner is very picky."

"Just give me the house. Why would you say no?"

"Well, say, if you're a serial killer, or you burned down your last house."

"No and no."

"Or you have ten dogs, or you're bankrupt."

"No and no."

"Or you've maxed out a credit card sometime in the last five years."

"Oh. That matters?"

"Or your last landlord says you trashed the house."

"Don't listen to him. He's a jerk."

205. No Social Security Number

"We've received your rental application, but you omitted some info."

"Like what?"

"You didn't give your social security number."

"I'd rather not. Identity theft is everywhere these days."

"We can't run your credit without it."

"My credit report is private."

"Then we can't process your rental application."

"I filled out most of the form."

"You didn't give us your employer's contact info."

"What for?"

"We need to verify your employment."

"I wrote down my job title and company name."

"We have to make sure it's true."

"Who would lie about that?"

"Last year a guy told us he was a store manager but he was really a sales clerk."

"What's the difference?"

"Thirty thousand a year."

"Do you guys really snoop around like that? Is that ethical?"

"If I rent you the house, will you let me move in with you?"

"I don't even know you."

"That's how we feel. We just want to get to know you."

206. Condensate Line

There was a leak in the basement of a rental. The tenant called and a contractor was sent.

The contractor found the condensate line on the HVAC unit was clogged and leaking. Water was everywhere. He unclogged the line. The owner was billed. The owner called the property manager to protest the charge.

"What's this about a hundred fifty dollars for some water pipe thing?"

"The condensate line was clogged. The basement flooded."

"What's a condensate line?"

"I think it's a pipe that carries condensation from the AC coil to the sump pit."

"What's an AC coil?"

"I think it's sort of like a car radiator, with lots of little pipes and fins, to radiate heat out of circulating fluid."

"What's a sump pit?"

"I think it's that hole in the basement floor with a pump inside that pumps excess water out of the house into the yard."

"Why on earth would my condenser coil sump things break?"

"Nothing broke. I think the line clogged."

"With what?"

"With lint or dust or stuff in the air."

"Where does the dust stuff come from?"

"I think your AC sucks air in those vent things in your house and cools it off and blows it all around the house through other vent things. But it has to go through a filter first. The filter gets clogged with dust and stuff in the air. Then the clog makes the condensation water flow down and flood the floor."

"What's that filter thing?"

"It's like a fiberglass screen in a cardboard frame that you change in your HVAC unit. You change it every month or so. You just slide it in the slot. So stuff doesn't clog the line."

"I never heard of that. I never changed any filter thing."

"That's probably why the dust stuff clogged the filter thing and the pipe got clogged and the water spilled on the floor."

"How do you know all this?"

"I'm Googling it as we go."

207. Worms on the Ceiling

The tenant called the property manager with an unusual problem.

"Hello? I think I have worms on my ceiling."

"I never heard of that."

"Send a pest guy quick."

"Right away."

The pest guy went out.

"Look at my ceilings. What are those things? Gross. Is it dangerous?"

"No. They're probably just pantry flies."

"What's that?"

"Sometimes called cabinet flies."

"What?"

"Or pantry moths."

"I never heard of that."

"Meal moths. Like fly maggots"

"Oh. Gross. Where do they come from?"

"They come in food packages. Mostly dry pet food. They hatch, they fly, they lay larvae up high sometimes."

"How did I get them?"

"Look. Your dog food bag is wide open. That's a common source of pantry flies."

"I don't get it."

"You made a breeding ground, a restaurant for pests. You're lucky you don't have rats."

"Gross. Kill them all. And make the property manager pay."

"I think he'll want you to pay for it."

"It's not my fault."

"It's your neglect. Own up."

"So you're some kind of expert?"

"Yes. Pest expert. Doctor of Grossology."

208. My Dad Said

Friends of the property manager were looking to rent a house. He showed the couple and their son four houses on Saturday. They didn't like them. He showed them three more on Sunday. They chose one. He helped them fill out the rental application, because they were friends. He presented it to the homeowner. It was accepted. He helped them read and sign the lease. He met them for the move-in and inspected the house with them. He got some minor repairs done for them. They were grateful. He had done so much for them, because they were friends. They thanked him.

"Thank you so much for all of your time and patience."

"No problem. I'm just glad you found a house you like."

"We love it. We'll have to have you over for dinner sometime."

"That would be nice, but it's not necessary. I'm just doing my job."

"You gave up your weekend. We really, really appreciate it."

He left them in their new home and walked to his car. On the sidewalk he passed their teenage son, who was carrying some boxes in.

The teenage son said, "My dad said you're an asshole."

209. The Rent Check

The property manager inspected the house with the new tenant on her move-in day. As her moving van pulled up, he asked her for the first month rent. She said she didn't have her checkbook. He said he couldn't give her the keys without rent payment. She said she just forgot to bring it. The property manager said it was required. She said she was good for it, she was an honest person. He said he hated to be such a stickler, going by the lease contract and all. She said please, and put her hand on his shoulder. He twitched a bit, stepped back, and said rules are rules. She looked like she was going to cry. He suggested they go outside and tell the movers to hold up. She scowled, whipped out her checkbook and wrote him a check. He gave her the keys, thanked her and left. She followed him out to his car. As he was leaving she told him not to deposit the check for a week, or it would bounce.

210. Seal the Deck

The landlord asked the property manager to have the deck sealed. He hired a contractor. When it was done the property manager received a bill. He paid it out of the landlord's account.
A month later the landlord drove by and saw the deck. It looked the same as before. He called the property manager.

"Hey, what's the deal with my deck?"

"It was sealed. You saw the payment on your statement."

"Yes, I did. But the work wasn't done."

"What?"

"I drove by. It looks the same."

"I'll call the contractor. This is not acceptable."

The property manager called the contractor.

"Did you seal the deck?"

"Yes, over a month ago."

"The owner is unhappy. He said it looks the same."

"We sealed it with a clear deck sealant, the most popular one on the market."

"Clear? That's why it looks the same as before?"

"It's supposed to look the same as when it was new. We pressure washed the mold and leaf stains off, sealed the wood, made it like new. We prevented rot for years to come. We stand by our work."

"The owner is unhappy that it looks the same."

"Listen. You didn't ask for stain. Stain has pigment. Sealant doesn't."

"Oh. I get it."

"The other decks in the neighborhood aren't stained. If you stained this deck it would stand out like a sore thumb."

"Ah. And that would mean an HOA violation."

"Yes, it would."

The property manager called the landlord and explained the situation.

The landlord asked, "Why seal it if it still looks the same? Why should I pay for something I can't see?"

211. Lawn Maintenance

The property manager got a lawn maintenance service contract at the landlord's request. All spring, summer, and fall the lawn workers were to mow, week, de-grub, fertilize, trim and mulch. They got the address wrong and took care of the lawn across the street. The owner of the house across the street did not complain. He just let them do it. In October the landlord drove by the house and saw his lawn. Long grass, weeds, overgrowth. It was a disaster. He called the property manager.

"Why am I paying you all year for landscaping and you do nothing?"

"They told me they were doing it. I didn't go look at it."

"Well I want a refund and I want you to fire the lawn company."

"We will repay you. We will fire the lawn firm. I am so sorry."

The landlord added, "And next year I want you to hire the company that does the lawn across the street. Theirs looks fantastic."

212. Foreigners

In the middle of the lease term the property manager and the landlord toured the rental house and met the tenants. Afterward the landlord and the property manager spoke on the sidewalk out front.

"You didn't tell me they were foreigners."

"They're not. They're U.S. citizens."

"They don't look like it."

"They gave us social security numbers."

"They have accents."

"That's a New York accent."

"I wanted Americans."

"They're second generation, born of legal immigrants. Their parents were nationalized fifty years ago."

"Can I see their papers?"

"No. They don't have to show anyone any 'papers'."

"When I bought this house years ago, the neighborhood was a lot different."

"What do you mean?"

"Everyone was white. Everyone was Christian. We were all the same."

"Did you love your neighbors back then?"

"Hell no. Their kids played ball in the street. Their dogs dug up my azaleas. They played that loud rock and roll."

"So, those were the good old days?"

"No. I'm just saying. At least I understood what was going on back then."

213. A Good Week

Monday the property manager settled an argument between neighbors over a trampoline.

Tuesday he took pictures of dog poop on a playground and wrote mildly threatening letters to the dog's owner.

Wednesday he inspected a rental house and found five semi-automatic rifles proudly displayed on a gun rack in the rec room. He wrote a polite note to the tenant suggesting they should be unloaded and locked up out of sight.

Thursday he wrote a letter to four college-aged tenants because all of their neighbors had complained of the smell of marijuana.

Friday he helped an elderly tenant get her car out of the impound lot after it was towed away for having no inspection sticker. She invited him in for tea. He accepted and spent a half-hour in her kitchen talking about how the old black-and-white movies were so much better than those new ones.

He didn't go back to work. It was Friday. Everyone at work was so busy on last minute phone calls that they didn't know he was missing. All in all, a good week.

214. No One Wins in Court

The property manager helped the landlord sue the tenant for knocking down a bedroom wall, creating a master suite, and installing a new shower and a Jacuzzi tub. It was a great improvement, and the landlord liked it, but he wanted retribution for the unauthorized work. He had neighbors as eyewitnesses, an expert witness in construction and remodeling, and an expert witness in real estate assessment.

In court, the case was argued over the terms of the lease prohibiting material changes to the property, whether the work was up to code and inspected, and whether the value of the house increased or declined. The key piece of evidence was an email in which the landlord had said he wouldn't mind if the tenant did a few handy things around the house. The trial lasted eight hours. The judge grew angry and the attorneys grew tired. The judge highly recommended they go out in the hall and settle up on their own or he would make a judgement both sides would regret. The landlord agreed to accept the improvements and the tenant agreed to pay the attorney's fees. The judge dismissed the case and told the property manager to do a better job inspecting his properties.

215. Suicide

A tenant committed suicide in a rental property. The property manager talked to the next of kin, police, and first responders. He contacted the insurance company and an attorney. He learned the method and cause of death. He talked to the family and learned the tenant had been treated for depression. He invoked the clause in the lease terminating it in case of death of either party. He worked with the movers and a storage facility. He talked to the neighbors and learned about the tenant's demeanor and downturn. He recommended a funeral home. He told the family to give him a copy of the death certificate so he could document the reason for lease termination. He had the house cleaned, painted, and re-carpeted. The house was rented again, for a lower rent amount because people talked about the event. When all was done, the property manager knew the whole long sad story.

The owner, who didn't know it was a suicide, asked him for the story.

"No story. Poor guy died."

"What do we know?"

"Not much. The family took care of arrangements."

"What did the police say?" What about the doctors?"

"I don't know. They just did their job. I tried to stay out of it."

"Don't you know anything?"

"Self-inflicted is all. More stuff you don't want to know."

"Was it that bad?"

"Yes. I can give you all the gory details. I spent a week on this. I'm exhausted and upset. This is what you hired me for. Anybody can collect rent and plunge toilets."

216. Can I Move in with My Tenants?

A landlord returned from overseas early. He wanted to move in and kick out his tenants, two young women. The property manager said no, their lease was not up for another year. The landlord asked if he could move in with them. The property manager said no. Could he live in the spare room? No. But it was his house. No. Couldn't he just ask the tenants? No.

The landlord bypassed the property manager. He went to the property and introduced himself. He asked if he could live in the spare room. They said no. He said he would reduce the rent. No. He said they could live there rent-free for the rest of the year. They said yes. He moved in. He called the property manager and terminated his services. He would take over from there.

217. Pedophiles and Rapists

The property manager got a letter from a tenant:

"Dear Property Management Services,

This neighborhood you put me in have rapists and pedophile. I have a power to make you uncomfortable. My best friend has lawyer husband. This is a permanent damage situation to me and my children who are scared. I don't want you to suffer but I want to make an example. I work at offices and I told about you to my superiors.

Also, the dishwasher has a funny sound and you should fix it."

The tenant didn't provide a name or property address.

218. Fourteen Million Dollars

The tenant was often late paying the rent. He incurred late fees. He bounced checks and had to pay bank fees for insufficient funds. His car was towed and he had to pay the towing company's impound lot to get it back. He broke a window and had to pay for the repair himself. He had enough. He sued the property manager for fourteen million dollars.

The property manager received a subpoena and contacted an attorney.

"I'm being sued in small claims court for fourteen million dollars."

The attorney asked, "Who did you kill?"

"No one yet."

"Don't sweat it. The most he can pursue in Small Claims Court is five thousand."

"Oh. Good. I don't have fourteen million."

"What reason does the subpoena give for the suit?"

"Harassment."

"What does he mean? I can't believe it even got past the Clerk of the Court."

"I can't believe he's suing me. I'm a saint."

"You still have to show up in court. Always show up in court. Always."

"What will happen?"

"The judge will dismiss it."

"And I don't need an attorney?"

"You can't have one in small claims. Either can he. It's a zoo."

The property management showed up for zoo court, with no defense, without any idea what would happen. The judge called the case and looked at the plaintiff.

"It says here you're suing for fourteen million dollars for harassment?"

"Yes, your honor."

"You can't sue for fourteen million dollars in my court. Would you like to reduce your claim?"

"How about ten million, your honor?"

"Just for my entertainment, what do you claim the defendant did?"

"He charges me for this. And that. And everything. Then he harasses me on the phone. He writes me letters."

"I'm dismissing the case. Would the defendant like to say anything?"

The property manager said, "I would, but I better keep it to myself, your honor."

219. A Happy Client Comes Back for More

The property manager went to see two former clients who wanted to hire him to rent out their house again. They walked through the house and discussed painting and cleaning it for showing. They asked him if they should get new carpet or countertops. He told them his priority formula: Upgrade the kitchen and master first. Then bathrooms and living room. Small rooms last. Cleaning and painting give the most bang for your buck. Don't install marble countertops or stainless appliances if you don't want to see them dinged. Just his opinion. They asked what they could deduct and what to depreciate, tax-wise.

He gave them his pitch: They were the best firm for them. The competition was not keeping up with the technology and service trends like he was. He would love to manage their home again. They said he did a good job the first time around and they would definitely hire him. But they just wanted a refresher. They had never understood how he operated. Last time they had just received rent proceeds and paid for leaky faucets. What was it he did again? He began to recite a list for them one hundred things he did, from inspections to collections. They said no thanks, no list, where do we sign?

220. Double Occupancy

The tenants' lease expired July 31. In June they gave notice they were moving out on that day. The house was marketed, a new tenant was found, a new lease signed beginning August 1. In mid-July the old tenants changed their minds. They said they could not move. They would need to stay another month to the end of August. The property manager said no, a move-out was scheduled July 31 and a new move-in would occur August 1. The tenant said it was impossible, they would have to stay the extra month. Eviction was useless because it would take two months. The property manager called the new tenant and told him the bad news. The new tenant insisted he had his rights. He told the property manager he had to have his kids in the new school district before the last week in August. The property manager's hands were tied. He asked if the tenant if he had friends or family he could stay with. No. Could he afford a hotel? No. Did he want to look for another house? No, it was too late. The new tenant called every day, sometimes with the sound of crying children in the background. The property manager called the old tenant daily asking if they could please move out on time. No. Could they move into a hotel? No. Did they have friends or family they could stay with? No.

The new tenants lived in their car for the month of August, parking in shopping centers and eating at fast food restaurants and convenience stores. On September first the move-in occurred. The house was not clean, it needed painting, and it smelled funny. It was a long, sad move-in. Profound apologies and legal threats were exchanged. It was the property manager's first summer in the business. He lost weight. He lost sleep. Other property managers told him it wasn't his fault, don't take it personally. Then they laughed and laughed and thanked God it wasn't them.

The old tenants called the property manager in September asking where their security deposit was.

221. The Missing Refrigerator

The tenant called. The refrigerator was breaking down. It wasn't cold enough. Food was going bad. The freezer was melting and dripping. When would it be fixed? Who would pay for their spoiled groceries? The property manager called an appliance repair and replacement company. The technician went to the house. They refrigerator was twenty years old. It could be fixed temporarily but needed replacement soon. The property manager called the landlord. The landlord said replace it, even though replacement costs much more than repair. The new unit was authorized and the landlord paid fifteen hundred dollars for the fancy new refrigerator.

A year later the landlord returned to town and asked to see their house. The property manager met the landlord and they walked through the house together. When they came to the kitchen, the landlord's jaw dropped. The old refrigerator was there, humming and rattling. The landlord glared at the property manager and asked why he had paid for a new refrigerator a year ago when the old one was still there. The property manager frowned and said there must have been some kind of "mix-up." The landlord said, "Mix-up?"

The property manager called the maintenance director, who called the appliance company. The refrigerator was ordered but never delivered because the tenant did not return call after call and no appointment could be made. The appliance company said it wasn't their fault. The maintenance director said it wasn't his fault. The tenant said it wasn't his fault. The property manager had to take the blame. The account was taken from him and given to another manager. The landlord demanded a free refrigerator and a fired property manager. The new refrigerator was installed. The old one was removed and discarded. The tenant was upset. He wanted the old one kept in the garage for extra beer space. The landlord was disappointed. She also thought she'd end up with an extra refrigerator for when she entertained. The property manager called the appliance firm. Did they still have the old refrigerator? They did not, but they picked up old ones every day. What color would he like? Would they like one with an ice maker? Fifty for the refrigerator, one seventy-five for delivery.

222. Noise Falling Down on my Head

The tenant called the property manager and complained about noise from the condo above her. She spoke in a thick accent and had a hard time explaining.

"My noise is in my house."

"You have noise in your condo?"

"Yes, from the people up there."

"The people upstairs?"

"Too much noise."

"I'm sorry. Have you talked to your upstairs neighbor?"

"I move out."

"Have you filed a noise complaint with the police?"

"No. I move."

"I can call the condo management."

"I already move."

"You will need to keep paying rent until we find another tenant."

"The noise is falling on my head."

"It's falling on your head?"

"Yes. On my head."

"I don't understand. But you can't just break the lease because of noise."

"Why don't you help me?"

"You need to read your lease."

"I can't because my English. You ashame."

"I want to help you but we have a written agreement."

"Where is my money back?"

"Your money?"

" I give you money. You give it back."

"Your deposit?"

"I need deposit."

"You get your deposit back at the end of the lease, if terms are met."

"Don't make fun."

"Is the condo empty?"

"Yes."

"Can I have the keys?"

"I don't have."

"I will go in with my keys and call you back."

The condo was vacant. The kitchen was dirty. There was a mural on a bedroom wall. There was trash in the dining room. The property manager changed the locks and kept the deposit for repairs.

The tenant sued the property manager in small claims court for the deposit. She told the court there was noise falling on her head. She said pay her money now. The property manager handed move-out photos to the bailiff, who handed them to the judge.

The judge looked at the docket. Thirty more cases to go. "Case dismissed. Next case."

223. Don't Blame the Agent

A tenant moved out of a rental property and left it in "Okay" condition. The move-out inspection was done and the property manager reported to the owner that the condition was "Okay." The landlord demanded to know what "Okay" meant. The property manager said the house needed painting and cleaning. The landlord told him to keep the deposit and pay for cleaning and painting. The property manager replied that the house was also only "Okay" at move-in. It had not been cleaned or painted before the tenant moved in. The landlord didn't remember. He said to keep the deposit.

The tenant sued the property manager's firm, not the homeowner. The property manager represented the firm as a defendant in court. The judge heard the tenant's claim and asked for the property manager's response.

The property manager said, "Your honor, we ask that the tenant re-file the case against the proper defendant, the landlord. The lease is a contract between the landlord and the tenant. It states that the property manager acts solely as an agent for the landlord. It says we administer the lease but are not a party to the lease."

The judge asked the tenant if he agreed. The tenant addressed the judge.

"In the beginning I paid the deposit to the property manager. He should return it."

The judge asked the property manager, "Who holds the deposit?"

"We kept it in an escrow account in the owner's name. We disbursed it to the landlord at his insistence. We told him the house was 'okay.'"

The judge asked, "Do you have the landlord's address to turn over to the tenant so he can take action against the landlord?"

The property manager replied, "Right here, your honor."

The judge asked, "Did you ever withhold the address from the tenant, preventing him from filing against the correct party?"

The property manager replied, "No sir. The plaintiff never asked for it, or for anything in our files. He filed no bill of particulars. There was no subpoena for documents. I don't know why he chose to file against our firm."

The bailiff took the document with the address on it and handed it to the judge. The judge handed it back to the bailiff and instructed him to hand it to the tenant.

The judge looked at the tenant. "You understand that you should file against the landlord next time?"

The tenant said, "The property manager withheld the deposit. He hired out the repairs. He sent the notice about the deposit deductions. He was my only contact."

The judge said, "I have to find for the defendant, the property manager. He correctly states that you filed against the wrong party."

The property manager met the tenant in the hall as they left the courthouse. The property manager asked, "Are you going to re-file the case against the landlord?"

The tenant said, "I don't know. I was sure I'd win in court today."

The property manager said, "We usually win in court."

The tenant asked, "Why is that?"

The property manager explained, "We wrote the lease in our favor. We spent years writing and improving that contract. How long did you take to read it before you signed it?"

The tenant said, "Maybe a half hour."

The property manager said, "It's not about right and wrong. It's about the lease."

224. The Leaky Shower

The tenant submitted a maintenance request. The master shower tiles were loose. The dining room ceiling below the shower had a small water stain. Water was getting inside the wall to the downstairs. The property manager got an estimate for two thousand dollars to re-tile the shower enclosure and repair the ceiling. The landlord did not have that much money. His mortgage was higher than the rent. He was barely getting by. The property manager told the tenant not to use the shower until the owner could afford to repair it. The tenant said he was paying good money and deserved to have the shower working. The property manager asked if the tenant could use the hall bath shower for a while. The tenant said he was not happy.

The property manager told the landlord that the shower repair was necessary. The tenant might not sign up for another year lease extension. The owner could lose more than the two thousand in marketing and decorating costs for a new tenant. The landlord still did not authorize the shower repair.

The tenant asked that his rent be reduced since he did not have full use of the property. The property manager said that such a remedy was not found in the lease or the law but he would ask the landlord. The landlord said no. The tenant demanded a rent reduction again. The property manager said the rent was twenty-five hundred a month and, coincidentally, the house floor-plan was about twenty-five hundred square feet. The bathroom was eighty square feet. He asked if the tenant was requesting a corresponding eighty dollar a month reduction in rent. The tenant said no, the bathroom was more valuable because it was a bathroom. He wanted a five hundred dollar reduction in rent or a suspension of all rent until the shower was repaired. The landlord did not agree.

Attorneys were consulted. The tenant's attorney sent a demand letter for a steep rent reduction. The property manager's attorney replied that the house is either habitable or not habitable but that there is no formula in the lease or the law for partial or limited use of the property.

The tenant told the property manager he would see him in court. The property manager replied that landlord-tenant court is on Fridays from nine to three. There would be up to a hundred hearings on the docket. The property manager recommended the tenant arrive early if he wanted to get a good seat.

225. The Bad Paint Job

The landlord and the tenant were friends. They agreed the condo would be painted. The property manager got an estimate for painting. The price was over two thousand dollars. The landlord said that was way too high. The property manager got another estimate for nine hundred but warned the landlord that the cheaper painter would do a cheaper looking paint job. He recommended the higher price. The landlord accepted the lower price.

The work was done. The tenant moved in. The tenant complained directly to the landlord that the paint job did not look good. The landlord told the property manager not to pay the painter. The landlord said she had expected better work. The property manager reminded her he had recommended she not go cheap. The landlord refused to pay. The property manager went to the house and looked at the work. It looked like nine hundred dollars worth of painting. The tenant pointed out that the closets had not been painted, nor the ceilings. The property manager showed him the proposal that did not include closets or ceilings. The lower price was a walls-only bid, clearly put in writing. The landlord had been sent both proposals as attachments to emails before the decision had been made. The tenant was angry. The property manager called the landlord and explained the "mix-up." The lower bid did not include closets and ceilings. The landlord had received the bids as email attachments but said she had not read them thoroughly. The unpaid cheap painter was irate and filed a lien on the property. The landlord called the property manager and threatened to sue him. The property manager told her that the landlord's property management contract contained four hold-harmless-and-indemnify clauses to keep the landlord and manager on the same side in all legal disputes. She couldn't sue him. The landlord said she had not read the whole contract. She said the tenant was her friend and the property manager was not. The property manager said he would like to be her friend too, if it was not too late.

226. Keys Locked in the Car

The property manager arrived at the scheduled time for the annual inspection of a townhouse rental. The tenant was just leaving. She had chosen not to be present for the inspection. She started her car and then went back to the house. It was locked. She went to the car to get the keys but she had accidentally locked that too. The engine was running and her baby was inside on the back seat. She looked in the car, panicked and began to cry out. Her purse was locked inside with her cell phone. The property manager arrived on the scene and offered to help. He called a locksmith but the locksmith would take an hour and a half to arrive. He asked the tenant if she had a coat hanger he could use to try to break into the car. No, all her coat hangers were locked inside the house. He asked if she had left any doors or windows open. She said no. The property manager got his the lug wrench from his trunk. He ran around to the sliding glass door. It was locked. He put the flat prying end of the lug wrench under the sliding glass door and popped it off its track. He set the heavy glass door aside. He ran inside and opened the front door from the inside. He yelled to the tenant to enter and look for spare car keys. He grabbed a coat hanger from a closet, untwisted into a straight wire, hooked one end, and forced it between the car window and frame. The tenant went inside, couldn't find keys and ran back to the car, unwilling to leave the baby unattended. The property manager pulled the lock button up with the coat hanger and opened the car door. The tenant jumped in the car and drove away in a hurry, horrified and ashamed, unable to speak to the property manager. The property manager inspected the house, put the sliding glass door back on track, locked the front door, and drove away to his next inspection. The tenant and property manager never spoke again.

227. No Water, no Electricity

The property manager met the new tenant at the house for the move-in inspection. When they entered they found the water and electricity turned off. The property manager tried the water main and the breaker box, to no avail. He called his office. There had been a "mix-up." "Mix-up" was code for "Oh no. We forgot." He called the power company and water company. It would take a day to get service back on. The tenant said it was okay, he was not moving in until the weekend. They performed the inspection with a flashlight. Scheduled cleaning and painting touch-up had not been done because there was no water or electricity. The house was not ready. The property manager called the painter and cleaner to re-schedule. The tenant said it was okay, he could wait. The property manager apologized profusely. The tenant said no problem; he was still delighted to get the house. The tenant said the cable company was supposed to arrive between noon and four. He couldn't meet them because of work. The property manager said he could leave the door open and put a note on the door for the cable company saying come in, with his cell number if help was needed. The tenant asked if he was responsible for the security of the house while it was open. The property manager said no, he would retain keys, possession and liability. The tenant thanked the property manager and went to work.

When the property manager got back to his office he got a call from the landlord asking how the move-in went. The property manager said the move-in was delayed by a day or so. The landlord asked why. The property manager said there was a "Mix-up."

228. Empty

The tenant apparently moved out early without notice. The house was empty with no utilities for weeks. The neighbors called the property manager and told him the newspapers were piling up in the driveway and the grass was long.

The property manager went to the house and picked up the newspapers. He photographed the long grass and the neglected landscaping. He entered the property. There was a horrible smell. The electricity was off. The refrigerator was full of rotten food. There were maggots in the freezer. There were open cereal boxes and potato chip bags in the cupboards. There were ants on the counters. The toilets had not been flushed because the water was off. There were dirty mattresses in the family room. A window was broken and a bird was flying from room to room trying to find a way out. There was a pile of trash in the driveway.

Calls were made to utility companies, a cleaning company, a hauling company, a painter, a handyman, a glass company, the landlord, and to the tenant. The property manager emailed the tenant, accusing him of abandoning the property and leaving behind hazardous neglect. The tenant said he had not moved out yet, he was still living there, he resented the idea that the conditions were substandard. He said GET THE HELL OUT OF MY HOUSE. He said he wasn't leaving. He was just on tour with his band.

229. The Leak Ruined My TV

The tenant saw a water leak coming from the ceiling in the living room in his condo. There was a steady stream of water pouring onto the carpet. The flooring was soaked. The tenant called the property manager and demanded immediate repair. He would hold the landlord responsible for any damage. The tenant moved his big screen TV and located it under the leak. Then he moved his living room furniture under the leak too. He brought a computer from the bedroom and situated it so it would be ruined too. He thought anything ruined by the leak would automatically mean he got a new one free. The plumber arrived and determined that the leak was in the unit upstairs. The condo association held the upstairs owner responsible. The leak was stopped, but not before ruining everything. The property manager walked through the condo with the tenant, shaking his head and expressing genuine concern. The tenant said he expected a new TV, computer, and furniture. The property manager told him to call his tenant insurance firm. The property manager said the landlord's insurance covered the condo property but not personal property. The condominium insurance covered damage between units and in common areas, but nothing else. If the upstairs unit's owners were responsible the tenant could sue them. The tenant should call his tenant insurance firm and file a claim. His insurance firm could subrogate the claim to the upstairs owner's insurance firm. The tenant said he had no renter's insurance and this was the first he heard of such a thing. The property manager said tenant insurance was a condition clearly required in the lease that the tenant had signed. The Personal Property Clause in the lease waived the landlord's liability for lost or damaged personal property. The tenant accused the property manager of fraud and malfeasance. The property manager showed him the lease and the pertinent clauses in the lease. The tenant said he would never pay for it. The property manager said it was okay, he would not force the tenant to replace his own TV, computer and couch, but no one else would replace them for him. The condo itself would be repaired by the landlord. The property manager asked the tenant if he had tested the TV and the computer to see if they still worked? He had not. The property manager told the tenant to do his homework, read the lease, and take whatever course of action he deemed necessary. The tenant contacted an attorney. The attorney asked to see the lease. The attorney went straight to the tenant insurance clause. He wouldn't take the case.

230. Abandonment

The tenants stopped paying rent. They did not return phone calls or emails. A letter was sent by snail-mail requesting a reply. A written notice was sent via certified mail giving proper notice that the property manager would be entering the property in three days, at noon. The property manager went to the house, rang the door bell, and knocked on the door. No answer. He entered with his key and called out his name and his firm's name. He called out the tenant's name. He walked through the house. It appeared the tenant had moved out. There was little furniture, no food in the refrigerator, and there were no clothes in the closets. The property manager put a notice on the door stating that it was abandoned according to the lease and the law, and notifying the tenants that if they were out of the property for over two weeks without notice, possession could be obtained by the landlord. The property manager put strips of clear scotch tape inconspicuously on the exterior doors so he would know if anyone had entered. He emailed the landlord and advised him of the situation and what remedies could be had.

After two weeks the property manager called and emailed the tenant again. Receiving no response, he went to the house. There was a car in the driveway. He rang the doorbell. The tenants were inside. He talked with them in the kitchen.

"I'm relieved to see you home. I thought you had left town for good."

"Why would you think that?"

"You stopped paying rent, responding to phone calls and emails, and you have no food or clothes here."

"How do you know we have no clothes or food? Have you been snooping around?"

"Yes. I had to. I sent notice and followed all the rules. The landlord's representatives have the right to access the property."

"Well we still live here. We just have another house. We moved everything there. We live there half the year."

"That explains it. When can we expect to receive rent?"

"We have to pay for two houses. Things are a little tight right now."

"I will tell the landlord. He may want to kick you out if you don't get back in compliance with the lease."

"Kick us out?"

"Yes. He can evict you as a last resort."

"What if we move out? Do we still have to pay rent?"

"Yes, until we find a new tenant and you pay all related costs."

"Well, you know dishwasher is broken. And the weather-strip is coming off the door. We don't have to pay rent for a run-down house."

"Did you request repairs?

"No. We don't live here."

"Does anyone live here?"

"My niece and her boyfriend live in the basement. But they're not responsible for anything. They're not on the lease. They're just our guests."

"Why don't you give me the keys now and walk away. We can call it even. Don't leave any personal property or people in the basement that you don't want us to set on the curb."

231. Civil Trespass

The tenant stopped paying rent and no longer responded to phone calls, emails, or letters. The property manager went to the house and knocked on the door. The person who answered the door was not the rightful tenant. The occupant said he paid rent to a man who lived in another state. The property manager asked the name of that out-of-state person. The occupant named the true tenant, whose name was on the lease. The property manager told the occupant he had no legal or contractual right to reside on the premises. The occupant didn't get it. The property manager said that the lease prohibited subletting the property. He still didn't get it. The property manager said the occupant had to leave, get out, go away, please. The occupant refused. The property manager told the occupant he would return and post a notice of civil trespass on the door, advise the sheriff's office of the action, and pursue civil remedies. The occupant glared. The property manager said GET OUT or he would return and take the house back and set the furniture on the curb. The occupant didn't understand what was happening, but he was trembling a little. The property manager went back to his office, called the sheriff's office, called an attorney, and returned to the house with a civil trespass notice three days later. The occupants were gone; the furniture was gone. There was a mattress in the family room, an aquarium full of dead fish in the rec room, and a note on the kitchen counter providing an address where the occupant would like the property manager to send the security deposit.

232. Twenty-One License Plates

A large house in a nice neighborhood was rented to four males in their mid-twenties. Two months later the neighbors complained that there were too many cars. Cars in the driveway, cars in the street, sometimes cars on the grass. The property manager drove by and counted two Camaros, a Corvette, a street-race modified Nissan, a Maserati, a Lexus, and a Hummer. All were recent models, loaded with extras. The open garage contained a stack of alloy wheels, a hydraulic jack, and a work bench full of pneumatic tools. The property manager went back to his office and called the tenants.

"I drove by your house and couldn't help but notice a lot of cars. A lot of cars."

The tenant said, "We like cars."

The property manager said, "Your application has four tenants and lists four cars."

The tenant said, "We have friends. Sometimes our families visit too."

The property manager asked, "We have had complaints. May I visit and enter the house to count beds and heads?"

The tenant said, "Come by any time. Someone is usually here."

The property manager said, "I can be there this afternoon, okay?"

"Okay," said the tenant.

The property manager arrived and wrote down the makes and models of the cars, jotted down the license plate numbers, and knocked on the door. An occupant let him in. The property manager asked his name.

The tenant said, "Joe."

The property manager said, "There's no Joe on the lease."

The tenant said, "I'm just visiting."

The property manager walked through the house. He counted seven beds and ten toothbrushes. He saw women's clothes in two closets. There were twenty-one license plates on the work bench in the garage.

The property manager said, "It looks like there are a lot of people living here who are not on the lease."

The tenant said, "We have visitors and friends. That's all."

The property manager said, "Why all the new cars and why so many license plates?"

The tenant said, "It's just a hobby. We love cars."

The property manager said, "You are in breach of the lease in a number of ways. And the neighbors are up in arms. I'll send you a notice clarifying the lease violations. Can you give me the names of all occupants?"

The tenant wrote down a list of names. Two were names from the lease. The rest were not tenants. They were unauthorized occupants.

The property manager called the police and an attorney. He described the seven expensive cars and twenty-one license plates. He learned that some people ship cars overseas as personal vehicles, avoiding commercial taxes and tariffs. Especially exotic cars. He called the landlord. He called Joe and told him the police would drop by. The landlord authorized eviction based on the No Business Use clause in the lease.

The property manager posted a Cure-or-Quit notice on the door providing the violations of the lease, the required remedies, and the redress the landlord would pursue in court. Later he called the tenant again.

"Did you get my notice?"

"Yes. But I don't get it."

"The landlord wants his house back. You are in violation of the lease, community rules and zoning ordinances."

"Can you prove it?"

"I took pictures of all the cars, mattresses, license plates and toothbrushes. Do you see where this is going? If you move out promptly you can take all your stuff with you. If not, you may be locked out and your possessions removed, or worse. I asked the police to investigate but they asked me to file a formal complaint with civil court."

"I don't get it. We're paying rent. We take care of the house."

"You're not on the lease, Joe. So you should leave either way. You're first on my list. Nothing personal."

"Give me two weeks. Some guys have moved out. Other guys have moved in. Some girlfriends come and go. The cars are not a problem. We will sell them."

"Sell them on Craigslist? E-bay?"

"We have a friend in the business."

"That friend, that's the guy police should talk to, or the state's attorney. What's his name?"

"Let me get back to you. Give me a few weeks."

The property manager drove by the house every day on his way home from work. The cars disappeared one by one. Moving vans came and went. When the house looked abandoned he called a locksmith. He posted notices on the door. He called the landlord.

"The tenants are gone. No idea where they went. We are taking possession after we exhaust all means of contacting the tenants."

"What about the rent?"

"I doubt they'll keep paying."

"Why did you ever let these guys move in, in the first place?"

"We recommended you accept the other application from the accountant with her three kids. But she offered fifty dollars a month under list price."

"I did that?"

"You turned her down because she's divorced, a single-earner household."

"I did?"

"You accepted the four single guys after I told you the risks."

"I forget."

"We did everything we could in your best interest."

"Is there anything we can do to recoup my losses?"

"I can put you in touch with an attorney. We can call a collections agency. Maybe a skip tracer. It will take time and money. There are no guarantees."

"Shit. Shit shit shit."

"I agree."

233. Twenty People

A plumber was called to fix a leak in a rental townhouse. He called the property manager afterward and told him there were at least twenty people living there. The property manager drove to the house, parked on the street, and watched the house from five to seven that evening. He took pictures on his smart phone of everyone who entered and exited. He knocked on doors and talked to the neighbors. He photographed cars and license plates.

The next day he wrote up a report of his observations. He sent his report to the landlord and the tenant. He notified the tenant in writing that he would enter the property and inspect it after a required reasonable notice period of twenty-four hours. He arrived with another property manager. They wore ties and carried cameras and clipboards.

The tenants had prepared rapidly. The only people in the house were the couple on the lease and their toddler. The tool shed out back was stuffed with mattresses. There were locks on the bedroom doors. There were enough clothes and toothbrushes for three or four families. The property manager stood in the living room and told them how eviction worked. When the female tenant started crying, they handed her husband a thirty-day Cure or Quit notice and left. It required that the breach be cured or possession would be taken.

The property manager drove by the house daily. Pick-up trucks came and went. Dozens of trash bags were set by the curb. In thirty days he inspected again. The house and tenancy miraculously appeared to be in compliance. All the extra people and their mattresses and clothes were gone. The small family that remained smiled and offered him a cola.

He felt no satisfaction, no job well done. He returned to his office and called the landlord. Mission accomplished, he said. But his delivery was unconvincing. The landlord was angry. He said he could never trust Those People again. The property manager had lost trust, too, not for Those People but for all people. He had begun to believe that everyone breaks rules, lies about it, and covers it up.

234. Ice Waterfall

Three young men with engineering degrees rented a townhouse. They earned a combined income of over three hundred thousand a year at local firms. They had good landlord references from apartment buildings out of state. When they went home for the holidays they turned off the heat to save money. The pipes in the upstairs hall bath froze and burst. That bathroom was over the foyer and front door. Water flowed down the front of the house, covering the front door in several inches of ice. It looked like a glass waterfall cascading down the house, flowing down the sidewalk. When the sun hit it, it was beautiful. The neighbors didn't report it. When the engineers returned they could not get into their house because of the ice wall. The called the property manager.

"There's something wrong with our house."

"What do you mean?"

"The front door is frozen over."

"When did this happen?"

"We've been out of town. We don't know when it happened."

"Oh. I think I've seen this kind of thing before. Can you get inside?"

"No, it's frozen over. It's like an iceberg."

"I can be there this afternoon. Let me call some guys with sledgehammers, pick axes, and shovels. Maybe a locksmith too."

"Are you going to fix this quickly? We need to get back in today."

"Did you leave the heat on when you left town?"

"No. Why?"

"Did you turn off the water main?"

"No."

"Did you ever read the lease?"

"I didn't have time. We were in a hurry to move."

"I'll bring a copy of the lease. You should find a hotel or something."

"When can you fix it?"

"Can you write us a check to get repairs started?"

"I don't get it."

235. My Dog Died Too

The tenant stopped paying rent. The property manager called him.

"Good morning. I haven't received the rent yet. Is everything okay?"

"No. My wife died."

"Oh, I'm so sorry. Are you okay?"

"No, I can't pay the rent anymore."

"Why not?"

"My wife died in South Africa. I flew there and tried to get her body. The red tape took forever. I stayed there a month. Then I was out of state for another month with funeral arrangements and family. I lost my job. Now I can't pay the rent."

"Can you make a partial payment?"

"No."

"Would you like to move out and find a place you can afford?"

"No. I can't afford to move."

"Do you have family or friends who can help you? Pay rent for you? Take you in?"

"No. I'm all alone. Just me and my dog."

"We don't want to evict you in your time of grief, but you can't stay for free."

"But my wife died. I don't care what happens to me."

The eviction process was slow. The courts were backlogged. Sixty days later there was a court hearing. The property manager presented a claim of three months' rent past due totaling six thousand dollars, plus attorney's fees, late fees, and court costs. He also sued for possession. He presented the lease, the accounting, and sheriff's notices to the judge. The judge addressed the tenant.

"Do you dispute the plaintiff's claim?"

"Your honor, my wife died overseas. I lost my job."

The property manager's attorney objected. "Your honor, we stipulate to the tenant's tragedy, but he has not contested our claims and we assert that his life story is not in dispute."

The judge said, "I'll allow the tenant some leeway but the claim for damages is all we are hearing today."

The tenant blurted out, "But my wife died. I don't have any money." He had no further testimony.

The attorney for the plaintiff said, "Your honor the landlord seeks immediate possession of the property. We will file a motion to seek garnishment of wages and bank accounts for the monetary damages."

The judge ruled: "The court grants the plaintiff's claim of damages. A Writ of Possession shall issue to the sheriff. The defendant shall vacate upon enforcement of the writ. We sympathize with the defendant's plight but his personal situation is immaterial. Judgement for the plaintiff."

The tenant cried out, "And my dog died too."

236. Identity Theft

The tenant applied to rent a house, was qualified, and was accepted. He met the property inspector at the move-in inspection. Six months later at the mid-term inspection the inspector saw that the occupant was not the tenant who was on the lease, or at the move-in. Sometimes people with bad credit used other people's data to apply and qualify for rent.

The property manager called the original tenant. The tenant confessed it was his son in the house, not him. He would straighten it out. The tenant's son stopped paying rent. The property manager called the father and told him it could lead to eviction, collections, and credit problems. The father said he would take care of it.

The rent continued to be delinquent. The property manager went to the house and knocked on the door. There was a different occupant, a woman who was also not on the lease, who would not give her name or grant access to the property.

The landlord filed suit for back rent, possession, attorney's fees, and court costs. The original tenant, the one on the lease, appeared in court with a handwriting expert who testified that the signature on the lease was not his. The property manager and landlord could not prove who signed the lease or who lived in the house. They had executed the lease by email. They had not met the tenant before signing the lease. They had not gotten a photo ID.

The judge ruled that the defendant was probably lying to cover his unauthorized sublet to his son. The judge said the landlord and property manager were credible. But the judge said that the defense argument that the lease signing was not witnessed or confirmed stood. The expert handwriting analyst was not refuted. Judgement for the defendant.

The landlord's attorney offered to refer the case to the state's attorney for prosecution for fraud, a criminal case against the occupant for defrauding both his father and the landlord. The landlord refused. He had lost six thousand dollars in rent and attorney's fees. He had also lost confidence in the courts and the property manager. He sold the house, fired the property manager, and wrote bad Yelp reviews about him.

237. Identity Theft 2

The applicant had excellent credit, salary, and employment history. He provided a lengthy collection of pay stubs, a tax return, social security number, addresses, next of kin, homes owned and rented. He was unable to come in to sign the lease so he signed it by fax. Real estate contracts of sale and rent are commonly executed by mutual facsimile. The signed lease was faxed back and a move-in scheduled. When the property manager arrived for the move-in inspection the tenant was not there, but his daughter was. She took the keys and said she would give the keys and inspection paperwork to her father.

After the move-in and the first rent, no further rent was paid. Notices were sent by mail, email, fax, and phone. No reply. The property manager went to the house and entered, after proper notice. The house décor and furnishings, and clothes in the closets, indicated it was occupied by a young woman and two small girls.

The property manager returned to his office and paid an online name-search website to find better contact info for the lease signor, who was a fifty-five year old male according to the application. When he reached him, the "tenant" was shocked. No, he had not applied to rent. No, he did not live there. No, he knew nothing of it. But he admitted he had a sneaky, dishonest outlaw of a daughter with his two precious grandchildren who he adored. She had, no doubt, duped him again. He asked for time to straighten it out, and that his credit not be affected, and his daughter not be charged.

The landlord filed Unlawful Detainer through the property manager. Six weeks later they met in court. The defendant did not show up, but the daughter had called the court and claimed she had a sick child. The judge was sympathetic. The "second bite of the apple" rule applied. Especially with sick children. The case was continued for two weeks.

After the court continuance the father came to the property manager's office and paid the debt. He moved his daughter out of the house. The landlord took possession of his house again. He re-rented it through the same property manager. When a good application was received, the landlord asked to meet the tenant before signing a lease, and to see the credit report and all financial and personal references in person. And he asked to see a photo ID.

238. One Year Rent Cash in Advance

An unqualified tenant wanted to rent a poorly maintained townhouse. It was a good match. The tenant had terrible credit, insufficient income, no manners and no clue. He offered to pay a year rent in advance in cash. The owner agreed. What could go wrong? Everything was paid up front. The tenant moved in and began offending neighbors. He broke HOA rules. He broke a window. He let the grass grow long. The landlord and property manager asked him to move out, but he had paid all the rent so it would be hard to force him out. Eviction for non-payment is open and shut. Eviction for material breaches of the lease, like neglect and destruction, turn into he-said she-said arguments. They required a higher standard of proof. They required the tenant be allowed time to cure the breach and comply with the lease.

The tenant finally agreed to move out if his remaining rent was refunded. The landlord said no, that money was gone. The tenant stated that the rent should have been kept in escrow and paid out in installments as payments came due. The property manager asked his attorney. She said yes, unless the contract stipulates otherwise. He asked his accountant. The accountant said yes, that's standard accounting procedure in a prepaid account. The property manager told the landlord. The landlord said no, he would keep the money, it was already spent, get the tenant out. They bullied and badgered the tenant out of the house with vague promises of reconciliation of the account. When the tenant moved out the landlord kept the rent, fired the property manager, and sold the house. The tenant called the property manager and threatened him with bodily harm. The property manager called the police. The police said he could file a toothless complaint but they couldn't do anything until after the bodily harm occurred.

239. People Living in the Shed

A neighbor called the property manager to complain about the tenants. There were up to twenty people living in the house. People were living in the back yard. A dog was barking at all hours. There were too many cars. The property manager went to the neighbor's house and talked to him. The neighbor said he recalled the old days when everyone knew everyone, when neighbors worked together, when times were simpler. He refused to make a complaint for the record or put anything in writing for fear of retribution.

The property manager knocked on the tenant's door. She said, yes, she had visitors, friends and family, doesn't everyone? She said no, she had no dog. There was a dog in her living room as they spoke. It wasn't hers, she explained, it was just a friend's dog visiting. No, no one lived in the back yard, how ridiculous.

The property manager inspected the house. He counted twelve toothbrushes and six beds. There were only two people on the lease. He found two mattresses and a TV in the tool shed. He asked the tenant about the shed. She said it was just storage. He showed her the TV in the shed, how it was plugged into the house. It had a cable box and a remote. He turned the TV on. She smiled and said it must have been that way when she moved in.

A week later the property manager went by the house on his way to work in the morning. He sat in his car reading the paper. He took notes and photographs of persons and cars leaving for work in the morning. He returned to his office and sent a full report to the tenant and the landlord. He described the avenues the landlord could use to remedy the violations of the lease and zoning regulations. He explained Unlawful Detainer, Cure or Quit, eviction, possession, sheriffs and locksmiths. He did not threaten any action, having been warned by counsel not to threaten any action that was not imminent or in process.

The tenant agreed to move out, but she needed a letter of recommendation from him in order to rent another house. He could not honestly recommend her overall performance so he wrote a letter pointing out her positives. She had two ongoing small business enterprises, house cleaning and handyman services. She kept the house immaculate and in good repair. She kept the lawn neat. She charmed her neighbors. The neighbor who originally complained withdrew his complaint. She had brought him casseroles. The property manager swallowed his pride and provided the letter of recommendation to a potential new landlord the tenant had found. The tenant was approved, moved out, and left the house like new.

The tenant called the property manager a month later and demanded the return of her security deposit. The property manager explained that the landlord had applied the deposit to pay attorney's fees and marketing expenses. The tenant didn't get it. She had been a good tenant. She had a letter to prove it. She threatened to call the police. The property manager encouraged her to do so. He knew they would listen. They might make a routine report, and do nothing more.

240. The Sick Child

The rent was late. The property manager called the tenant. She had a sick child. A month later there was a kitchen fire. The property manager told the tenant she had to pay for the damage. She said she had no money, she had a sick child. Six weeks later the HOA sent a notice threatening fines if the tenant did not mow the lawn. The property manager called the tenant. She said she didn't have time to mow, she had a sick child. At the annual inspection the inspector reported that garbage in the back yard was attracting vermin. The property manager asked her to clean the back yard. The tenant said no, she had a sick child.

At the end of the lease the tenant moved out. The security deposit was used to repaint the kitchen, clean out the back yard, pay HOA fines, and offset late fees. The tenant demanded her deposit to help pay for her sick child's medical expenses. The property manager asked if she could provide the child's medical bills as proof. The tenant said no. It was private. That would violate her HIPAA rights. The property manager told her she should switch it up once in a while. Use the "sick child" thing once. Use the "grandma died" thing the next time. Throw in "I was laid off" once in a while.

241. Patched Doors

There were two tenants, one male and one female. They appeared to be boyfriend and girlfriend at the time of the application and move-in. During the tenancy the young woman called the property manager and asked him to lock the male tenant out. The property manager couldn't remove a signatory or tenant without written consent of all parties, but told her she could petition the court for a restraining order. The male tenant called the property manager and said his ex-girlfriend was not paying her half of the rent, could he kick her out? The property manager explained that leases treat all tenants as one entity, equally and severally liable for all damages. Terms and conditions applied to all parties. The tenants fought. The neighbors complained. Police were called about noise, but no violence was detected. No citations were issued or arrests made.

By the time of move-out the tenants were living in separate rooms, separated by a locked door. The house looked good overall. The tenants received a full refund of their security deposit.

The landlord returned and moved into the home. A few months later the he slammed the door between the two bedrooms. It cracked and fell in pieces to the floor. It had been battered to pieces by the fighting tenants, patched and glued back together like a puzzle, then sanded and painted over. It had been hanging there, waiting to fall apart, for months.

The property manager called the ex-tenants and asked for compensation. They said they didn't know what he was talking about. They told him to stay out of their personal lives.

The landlord demanded the property manager pay for a new door due to negligence in inspecting the property. The property manager offered to remove the door and hinges, patch the hinge screw holes, and let the second room be a den or dressing area instead of a second bedroom. The landlord said he would agree, if the property manager paid him the value of a new door. The property manager got a price from a carpenter for five hundred dollars to replace the door with a similar hollow-core flat door, like all the other doors in the house. The landlord got a price on the internet for two thousand dollars to replace the door with a hardwood-paneled door with brass hardware. The property manager said that for two thousand dollars he would have to be there witness the installation and get a copy of the itemized invoice. The landlord said no, he wasn't really going to replace the door, he liked the new layout. He just wanted the money.

242. Noise

A condominium tenant called the property manager to complain about the upstairs neighbors walking loudly on the floor above him. He could not sleep. The property manager told him that noise is not covered by the lease or regulated by the property management firm. The tenant could call the condo association or the police to see if they would accept noise complaints. The tenant said he would rather confront the upstairs occupant. The property manager said a courteous conversation was a better place to start.

The property manager found the name of the upstairs owners through public tax records. He called them and asked if they were aware if the problem. They said yes, they had been courteous with the tenant below, but he had threatened them in the hallway.

The property manager called the tenant and asked him to talk to his neighbors in a more courteous manner. The tenant refused. The property manager told the tenant that after 10PM the police may be able to enforce noise ordinances. The tenant replied that he works nights so the noise problem is during the day when he is trying to sleep. The noise ordinances did not apply in day time. The police were not helpful. They found him rude and discourteous.

The property manager made an appointment with the upstairs owner and the downstairs tenant to meet at the condo, walk on the upstairs floor while the tenant listened below, and then listen downstairs while the upstairs owner walked on the floor. After he had done so, he expressed his opinion to the tenant that the amount of noise seemed normal for a condo. The property manager had lived in apartments and condos and had to deal with similar noise levels. The tenant didn't get it. He had lived his whole life in a detached house on an acre lot, with neighbors more than fifty feet away. The property manager suggested that was the problem, the tenant had chosen to live a couple feet below neighbors without considering the consequences. The tenant threatened to contact Yelp, the Better Business Bureau, and Channel Seven News. The property manager recommended the tenant be cautious while asking for help in harming others' reputations, to avoid risking libel and slander suits.

243. Noise 2

The property manager received a complaint from the tenant's neighbor. The tenant's dog was barking a lot. It was disturbing the entire neighborhood. The property manager asked which house the complainant lived in. It was the house directly behind the tenant's.

The property manager went to the neighborhood and knocked on doors. He met the neighbors to the right and left. He talked to the neighbors across the street. He couldn't find anyone who had heard any barking. He knocked on the tenant's door. The tenants introduced him to the dog in the back yard. The dog did not bark when the property manager, a stranger, entered the yard.

The property manager looked out behind the back yard at the house of the complainant. There were trees leading down a ravine to a stream and flood plain. Across the stream was the complainant's house, barely visible through the trees.

The property manager walked around the block, measuring distances at two feet per pace. The rear neighbor who had complained appeared to live eighty to one hundred feet away from the tenant and dog.

The property manager wrote a letter to the landlord, describing the noise complaint, identifying the house numbers and distances involved, and identifying those neighbors who had given him their names. He sent the report by email to the tenant and the landlord. He sent a hard copy by regular mail to the complaining neighbor. He summarized that the noise problem could not be verified through normal observation. His recommendation was that the offended neighbor call the police promptly when barking occurred after 10pm, when noise ordinances applied. He warned that most police officers will not write citations for noise violations, that the police don't like being called for such affairs, that the police are generally annoyed and recommend neighbors work things out together.

The landlord and tenant thanked the property manager. The offended neighbor did not reply. The police were not called. The offended neighbor bypassed the property manager and contacted the landlord directly and told him the property manager was taking sides. The landlord said he hoped so.

244. Noise 3

The tenant's neighbor called the property manager and complained that the tenant was playing loud music late at night. It was a townhouse so the sound came right through the walls. The tenant said he had a rock band. They practiced in the basement. The basement had a concrete floor and walls with no windows. The tenants had soundproofed the basement with foam panels. The property manager asked them to stop playing after 10pm. They agreed.

The same neighbor called the property manager again and complained that the tenant started his motorcycle every morning, disturbing the peace. The property manager asked what time it occurred. The neighbor said 7:30 am. The property manager said county noise ordinances govern excess noise from 10:00 pm to 7:00 am. The lease did not govern noise at all. He asked her to talk to her neighbors, work things out in person. She said no, she was afraid that young men with drums and motorcycles would retaliate.

The property manager called the tenant again and asked him if he got along with the neighborhood in general. The tenant said all of the neighbors liked him except one, the house to the right, who never spoke to him. He assumed that was the one complaining. He said he would talk to her. The property manager told him she was already intimidated, please tread lightly.

The property manager did not hear any more about the problem. He waited a month and called the neighbor. She was very unhappy that she had been forced to speak to the person she complained about. She accused the property manager of ratting her out. The property manager thanked her for talking to the tenant. He told her about the good old days when he was growing up when neighbors talked to each other and solved problems together. She said she wanted to talk to his boss. He said that was a good idea, talk to his boss, talk things out, get it off her chest. She hung up.

The property manager called the tenant. He told him that when the lease ended in three months he could help him find a detached house, further from nosy neighbors, if he would like that.

245. Noise 4

A new tenant moved into a one-bedroom condo. She moved her possessions in, turned her radio up loud, and disappeared for a few days. Neighbors complained about the loud radio to the condo association, to the property manager, and to the police. They banged on her walls and knocked on her door.

The property manager called her cell. She told him she had turned on the loud music and moved out for several days to scare away evil spirits. She said she had lost the keys and couldn't get back in so she was staying with a friend. She asked for more keys. He told her to call a locksmith and pay for new keys.

He told her he would enter the property in twenty-four hours if she had not turned off the music. She said that if he entered her condo alone he could be in grave danger if it was not purified. He asked her if she could please put that in writing. He entered the condo and turned off the radio. On his way back to the office he got a flat tire. He guessed it was caused by the curse of the evil spirits. He wrote it down in her file and kept the receipt for the new tire. He called her and told her she would be held responsible for the tire damage incurred by her spirits, including his tire, if she didn't lift the curse. She was pleased and grateful that he admitted there were spirits.

246. The Goat

A neighbor of the tenant called with a complaint. On Saturday nights the tenant had big parties in the front yard. There was music and drinking. Noise until 2:00 AM. The property manager asked if the neighbor had called the authorities. She said, "No. I'm calling you."

The property manager called the tenant. She did not deny it. Sure, she had visitors, and friends, and family too. She said that's a good thing. She accused the neighbor of having no friends or family and not understanding those things.

After the next party the neighbor called again. Saturday night there had been another party. There was a goat rotating on a spit over a fire in the front yard. Food was being sold. Cars were parked all over the street. No English was being spoken. The property manager said business uses were prohibited in the residence. He would call the tenant again. He would call the county about unlicensed businesses.

The tenant said the problem was just a cultural difference. She expected more tolerance in a metropolitan area and a diverse suburb. The property manager said he would have to drive by on Saturday night, witness the violation, call the police or zoning, or the department of health, or whoever would listen.

The property manager called the offended neighbor again and told her he was doing everything he could. He would be forced to drive by on Saturday night. He didn't want to. It was not his job. The neighbor recommended he try the goat. It was superb.

247. One Inch of Mold

A tenant called the property manager and said he had mold in his unit. The property manager went to look at it. It was a black discoloration in a one-inch strip of caulk around the dining room window. The property manager laughed. The tenant produced a note from his doctor that used the word "mold." The property manager called the landlord, who agreed to mold testing. The mold testing firm tested the air in the unit. They tested the exterior air for a baseline. The test revealed elevated levels of a group of molds called Penicillium Aspergillus. It was above recommended levels, in parts per million. They proposed four thousand dollars worth of remediation. The owner felt cornered and agreed.

They removed the caulk and window trim, the adjacent drywall, and the insulation. They put a blower on the air handler and cycled the interior air rapidly. They created negative pressure in the unit with suction, to isolate the area. They filtered all the air in the unit through HEPA-filters. They treated all furniture and personal possessions with an EPA approved mildewcide. After the parts-per-million of microbes in the air was deemed acceptable, they left. The tenant felt much better.

After the treatment the property manager inspected all the resident-accessible hallways in the building, and all storage rooms, the laundry room, and common areas in the building. He found black powdery discolorations of apparent mold growing everywhere. He found the building's website, found contact info, and wrote a letter to the association, copied it to the management company, on-site manager and maintenance director. He sent them all photographs and documented the remediation costs incurred by the landlord. He suggested the association may be responsible for compensating the owner for those costs. He received no response. He did a little digging and found the names of the association board members, found their home addresses on public tax records, and sent them his findings as well. Several months later he walked the common areas in the building again and discovered all the mold had been painted over, not remediated. Mold loves paint. Paint is one of mold's favorite foods. The mold would be back and so would he.

248. The Toilet Tank

The tenant filed suit against the landlord and property manager in small claims court. He claimed that the powder room toilet did not work and had not been repaired.

The property manager said, "I sent a plumber. He said it was cracked by someone hitting it or falling on it. Significant force had been applied. The tenant should pay to fix it."

The tenant said, "I was on vacation when it cracked. It must have been spontaneous."

The property manager entered into evidence an invoice by the plumber that included the words "Tenant broke toilet."

The tenant had a receipt from a rental car company showing he was out of town for two weeks right before reporting the breakage.

The tenant stated he did not have full use of the property because he was short one toilet, and therefore should not have to pay the full rent.

The judge asked, "How much rent should be deducted to compensate for the loss of use of one toilet in one bathroom?"

The tenant said, "I shouldn't have to pay any rent for a partly usable house."

The property manager said, "The powder room is one fiftieth of the house in square footage and its value is no more than fifty dollars a month."

The judge said, "I've never heard of spontaneous toilet tank breakage. But the landlord should have repaired the toilet and debated the cost later. Please don't ever bring your toilet problems into my courtroom again. Take them to arbitration or settle them out of court. The landlord shall repair the toilet, having failed to provide any toilet tank crack expert."

The case was settled. The judge called the next case. The next plaintiff was suing his son for refusing to pay rent or move out.

249. The Hostage

The property manager met the landlord at the house after the renter had moved. The landlord complained that the house was not clean, the chandelier was tilted, the vinyl flooring was dull, the walls had nail holes, a window screen was bent, and the sliding door was off track. As they walked through the house the owner named more minor damage in each room. The property manager dutifully listed the damage on an inspection sheet. He told the owner how much the security deposit was and how many items it might cover. When they reached the last room, the master bedroom, the wife lectured the property manager for forty-five minutes while the husband stood in the bedroom door with his hands on his hips, elbows to the door frames, blocking the only exit. The AC was not on. The room temperature was over eighty degrees. The property manager sweated profusely while taking copious notes. After the owners got everything off their chests the husband turned and led the property manager downstairs and out the front door, with the wife following the property manager describing how the house used to look, before it was rented out.

Standing in the front yard the property manager explained that the wear and tear was relatively normal for a rental. He apologized that he had not fully explained the risks of landlording.

The owner told the property manager that he had expected the house to be returned in the same condition as it was delivered to the tenant. The property manager said that no rental property is ever returned in identical condition. Wear and tear is unavoidable. He defended the tenant.

The owner explained that he was the customer and the property manager worked for him. He said he would contact the property manager's employer and tell him about the shabby treatment he had received. The property manager said that his boss would appreciate and act upon such negative feedback.

The property manager returned to his office and wrote a four-page email describing the entire two-hour walk-through and discussion in detail from his notes, and sent the documentation to the owner and to his boss. He included an attached email from two years previous in which the property manager had described the risks and rewards of being a landlord, and defined normal wear and tear. He did not mention being held hostage in the master bedroom for forty-five minutes. Maybe he had imagined it.

250. The Hostage 2

The property manager met the landlord at his house as he was returning to it after renting it out for four years. The landlord complained that he had knocked on the door a week earlier and the tenant would not let him in. The property manager explained that the tenant had owned possession at that time and was owed proper notice prior to the owner's access. The owner protested that it was his home. The property manager explained that the lease and the law granted that it was the tenants' home, and not the owner's, for the duration of the lease. The owner growled and led the property manager through the house, pointing out damage in each room. The property manager wrote down every detail.

When they reached the basement utility room the property manager stood in the middle of the room while the owner stood in the only doorway, with his hands on his hips and his elbows inches from the door jambs, blocking the exit. He maintained that position while he ranted for fifteen minutes.

The owner complained that the HVAC unit was making an irritating little sound. Could he charge the tenant for that? The property manager assumed it was a bearing in the blower fan motor and could not have been caused by the tenant. The owner reiterated that it must be the tenant's fault because it was not there when he left. The property manager said that the tenant would have had to remove a sealed metal panel from the unit and damage the bearings with some degree of skill, then reassemble the unit. Most tenants would just kick it and leave a dent in it. They were not that subtle. The owner pounded his right fist into his left palm repeatedly, repeating his accusations about the tenant's maliciousness, blocking the door.

After fifteen minutes of point-counterpoint the owner heaved a sigh, moved out of the doorway, and led the property manager out of the house. They stood in the front yard for twenty minutes while the owner complained about how the neighborhood had changed. How the regular neighbors had moved out and "international" people had moved in. The property manager nodded his head as if in agreement, and shook his head as if it were all a shame how the world was changing. He looked at his watch and mentioned that he was late for his next appointment. The owner thanked the property manager for his patience. The property manager went home early and drank.

251. The Hostage 3

The tenant called the property manager and said his AC was not working. He demanded immediate repair. He said otherwise his children would suffer terrible consequences.

The property manager called the heating and cooling repair firm. He said he needed an air-conditioning repair estimate as soon as possible. The contractor scheduled an appointment with the tenant.

The AC mechanic arrived and diagnosed the repair. He told the tenant he would have to give the property manager an estimate before returning to do the work. The tenant said he better fix it now or else. The mechanic called his office.

The AC firm called the property manager. Their mechanic was being held hostage by the tenant. He would not be allowed to leave without doing the repair. The property manager asked how the tenant could keep the mechanic from leaving. It turned out the tenant was standing in the only doorway blocking his exit. The tenant had moved his car to block the work van's exit.

The property manager authorized the repair. He called the owner and told him he had authorized the payment due to the seriousness of the situation. The owner said he would not pay for the repair. Air conditioning was a luxury. He had grown up in the 1930s without it.

252. The Hostage 4

The property manager walked through the house with the tenant at the annual mid-term inspection. He noticed there were four beds but only two tenants on the lease. He asked who lived in each room. He asked for names. He described the lease clauses prohibiting subletting and requiring all occupants be on the lease.

The property manager photographed each bed and bedroom. He counted toothbrushes and looked at the calendar, photos and notes on the refrigerator. He glanced at a pile of mail on the counter, noting the names. When he entered the master bedroom, taking notes and pictures, a large young man got out of bed and demanded an explanation. The inspector asked his name and told him he was not on the lease. Either the lease could be renegotiated or the tenancy terminated. The large unauthorized occupant moved to the master bedroom doorway in his briefs, blocking the only exit. There was no room to squeeze by and the body language was clear. The property manager talked and listened and took notes while the occupant argued and puffed out his chest and made vague threats of bodily harm. The property manager continuously scribbled notes, taking direct quotes and reading them back to the occupant. Neither party moved forward or back, their feet staying in place while words flew back and forth for ten minutes.

After the conversation wound down and got boring, after the inspector turned it into a discussion of legal and contractual obligations and responsibilities, the occupant got irritated, unblocked the door, and told the property manager to leave.

The property manager exited and stood in the driveway. He wrote down the makes and models and license plate numbers of the cars in the driveway. He called his office, the landlord, and the non-emergency police phone number. He described and documented the threats of bodily harm, word for word. He asked the police how he could submit a routine online report, for the record, to be used in case of any future threats or assault. The police offered to meet him at his office and take a statement, just for the record. It was a slow day for real crime.

253. Dog Poop

The property manager was notified by the HOA that the tenant had not cleaned up the dog poop in the yard.

"Is dog poop prohibited?"

"Yes. In the common areas."

"Where is the dog poop in question?"

"In the yard, not common area, I know. But the neighbors complained. I have to do something."

The property manager called the tenant and asked about the dog poop.

"I have a report of dog poop in your yard. People complained."

The tenant said, "I have a dog, as it says in the lease. Where else should it poop?"

"I know. You're right. But the neighbors complained. I have to do something."

"The neighbors have dogs, too."

The property manager said, "I'll just send you a little warning, and you talk to the neighbors, and maybe it will all go away."

"I have an eight foot stockade fence. No one can see into my yard except from one little second story window next door. It's that nosy little old lady, isn't it?"

"I don't know. I don't want to know."

"I'll definitely talk to her."

The property manager went to the property and walked around the perimeter. There was no poop on the front yard, sidewalk, or common areas. There was no visible poop or poop smell anywhere. The back yard could not be viewed without a step-ladder, except from one neighbor's upstairs window.

The property manager returned to his office and called the community manager.

"Is dog poop prohibited in back yards?"

"No."

"Are there any written requirements regarding clean-up, or smell?"

"No."

"Are any real rules being broken?"

"No. Just complaints."

"One complaint or many?"

"One."

"The tenant figured out who complained, and he's going to confront her."

"Oh no. Shit. She's going to kill me. I promised it would be anonymous."

The tenant confronted the neighbor. The neighbor confronted the HOA community manager. The community manager called the property manager.

"What do we do now?"

"I'll ask the tenant to make a poop clean-up schedule. I'll tell him he scared the neighbor to death and she broke down and cried. I'll ask him not to talk to the neighbor anymore. You tell the neighbor we are badgering and threatening the tenant. You call me next time before you send my tenant a violation notice."

"So we do nothing, right?"

"Nothing. But make it look like something."

254. Dog Poop 2

When the homeowner returned to his home after leasing it out for several years, he walked through with the property manager to inspect everything. The house looked perfect. The tenant had paid rent on time, taken good care of the house, and not complained about a thing.

After walking through the entire house, mutually satisfied and agreeing to release the full deposit to the tenant, they walked down to the dark unfinished basement. It had bare bulb ceiling lights, concrete walls and floors, and a damp mildew smell that had been noted at move-in.

They were standing in the basement discussing how the basement could be finished. There was room for a rec room, a bedroom and a bathroom. It would benefit the owner at re-sale. Just then the owner looked down and said, "What's that?" The property manager looked down and said, "Oh, it's dog poop." He leaned over and took a picture of it. He promised to send the picture to the tenant who had moved out. The owner smiled and said, "Forget it. Just clean it up." The property manager kept a bucket in his car filled with rags, disinfectant, deodorizer and a scrub brush for just such occasions. He cleaned it up.

When he returned to his office he told his co-workers and added it to his Dog Poop file. They told him to look at his shoes.

255. Dog Poop 3

The Condo Association required all leases be subject to association rules. All tenants signed an agreement to comply with the community rules. The rules included a requirement that all occupants submit DNA from their pets to the association. There had been an epidemic of dog poop complaints in the common areas where occupants walked their dogs. Children played there and occasionally got dog poop on their clothes, shoes, or bare feet. Dog DNA databases were a trend in the industry that allowed associations to effectively enforce violations of dog poop rules.

The property manager received a notice that his tenant had not submitted a DNA sample. He called the tenant. The tenant had not read the lease or the condo addendum that he had signed. He said he had not violated anything. The property manager said that non-compliance was a lease violation that could lead to eviction through a Cure-or-Quit notice. The tenant got angry and accused the property manager of violating the dog's right to privacy. The property manager said there was no Bill of Rights for dogs. The tenant hung up.

The tenant went to the condo association's on-site office. He yelled at the receptionist and asked to yell at her superior. The manager called the property manager and allowed him to hear the angry yelling over the phone. The property manager apologized for the association manager's plight and said he would try to calm the tenant down.

The property manager called the tenant and asked him to move out at the end of the lease term. The tenant protested. The property manager asked him please, it's easier than eviction. The tenant asked if it would be okay if the dog just pooped inside, maybe in the kitchen instead of outside from now on. Nobody would see it. Then he would like to extend the lease another year.

256. Dog Poop 4

The property manager received a complaint from the downstairs neighbor below his tenant's condo. The tenant's dog was pooping and peeing on the balcony and the poop and urine were running down to her balcony. The property manager asked if he could see the damage before confronting the tenant. She agreed. She let him in and showed him the balcony. There was a strong poop smell. Urine stains ran down the balcony walls. Uric acid had etched and rusted stains into the metal door frame.

The property manager apologized profusely for the damage and promised that the owner of the upstairs unit would be implored to repair all damage. Before leaving he stood in her living room and looked at the clutter that was piled up onto the walls: piles of old newspapers, stacks of dirty carry-out containers, dozens of full black plastic trash bags. He peeked into the kitchen and saw filth and rotting food. He asked to use the bathroom. She declined. He put his hand on the camera hanging from a lanyard around his neck. She ordered him to leave. He promised he would not reveal her hoarding to the fire marshal or health department if she would be patient with him while he resolved the problem with the crazy dog poop neighbor upstairs.

Three months later the "Balcony Dog Poop Report" was moved from the "Poop Pending File" to the "Resolved File."

257. Dog Poop 5

When the owners returned to move back into their home, which had been a rental for a couple years, they had only one complaint. They pointed to dog poop deposits in the yard. The property manager dutifully photographed a half-dozen poop deposits, some old and dried out, some newer and still damp. The property manager pointed out that the tenant had moved out a month before but some of the dog poop was much more recent, fresher, it couldn't be the tenant's fault. The homeowners said so what, don't be ridiculous. They wanted compensation.

While they stood in the yard, the next-door neighbors came out of their house with their kids and two dogs. They were old friends of the owners. The two families hugged and laughed and talked in the yard while the property manager continued photographing poop. The neighbor's dog ran into the rental property's yard and pooped. The property manager looked his client in the eye and raised one eyebrow. The owner looked at the pooping dog, narrowed his eyes, and nodded almost imperceptibly at the property manager in a non-verbal agreement. The property manager went to his office and released the entire security deposit to the tenant. All poop notations were deleted from the move-out inspection report.

258. Dog Poop 6

The property manager received a complaint about dog poop from the tenant's neighbor, so he drove by occasionally on his way home from work to observe the dog, to see if it was allowed to run about unleashed. There was a leash law. He saw the dog on two occasions sniffing around the gardens. It squatted but produced no observable poop or urine because it was wearing a dog diaper. Dog diapers are available for under twenty dollars on Amazon. The property manager moved "Dog Poop 6" to the "Resolved File."

259. Weapon Brandished

The property manager received a report from a tenant's neighbor. She had called the police after she witnessed the tenants arguing in the parking lot. The male tenant produced a knife and threatened the female tenant. The neighbor called the police. The police arrived after the incident and questioned the tenants in their home. They denied it. The police asked the neighbor if she would testify against the tenants in court, since she was the sole witness. She said she feared retribution, couldn't the police testify? No, they were not witnesses. They could not be plaintiffs.

The neighbor called the property manager. The property manager called an attorney. The attorney asked for a copy of the lease. She said the tenant could not be prosecuted criminally if the neighbor would not be a witness to the crime. To evict the tenants would require a breach of the lease. The lease prohibited criminal acts on the premises, but not in the parking lot, which was not owned or managed by any of the parties involved. She suggested future leases be changed to include any and all criminal activity by any tenant or occupant, on or off the premises.

The landlord hired the attorney to negotiate an early termination of the lease, since eviction was iffy. The tenants agreed to move out early if they got a break on the last month's rent. The surrender of possession, rent payment, and deposit disposition were agreed to in writing.

The tenants moved out early and the house was marketed for rent again. The next tenants signed a newly modified lease and were asked if they understood the new clauses pertaining to prohibited activities. They did.

When the new tenants moved in, the neighbors came by, introduced themselves, and got to know everything about them.

260. Condo Fees Lawsuit

The community association management's law firm sent a court subpoena to the landlord at the rental address for non-payment of dues and attorney's fees. The overdues were eight hundred dollars and the attorney's fees were twelve hundred dollars. The landlord said it was unfair that the bills and notice were sent to the tenant's residence and not the owner. He would have paid on time if he had known. He said it was not his fault. But it was. He had failed to provide his forwarding address to the association.

The property manager asked the landlord permission to pay the eight hundred in dues immediately, from the owner's account, and ignore the legal fees, forcing the attorney to go to court solely for attorney's fees in a case where the original debt was satisfied. They were betting that the judge would not award attorney's fees over a paid debt. The owner agreed to the plan.

The property manager took a check to the attorney's office for eight hundred dollars with "Payment for dues only" written on the memo line. The attorney accepted the payment but said the attorney's fees would still be pursued.

The court date passed. Court records showed it was dismissed. It was never reflected on the court docket or on the online court cases records. The attorney had dropped the suit for attorney's fees, as the property manager hoped. The property manager called the landlord and said it was a twelve hundred dollar victory. The landlord said it was an eight hundred dollar loss. The landlord fired the property manager for failing to forward the mail.

261. Eviction

The tenant stopped paying rent. Her boyfriend had left. She lost her job. She had two kids and lots of bills. The landlord sued for possession, back rent and attorney's fees. It would take thirty to sixty days before a court date. Winter was coming. Eviction would occur after Thanksgiving, perhaps near Christmas. The property manager and attorney would present the case as representatives for the owner. The owner was advised not to attend the hearing. There might be an emotional component, it being the holidays and all.

The tenant arrived with her brother as a translator. He said she could not speak English. He was lying. The property manager had spoken with her several times in English. She was fluent in English. The brother was acting improperly as her advocate.

The judge said, "I'll allow your brother to translate, but he may not speak for you, he may only translate. Do you understand?"

The tenant said, "Yes." She had bypassed her translator.

The judge said, "Wait. You understood my English?"

"Yes, your honor," she said.

The judge lost his patience and ruled summarily. "You've wasted the court's time. Judgment for the plaintiff. Possession granted pending a writ. Next case."

The tenant followed the property manager out of the courtroom. The attorney advised him not to talk to her. The tenant followed the property manager out to his car. She approached him. "Can you give me a ride? My car was repossessed."

"I don't know. It's not really proper."

"You just made me and my kids homeless. It's the least you can do."

"My attorney said I shouldn't talk to you."

The tenant said, "Come on, it's Christmas."

262. Eviction 2

The landlords found their own tenant. The property manager asked if he could do background screening, credit and references, but the landlord had already allowed the tenant to move in. After the first month the tenant stopped paying rent. He did not return calls or email. He was never home. The property manager did not know if the tenant was employed or had any income or savings. For two months no rent was paid. No calls were returned.

He called the landlord. "Would you like to pursue eviction? You're losing a lot of money."

"No, we don't want to be the bad guys."

"How did you find this guy?"

"On Craigslist."

Two more months went by. The tenant's overdue rent totaled eight thousand dollars.

The property manager called the landlord. "Are you sure you don't want to evict him? He's really ripping you off."

"Eviction is so drastic. We don't want to be mean."

"There's something really wrong with this guy."

"Give him a little more time."

At the end of the lease term the tenant hadn't moved out.

The landlord said, "Doesn't he have to move out?"

"We gave him notice to vacate but there's no sign of a move-out."

"Isn't the lease over?"

"Yep."

"Doesn't he have to move out?"

"Yes, but we can't drag him out of the house. We can't change the locks. There are laws."

"We want him out of our house."

"Do you want to evict him?"

"How much does he owe us?"

"Ten thousand dollars. Five months."

"Ask him for ten thousand dollars first. We don't want to be the bad guy."

263. The Missing Trash Can

The landlord hired the property management company to rent her five-bedroom house for three thousand dollars a month. A qualified tenant was found, a lease was signed, and the tenant moved in. The tenant paid over a hundred thousand dollars in rent over the course of a three-year lease. The tenant had no complaints and the house had only a few minor repairs during the lease term. It was an excellent landlord experience, on paper.

The landlord returned and walked through the house with the property manager. She pointed to worn carpet, worn wall paint, and worn vinyl flooring. All were normal wear and tear, not damage by tenant abuse, he said.

They walked through the main floor, the top floor, and finally the basement. The last room they looked at was the basement bathroom. The landlord was shocked.

"Where is the trash can?" she demanded.

"What trash can?"

"I left a small plastic trash can in this bathroom."

The property manager scratched his head.

She said, "It was black. It matched the wallpaper border."

He said, "It's not on our move-in sheet. It's not in our records."

"Why not?"

He said, "It's personal property. We ask our clients not to leave their stuff in the house."

"But they stole my trash can."

"How much did it cost?" he asked.

"How should I know? How much is a plastic trash can worth?"

The property manager said, "I bought three matching plastic trash cans for my house for six dollars each."

"Well mine was very nice. It was black with gold trim."

The property manager asked, "Would you like us to pay you six dollars or so?"

She said, "The tenant should pay for it."

"But he was a perfect tenant. And it was a used plastic trash can."

She said, "It's not about the trash can. It's the principle."

"May I pay you six dollars cash right now? I can call the tenant later for an explanation."

She said, "The tenant should pay."

"Okay okay."

They walked into the utility room and looked at the washer, dryer, and furnace. On the work bench in the corner sat a black plastic trash can.

"Oh, look," said the property manager, "The trash can. Thank God."

The landlord said, "Why on earth did they put it in here? Didn't they like it? It went perfectly in the bathroom. It doesn't make sense."

"Don't worry. I'll call the tenant and get to the bottom of this."

264. Mail on the Counter

The property manager arranged an appointment to inspect a rental townhouse. The tenant would be at work. He said the property manager could come by any time and enter with his key. The property manager arrived at noon and walked through the house. The house looked good but it looked like a lot of people were living there.

Before leaving, the property manager noticed a big pile of mail on the kitchen counter. He looked at it and saw there were letters, bills, and magazines addressed to a lot of different names at the same address. He leafed through the letters, feeling a little creepy and guilty, and wrote down all the names at the address. He saw a to-do list on the refrigerator that assigned chores to a number of people, many of whom were not on the lease. He looked at the calendar by the wall phone and saw appointments for people not named on the lease. He collected all names that were not on the lease. It appeared at least eight people lived there, with only two on the lease.

He knew that if he confronted the tenant about over-occupancy the tenant might accuse him of snooping. Snooping is exactly what he did on inspections, but there is an expectation of privacy that shouldn't be abused.

The property manager went back to his office and called his co-workers. They decided to send the tenants a letter notifying them of a breach of the lease. The letter would say that only those persons on the lease could reside in the house. Nothing more. If the tenant accused him of snooping he should just say a neighbor reported it. If the tenant asked which neighbor reported it, he could say it was an anonymous call.

The letter was sent. After the tenant received the letter he called the property manager and said only he and his wife lived there. They had visitors and friends over, but no one else lived there.

The property manager then wrote letters to the other six names he saw on the mail and on the refrigerator. He sent the six letters to the six names, all at the same rental address. The letters notified them of other rental houses he had available and asked if they were looking for a place to rent.

265. Phantom Breakage

The tenant called the property manager and said the kitchen sliding glass door had shattered for no reason. It was fine one second, broken the next. It cracked in a spider-web pattern, then fell to the floor in a million pieces. The property manager went to the house and determined that the glass had shattered inward, due to some external force. He called a glass company. They told him sometimes on a hot day, cool rain can cause it. Or the door may have been installed with a slightly twisted frame and the glass was always distressed, just waiting to break. Or finally, it may have been "spontaneous breakage," a rare thing, but something known to glass companies.

The property manager sent photos and opinions to the landlord. The landlord didn't believe the spontaneous breakage thing and said it must have been the tenant's fault. The property manager said that the door opened onto a deck that had no other access, no stairs to the ground, so the tenant would have had to go outside, locking the glass door behind her, break the glass, then crawl back into the kitchen through the window over the kitchen sink. Or else she jumped off the deck. The landlord said, "So?" The property manager said the tenant was about two hundred and fifty pounds and probably couldn't have fit through the window or survived a leap. The landlord said she must have broken it and then walked back through. The property manager said that from his inspection and the photos it appeared that the broken glass was perfectly distributed over the vinyl floor, undisturbed. If she walked through it she must have carefully rearranged the shards afterward. He believed the glass had broken spontaneously. The landlord accused him of taking the tenant's side. The property manager agreed, he was taking the tenant's side just this once. If another glass door or window broke, he would raise holy hell with the tenant and demand restitution.

266. Mold Conditions

The property manager went to meet the tenants at the house after they complained about mold. He inspected the house and asked the tenant some questions.

"When you shower do you use the bathroom vent fan?"

"No, it's too noisy. I want to hear if the phone rings."

"Do you use the range hood fan when you cook?"

"No, too noisy. We talk while we cook."

"Do you clean the house with any bleach-based or mildewcide cleaning agents?"

"No."

"Any Lysol, Clorox, Tilex?"

"No."

"I see the AC is off. Do you run it often, or run the fan on auto?"

"We leave it off to save electricity."

"Your shades and drapes are all closed. Do you leave them that way?"

"Of course. So the neighbors can't see in."

"Do you ever open the windows to air out the house?"

"Why would we do that?"

"Well, mold is everywhere. My house, your house, indoors and out. It only germinates in moist conditions. Mold doesn't like air circulation, or light. You have made this house a mold heaven. You should use the bath and kitchen fans, run the AC or furnace fan, let some sunlight in, let some air in."

"Are you saying we're dirty people? Is that what you're saying?"

"No. It's not you. Not personal. But it's like a swamp in here. Let's talk outside."

267. The See-Snake

The basement flooded when the washer broke down. After the water was removed the basement looked good but the tenant said she smelled mold. The property manager inspected and found no visible evidence of mold. The tenant said, "So what?" The property manager said that "visible evidence of mold" was the term found in the state law, the lease, and in the EPA website. Visible evidence of mold would obligate testing. The tenant disagreed and said the mold was probably inside the walls. She couldn't sleep at night wondering what was in the walls.

The property manager returned the next day with a drill and a See-Snake, a plumber's tool. It was a small flexible fiber-optic conduit with a tiny camera on one end, and a monitor screen like a TV on the other. He explained to the tenant it was like a colonoscopy, but for looking inside walls.

He drilled a hole in the wall and inserted the camera end of the conduit into the wall. The screen showed white pine studs, clear gray drywall and clean pink insulation. The tenant was amazed and pleased. She said try it over there. They tried it on every wall in the basement until the tenant was relieved and she suddenly thought the house smelled better.

The property manager packed up his tools. The tenant said what about all the holes? The property manager didn't want to start patching all the holes, so he told her they had to leave the holes open for a while to allow the walls to breathe. It would assure dryness in the walls and allow them to look in the walls in the future. She bought it. He left.

268. Sidewalk Confrontation

The property manager met the landlord at her house after she returned to live in it. When he arrived she was already inside and came out of the front door fuming. They stood on the sidewalk and talked.

"My house is trashed!"

"Oh, my. Is it dirty?"

"You bet it's dirty."

"Let's look inside."

"Not on your life. The walls are scuffed up. The carpets are stained."

"Let me take pictures of the damage, to add to the move-out inspection."

"You stay out of my house. You've done enough."

"When are you moving in?"

"Tomorrow."

"Do you have time to clean and paint and re-carpet?"

"No, we're not doing all that."

"You're going to live in a dirty run-down house?"

"How dare you say my house is run-down!"

"Let me take a peek. The move out inspection shows it was in similar condition at move-out as it was at move-in."

"It was immaculate at move-in."

"The paint and carpet were old at move-in. I was here."

"You're insulting."

"You left dirt and debris in the house because you were in a rush. Remember? We emailed back and forth about it for a month while the tenant called the Better Business Bureau on me."

"You're avoiding responsibility. You screwed up."

"You emailed me recently thanking me for going above and beyond the call of duty."

"I'm going to tell everyone how bad your company is."

"I apologize if you had a bad experience. I didn't know."

"I'm going to ruin you with internet reviews."

"Oh. Well. I don't know what to say."

"Get off my property."

"But we're on the sidewalk."

"When my husband gets here he's going to go ballistic. You better be gone."

"But…"

"Now!"

"Okay. Bye-bye."

The next day the husband called the property manager.

"We're moving in. The house looks good."

"It does? Your wife wouldn't let me in."

"Don't you have keys?"

"I had keys with me but I was ordered off the property."

"My wife is stressed out. She thought we left the house in great condition."

"Yes, she said immaculate."

"Well, you did a good job, considering."

"Considering?"

"Considering we didn't do the cleaning and painting you recommended. And we turned down the first good application and took the one you recommended against."

"Well, I had the keys with me yesterday, and I had the inspection reports and repair requests. But she cut me off. I have keys and a bunch of documents you may want."

"Just mail them to me. Sorry my wife was so stressed out. We were in a country for two years where women have to cover their heads and can't drive. She was ignored and disrespected in diplomatic circles. She pretty much hates men now."

"Oh, now it all makes sense. She was the diplomat and you were the spouse, and everyone treated you like royalty and treated her like a servant."

"Exactly. You nailed it."

"I've seen this before. I don't blame her. I feel bad just being a man."

"I'll tell her that. She will appreciate it. Thanks for all your help."

"Good luck, dude."

269. Five Unrelated Adults

A landlord hired the property manager to rent out his five-bedroom house. It was two miles from a college so the property manager warned the landlord that they would get applications from groups of students. The landlord said he didn't want students, he wanted a family. The property manager said he could not rule out tenants based on marital or familial status, so he would just make sure all the applicants qualified financially. Students usually had little income and could not qualify without cosigners. Even their parents would be leery of cosigning.

The first application was from a group of five students. They had a lot of money and some great references, like All-American this and National-Scholarship-Finalist that. The owners wanted to accept the application. The property manager said the county zoning regulations prohibited more than four unrelated adults in a single-family home. The owner met with the applicants without the property manager's knowledge. They changed the application to four tenants and resubmitted it. The property manager said no, but the landlord said yes and accepted the group of students.

A month later a neighbor, a friend of the landlords, called them directly and told them that the house was one big party, loud music and public drinking, like Animal House. The landlord called the property manager and demanded to know what he was going to do about it. How was he going to get those damn people out of their house?

The property manager called the tenants and told them the landlord wanted them out of the house. But the tenants had moved out and sublet it to a group of friends. They were renting each room out separately, like a boarding house. They were making a profit. He asked the original tenants if they could get their friends out of the house. They said they couldn't go back on their word. It wouldn't be fair.

The rent was paid late. The lawn went to hell. The street was lined with cars. Police were called every weekend. The neighbors hated the tenants. They hated the property manager. They hated his firm. They hated the landlord. The landlord fired the property manager for allowing their home to become a frat house.

270. Complaints

The tenant moved into a small townhouse. She had only rented apartments before so she assumed she didn't have to take care of anything on the exterior. Her grass grew long. The neighbors complained. The HOA complained. The property manager told her she had to mow. She complained and had her father call the property manager to complain. She complained to the neighbors. She complained she hadn't read the lease. She complained that mowing was dirty and dangerous.

In the winter snow and sleet fell on her driveway. Her sidewalk iced over. She slipped and fell while walking to the mailbox. She complained to the property manager. He sent her a copy of her lease, underlining the clause requiring her to mow, rake, and remove ice and snow. She complained that she hadn't read the lease. She complained to her father. Her father complained to the property manager. He complained to the HOA. He complained to the Better Business Bureau. They complained on Yelp and Google reviews. No one shoveled her driveway or her sidewalk. She slipped again and broke a carpal bone in her wrist. She found an attorney. He read the lease. He wouldn't take the case. She found another attorney. He looked at her lease. He wouldn't take the case. She complained to the property manager's boss. She complained to the Board of Realtors. She complained to the state licensing board.

The tenant was not offered a lease renewal at the end of the lease term. The property manager gave her notice to vacate. The tenant applied to rent from another property management firm. That firm called the property manager to ask for a landlord reference. The property manager said she paid rent on time and cleaned the house. She had ample income and good credit. There were no other questions. He didn't mention her tendency to complain. He didn't mention he hated her and she hated him. She was accepted by the next property manager.

The landlord called the property manager and asked how he had let such a good tenant slip away. She paid rent on time and she took good care of the house. The landlord complained he had made a mistake. He complained to his boss about him. He complained to the owner of the management company. He complained.

271. The Hoarder

The annual mid-term inspection indicated a hoarding situation in one of his rentals. The house was full up to the window sills with rubbish, clutter, and debris. He made an appointment and met the tenant at the house. The tenant tried to clean up in advance but there was too much stuff. All the bedrooms were obstructed and could not be navigated. The kitchen was an impenetrable jungle of carry-out boxes, trash bags, grocery bags, newspapers, magazines, and piles of unidentifiable debris. The middle of the living room had been cleared out with just enough room on the couch to sit and talk. The tenant was impeccably dressed. He was a partner in an accounting firm.

The property manager said, "There's a county hoarding task force. They arrive with the fire marshal, health department and social services. They can escort you from the house. They can condemn the house."

The tenant said, "No. I won't allow it. I can't move. Ever. Look around. This stuff is my whole life."

The property manager pulled out his camera and began to take pictures. The tenant jumped up and said, "Leave. Please. Now."

On his way out he looked at the tenant's car. It was immaculate inside and out. It was detailed and shined, right down to the tires. He went back to his office and called the task force. They told him they were overbooked, that they were so backlogged that the county was going to have to discontinue the task force and leave landlords and property managers to their own devices.

The property manager asked the task force officials if they had noticed other hoarders who lived one life inside the house and an entirely different life outside of it. They said yes, it appeared to be a mental illness that was confined to the home, therefore almost impossible to diagnose.

He called the landlord and told him the bad news.

"The tenant is a hoarder. I can't even describe it, it's so bad. It's going downhill fast and the authorities are no help. We have to evict. Will you pay for a lawyer?"

The landlord said, "No. I don't want to go to court. Can't you just kick them out and change the locks?"

"No, that's not legal without due process. I can post notices, write letters, make calls."

"Threaten them. Scare them out."

"I can't. We can talk, notify, or sue. Threats are iffy. Collections laws suggest threats are actionable."

"Who says? It's my house."

"It's those pesky civil rights acts and fair housing laws they passed when I was a kid."

"The damn liberals."

"Yes. Those guys. They're everywhere."

272. The Hoarder 2

The hoarders had piled mountains of junk against the walls. There was only a narrow path through each room. It was like a maze. Windows and doors were blocked off, making egress in case of fire impossible. The property manager went down into the unfinished basement and looked at the underside of the floor joists. The plywood flooring was buckling.

He went upstairs and got on his hands and knees in the living room. He felt around until he found a wooden ridge under the carpet. The weight of the piles of junk against the walls was pushing the floorboards inward to the center of the room where they met and buckled upward. The structure of the house itself could be at risk due to the massive weight of hoarded material.

The property manager explained the danger to the tenant. She said nothing. He took out his camera to document the hazard. When she saw the camera she jumped straight up off the floor about two inches, in her sharp business suit and chic heels.

He sent the pictures to the landlord. The landlord asked, "Can I sue the tenant?"

"Yes you can."

"Can I sue you?"

"Yes you can."

"Which one is faster?"

"If you sue me, you're suing your star witness. If you sue the tenant, you're suing the person who is incurring your losses."

"Can I sue both?"

"Yes. But then your star witness will be testifying against you."

"Against me? What did I do?"

"You signed an agreement that says you're liable for anything having to do with your property and I'm not."

273. Carpet Cleaning Verdict

The property manager deducted the cost of carpet cleaning from the tenant's security deposit because at move-out there were many carpet stains not documented at move-in. In court the tenant arrived with twenty photos of the carpets, showing no stains. The property manager had only the hand-written inspection reports. Digital photos were being used in court more and more often. The property manager did not have any photographs, a fatal mistake.

The judge looked at the photos and saw no stains. He asked the property manager, "Why are there no stains in the photos?"

The property manager looked at the photos and replied. "The photos were taking from an oblique angle. If they were taken straight down they would show the stains. It's like looking at a cornfield. From the side you see the leafy crowns of the cornstalks. From overhead you see the soil littered with fallen ears. If the pictures were taken looking straight down at the stains they would show the true condition of the carpets."

"If? You have no pictures? You didn't take pictures?"

"No, sir. We took notes. Written contemporaneous documentation. We've done it that way for forty years."

The judge raised an eyebrow and glared over his reading glasses at the property manager. He thought the property manager was a lying weasel or a perjurer. The property manager knew from the judge's face that he had lost. He slumped his shoulders and lowered his head. He would never show up without pictures again. Judgement for the tenant.

274. Carpet Cleaning Verdict 2

There was another court case brought by another tenant over a carpet cleaning deduction from a security deposit. This time the property manager showed up with digital photos of dirty carpets taken with Nikon macro/micro/and wide angle lenses. He also brought in his brief case a one-square-foot piece of the dirty carpet he had removed from the house in question. He had close-ups of toilet bowls and countertops. He had a notarized invoice from the house cleaner vouching for every asserted deduction. The judge raised an eyebrow and glared at the property manager. It was the same judge he'd had before. The deductions were disallowed without explanation. The property manager hung his head and slumped his shoulders. Judgement for the tenant.

275. Carpet Verdict 3

The tenant sued the property manager and landlord over a security deposit deduction for carpet replacement. The tenant had witnesses who were willing to testify about the condition of the carpet. The judge gave credence to the witnesses and asked for the property manager's defense. The property manager told the judge that in addition to ruined carpets, the tenant had driven through the garage door. The property manager provided a case number the responding police had provided to the neighbors who called it in. He had three estimates for garage door repair, and an invoice for the completed repair. The garage door replacement cost more than the deposit. The carpet was an additional twelve hundred. The property manager told the judge he would gladly stipulate that the tenant was right about the carpet if they all agreed that the garage door repair cost was the tenant's responsibility.

The judge agreed. The tenant disagreed. Judgement for the Landlord.

276. Medical Issues

The tenant stopped paying rent. She had lost her job. She couldn't afford to stay and she couldn't afford to move out. The property manager went to her house. The tenant offered him a drink and they sat in her living room. She wanted to explain her circumstances. She had been hospitalized for exhaustion. Then she had a stroke. She fell and she sprained her wrist. She dislocated her shoulder. She couldn't drive to work. She was laid off. She got hooked on pain medication. She tried to get into rehab but her insurance wouldn't cover it. Then her insurance dropped her.

The property manager said he was very sorry, but he didn't know how to help her. His client, the landlord, needed to have the rent to pay his mortgage. He couldn't afford to let her stay for free. He didn't want to evict her but if she wouldn't move he would have no choice.

The property manager offered to contact the tenant's friends or family. She had no one. He asked if she had a church or a support group. No. She didn't know any of her neighbors. Could he help her apply for subsidized housing? She had tried that. He called the county homeless shelter. She wouldn't go there. He searched her references for next-of-kin, family, anything, and found nothing.

The property manager called the landlord and explained that eviction might be his only option. The tenant was stuck in the house with no way out and no future prospects. The landlord said he had met the tenant and he liked her. Eviction would break his heart and letting her stay would bring foreclosure.

The property manager asked the landlord to authorize the eviction and let him do the rest. The property manager would be the bad guy. The landlord would not appear in court. The property manager would do everything. If the tenant asked he would tell her that he was in charge of the eviction and the landlord was out of the loop. The landlord should sleep well at night knowing that the property manager was doing everything possible to help the tenant move on and avoid eviction. The landlord agreed and sent the property manager funds to retain an attorney.

Before the eviction date the tenant disappeared, leaving behind all of her possessions. She left no forwarding address. She did not respond to phone calls or emails.

The property manager met the landlord at the house. They inspected it and made plans for repairs. The landlord said he had to sell the house. He just couldn't go on being a landlord. He was too sad.

The property manager couldn't find out where the tenant had gone. He tried to find out if he was okay. She was gone without a trace.

He told the landlord that the tenant had found an old friend to live with. It was a lie. He said her life was getting back on track. It was a lie. He said she apologized for being so much trouble. He was lying. She had just disappeared. He couldn't find her. He didn't know what happed to her. The landlord felt better. The property manager felt worse.

277. Please Read the Lease

"Good morning. Have a seat in our conference room. Please take your time reading the lease before you sign it. If you have any questions I'm right here."

The tenants sat and began reading the twelve-page lease. They had questions.

"What's this about the rent being due on the first?"

"Rent is due on or before the first of the month."

"But we're moving in on the fifteenth."

"Yes, so you pay a prorated half month rent prior to move-in, and pay subsequent rents on the first."

"Can't we pay on the fifteenth?

"You can pay on or before the first."

"Can't you be more flexible?"

"This is our lease. Read the rest of it and see if you have more questions."

"What about here where it says we can't sublet. Can't we add roommates?"

"You can if they apply, they qualify and they are accepted by the landlord, then they are added to the lease in writing and have all the same obligations as you."

"That's a lot of trouble. What if we just let someone live in the basement rec room?"

"That's not a bedroom. It has no egress, no exit to the outside, so it is prohibited."

"Where do you get all these rules?"

"The fire marshal, zoning regulations, lawyers, courts, and also the lease."

"Our last landlord wasn't so picky."

"Read the rest of the lease. If you won't sign it we'll put the house back on the market and refund your deposit."

"Your lease says we can't run a business in the house. What about day care?"

"Day care requires local and state licensing, county inspections, and a waiver from the HOA. Protecting children from harm, and all that."

"We had day care in our last house."

"Was it allowed on your lease?"

"The lease was just two pages. Your lease is twelve. It seems like you're trying to run our lives."

"Well, you came to us and applied to live there. We accepted and we offered you a lease. We can't make you sign it. Please read the whole lease while I see how fast we can put it back on the market."

"No. We really want this house."

"And we really want you as tenants. But only if you agree to all the terms of the lease."

"What about this clause here?"

"Oh. That says if you don't pay rent on the first we give you a five-day notice and then we can start the eviction process. But it's a long slow process. You can stop it by paying rent."

"You would make us homeless if we can't pay the rent?"

"Yes. That's our lease boiled down to one sentence. Pay rent or leave."

"I don't know if we can sign your lease."

"Your last landlord gave you a good reference."

"Our last landlord was my mom and dad."

"Oh, now I get it. Are you on good terms with them?

"Yes, but they want us out by the fifteenth."

278. Blue and Orange Paint

A young couple hired the property manager to find tenants to rent their house. He went to the house to see the condition and value for marketing purposes. He walked through the house with the owners and commented on the paint colors they chose. The kitchen was pumpkin orange. The living room was deep sea blue. The bedrooms were painted in rich hues of yellow, pink, and red. He offered his recommendations.

"Do you plan on repainting?"

The owners said, "No. The paint is a year old. It's in good shape."

The property manager said, "I like the bold colors, but they are custom made for your taste."

"Yes, we love our colors," said the owners.

"Have you considered repainting in off-white? We find that most tenants prefer off-white."

"Off-white is boring, don't you think?"

The property manager said, "The odds are not good that prospective tenants will have furnishings that go with your color scheme."

The owner said, "We really don't want to spend thousands of dollars on painting."

The property manager said, "It will rent faster if it's off-white."

"But we love these colors."

"If it takes a month longer to rent than other off-white townhouses, you will lose thousands in rent," warned the property manager.

"But we want you to find renters that share our taste. People like us."

"Even people like you will be put off by bold colors when they walk in the front door. It's just the way it is. We've seen it a thousand times."

"Well, they have to rent it the way it is, don't they?"

"There are over forty houses for rent in your price range in this county. Potential renters will see no more than a dozen before they choose. You don't want them to remember your house as the one with the crazy colors."

"But our house is special. It's near the park. Shopping. The playground. It's on the best commuting route."

The property manager said, "There are two houses for rent in your neighborhood that rented recently. They were both off-white. They had new carpet and appliances. The competition is tough. There's a house a mile away from here like yours, with bold colors and bright carpet. It's been on the market for six weeks."

The homeowners asked, "How do you know all that? How can anyone know all that?"

The property manager said, "I showed some of those houses. I leased some of them. I met the owners and the tenants. I'm really into this whole marketing thing. I give you my recommendations from my own experience."

The owners asked, "How do you know there aren't people out there like us, who will love this house the way it is."

The property manager said, "Oh, there are. They're out there. But they're special, like you. They're rare and hard to find. It takes a long time to find them. I want you to get renters and make money as soon as possible."

"You sound like you know your stuff. Go ahead, find people like us soon. For top dollar. And make sure they love our colors."

279. The Sewer Line Camera

The sewer line was blocked under the front yard at a rental property. The toilets were backing up. There was sewage in the bathtubs. A plumber was called and couldn't snake out the clog. He said it must be in the yard. A specialized plumbing firm was called. They recommended a snake auger be used to clear the line. It would cost a couple grand.

The landlord had a lot of questions:

How could the sewer line be clogged?

Why now?

What caused it?

Do I have to pay for it?

Why doesn't the water company pay for it?

How do you know the tenant didn't put something down the drain that caused it?

Is it the previous owner's fault?

Why didn't the home inspector find it when the house was purchased?

What if the clog is in the town sewer?

What if it's the homeowner association's pipe?

Will insurance pay for it?

Why didn't you warn me this might happen?

The property manager talked to more plumbers. For several hundred dollars the sewer company could put a fiber optic camera on a flexible line and explore the sewer line from a toilet all the way to the municipal sewer line. It might answer some questions.

The landlord agreed. The plumber used the camera and videotaped the entire line. The video showed roots in the line about twenty feet away from the house. That corresponded to the location of a tree or two. The sewer break was on the landlord's property and was his responsibility. The landlord had questions:

How did the tree know how to find the sewer line?

Are trees attracted to sewage?

Which came first, the breakage or the roots?

Did the roots break the pipe or was the pipe broken first and attracted the roots?

How could a tree decide where its roots should go?

How long had the break been there?

If the camera could get through, why couldn't the sewage get through?

Did the video show anything the tenant had flushed something that she shouldn't have?

Do I have to pay for the video?

The tenant could not use the toilets for several days. She had questions:

Can I move out?

Will you pay for a hotel?

Will you pay for my ruined things?

Will you refund my rent?

Is this my fault?

280. Cold Basement, Hot Bedrooms

A tenant called the property manager and said her basement was cold and her bedrooms were hot.

He asked her, "What was the thermostat set at?"

"Seventy."

"What's the temperature on the main level?"

"Seventy."

"What's the temperature in the basement?"

"I don't know. It's cold."

"And the bedroom level upstairs?"

"It's hot."

"Can you check the temperatures with a thermometer?"

"I don't have a thermometer."

"Do you want to borrow mine? Or I can come by."

"I just want it fixed."

The property manager called an HVAC contractor, who said the difference between levels is often five to ten degrees.

He called a home inspector, who said it should be two to three degrees difference. A heating firm's website said four to eight degrees. He measured the temperature in each level of his own home and got a five-degree difference per level. He read some blogs on the subject, where he found nothing but complaints about temperature differences between floors. He called the tenant and told her what he had learned.

"The difference between floors varies by house. It could be two degrees, it could be ten."

"Well my house is uncomfortable."

"My house is five degrees between floors."

"I'm not talking about your house."

"I did an internet search. You can reduce the temperature difference by setting your thermostat to ON instead of AUTO, so the blower runs and constantly cycles your air."

"Won't that take more electricity?"

"Ceiling fans help too."

"That doesn't make sense."

"You can close off the vents or registers in rooms you don't use."

"Why?"

"You can move furniture that blocks heat registers."

"You're kidding."

"I moved my couch. It was over a vent. The vent was blocked."

"You're dancing around the subject. Why is this happening?"

"I hate to say it, but heat rises, cold air sinks."

"I've never had this problem before."

"Have you ever lived in a three-level house before?"

The tenant said, "No. I grew up in a one-story house. Then I moved to an apartment. What does that have to do with it?"

281. The Missing Security Deposit

When the tenant moved out, his rental house was clean and in good repair. The property manager refunded his security deposit of two thousand dollars in full. The tenant called the property manager and said there had been a mistake.

"Hello. You sent me two thousand dollars of my security deposit back, but I paid a double deposit. Where's the other two thousand?"

The property manager was puzzled. "According to our records we sent you the same amount that you originally gave us."

The tenant said, "I paid a double deposit. I paid four thousand dollars."

"Let me check the records and call you back."

The property manager looked at the lease. It said there was a two thousand dollar deposit. So did the accounting for the property. The date of the deposit corresponded with the beginning of the lease.

There was one anomaly. The property and account had been transferred from another property management firm. The other firm had done the advertising and tenant screening. They had collected a deposit. Their records showed a two thousand dollar deposit as well. But the previous property manager had also collected one month rent as a commission for the leasing agent. It had been recorded as a double deposit but paid out as deposit and one month commission. The money had been erroneously pocketed by the original agent as a commission. The tenant had paid the deposit and first month rent in one four thousand dollar check, which had been called a deposit. It could be considered commingling or fraud committed by the first property manager. If so, they had defrauded both the tenant and the current property manager, but they left sketchy records.

The property manager called the first firm. The agent who made the commission no longer worked there. The broker claimed they had forwarded all records and no longer had any interest or responsibility.

The property manager called the tenant.

"We only got the one deposit for two thousand. If you paid a double deposit it was to the previous real estate firm or agent. You should call them."

The tenant said, "I called you because you are my property manager. I can prove I paid a double deposit."

The property manager said, "We sent you the deposit and that's all there is."

"Don't make me sue you." threatened the tenant.

"Don't sue me. Sue your first agent. Please."

The tenant sued in small claims court, where there were no lawyers, just the tenant and the property manager. The tenant told the judge about the double deposit. The property manager said it was a single deposit.

The judge asked the tenant, "Do you have a cancelled check?"

"No, your honor, not with me."

"Do you have a receipt?"

"No, sir."

"Do you have any accounting, or a lease, or anything in writing?"

"No."

The judge asked the property manager if he had any documentation in his defense.

"Yes, your honor. I have copies of the lease, the tenant ledger, the accounting for our deposit and escrow account, and a copy of the check we refunded to the tenant. They all show a single deposit of two thousand dollars."

The judge said, "Hand them to the bailiff."

The bailiff handed the documents to the judge. The judge read them and saw the two thousand dollar amount repeated on each document.

The judge said, "I'm ruling in favor of the property manager. I don't know what funds were exchanged in the original transaction, but the defense has documented their position and the plaintiff has offered no evidence whatsoever of his claim to a double deposit. Judgement for the defendant."

The tenant said, "I object."

The judge said, "I have already ruled."

The tenant said, "I want to appeal."

The judge said, "You could have hired an attorney and gone to General District court in the first place. You can't appeal now. You need to seek counsel if you want to change the venue and re-file the case."

The tenant said, "I can get a copy of the check. I can get a witness or something."

The judge said, "Next case. Anderson versus Ace Property management. Come forward please."

The tenant stomped out of the courtroom. The property manager stayed and watched the next few cases. He had a hunch the tenant was outside the courtroom door waiting to talk to him. He knew how the conversation would go. He knew the tenant had been told he paid a double deposit by an inept realtor. But he didn't think he could explain it to the tenant. After an hour he walked to the rear of the galley and peeked between the heavy wooden doors to the hallway. The tenant was still out there, waiting.

282. I Want Twenty-Four Hundred a Month

The property manager met a prospective new client at his house. They listed all the appliances and fixtures, upgrades and improvements, room measurements, location and comparative value. The property manager searched the online real estate listings on his laptop in the prospect's kitchen. Similar houses in the area were renting for two thousand to twenty-two hundred a month.

The property manager recommended he start the advertised price at twenty-two hundred. If it didn't move in two weeks they would go down to twenty-one hundred. If the market was hot they would get competing bids and tenants might bid it back up to twenty-two or twenty-three.

The prospect said, "No. I want twenty-four hundred. I spent thousands on a new deck."

The property manager said, "Hmm. The competition all has decks too."

"But my house has the biggest lot on the block."

"The other lots are just a pinch smaller."

"My house has wood floors."

"Your builder put wood floors in all the houses in the community."

"Whose side are you on?"

The property manager said, "I just don't want your house to be overpriced and languish in a competitive market. There are dozens of houses for rent in the county. Most renters will only see eight or so houses before they sign a lease. I want them to see your house first. We need to attract the early birds, the active shoppers."

The owner said, "But won't the best tenants want the best house?"

The property manager said, "Yes, but look at my laptop. There are four houses for rent within two miles that are bigger and newer."

"Do they have all the crown mould and chair rail I have? Or the granite counter tops?"

"I have an idea. Let's go look at them. We'll pretend to be tenants looking for a house to live in, but we'll be spying on the competition."

"Isn't that a little excessive?"

"Twenty four hundred is excessive. We need to come to a compromise."

The owner said, "Compromise? If I hire your firm, you will work for me, right?"

"Sort of. Our contract makes us partners in this rental venture. You get the last word, of course, but we consider ourselves the experts and we want to use our skills to profit you."

"Well, let's say twenty-four hundred or I'll hire another property management firm."

"Okay. Let's test the market with twenty-four hundred and revisit the price after the first weekend. If we get twenty showings and two applications, you were right. If we get two showings and no applications I was right. Does that sound okay, or am going too far?"

The owner said, "I'm hiring that other firm, Home Rental Something. They said I could name my price."

"Good. You're a wise shopper. We know there are a lot of good firms for you out there. We still want you to think about hiring us in the future if you want to shop around again."

The homeowner hired the competition and listed the house at twenty-four hundred dollars a month. In the first weekend he got three showings and no applications. Fifteen other houses priced at two thousand rented the same weekend. The next weekend he got two showings and no applications. Ten competitive houses rented for twenty-one hundred. After a month all of the rentals in town were rented, except for those over twenty-three hundred and those in need of repairs. After two months, after losing four thousand dollars in rent he would have earned if he had rented in that first weekend, he lowered the rent to twenty-two hundred. It was August. The market began to slow. People were moving in time for school, or they were at the beach on vacation. The owner rented his house in September for twenty-one hundred a month. He fired his second property management firm for failing to get the price he demanded. He hired a third property management firm. He told the new firm how bad his first two choices had been. That third firm called the previous two property management firms and asked what had happened, what was wrong with this guy. They all agreed that the problem was the price and the owner's refusal to believe the market research. The third firm took over management, but they put a note in the owner's file to remind themselves that the next time the house went on the market they would probably be forced to overprice the house or be fired. They put the account on a list of at-risk or expendable clients. They had many clients who over-valued their houses and ignored their expertise. They knew they couldn't please everyone. They would give them a one-year trial period, then have a meeting and chart the best to worst clients, separate the wheat from the chaff, and fire the worst ones.

283. Lawn Mower Liability

At the landlord's move-out he asked the property manager if he should leave the lawnmower in the garage for the tenant to use.

The property manager said a tenant might like it, unless the tenant had their own mower, then they would want the landlord's mower gone. The landlord said he had nowhere to store the mower except the garage. The property manager said the tenant might use the landlord's mower and cut off his toe. Who would be liable in that case? The landlord said he couldn't believe such a simple thing could be so complicated. The property manager admitted that he always looked for the worst-case scenario. Other property managers said he was over-thinking it.

At the move-in the tenant was glad to see there was a lawnmower. He had read the lease and knew he was responsible for lawn care.

A week later the tenant called the property manager and said the lawn mower wouldn't start. He had pulled the cord, adjusted the choke, checked the gas, and cleared the air filter. The property manager called the landlord and told him what the tenant said. The landlord said he had the same problem. The lawnmower was old and unreliable.

The property manager told the landlord the tenant was under the reasonable assumption that the mower was provided in working order for his use. The owner said it was as-is. The property manager said the tenant could remove or dispose of personal property rather than store it in his house. The landlord said it was his house, not the tenant's. The property manager said the landlord owned the deed but the tenant owned possession via his leasehold interest, according to the lease and the law. The owner said the property manager was making a simple thing too complicated.

The property manager called the tenant and asked if he would repair or store the mower. The tenant said the grass was long, he couldn't wait, and he bought a new mower. He wanted the old broken one out of his garage. The property manager asked if he could come over and shove it in the crawl space under the house. The tenant agreed. The landlord agreed. The property manager put the mower in the crawl space.

A month later the tenant called and said he went to put some boxes in the attic but it was full of the landlord's boxes. He believed it was his space to use based on his lease granting him full use of the property within reason. The property manager called the owner and presented the situation. The landlord said it was just Christmas lights, boxes, an artificial tree and decorations up there. The tenant could surely use them. The property manager pointed out that the tenant might not observe Christmas. The landlord asked the religion of the tenant. The property manager said he didn't know and couldn't ask without risking losing his license. Federal and state fair housing laws prohibited conditioning housing availability on race, religion, creed, color, age, family status and sexual orientation. The landlord asked him if the tenant was Muslim or gay or what.

284. Ladder Liability

The landlord left a ladder in the storage shed behind the house. The tenant used it for cleaning the gutters and putting up a bird feeder. The ladder slipped and the tenant fell, fracturing his tibia. One of his friends said he should sue. The tenant called the property manager and asked if he should sue. The property manager said no, the ladder was used at his own risk. The tenant said his friend said he could sue. The property manager asked the tenant to read clause sixteen in the lease titled 16. Landlord Without Liability. It was a general waiver of liability. The tenant asked if that would stand up in court. What if the roof fell on his wife and child? What if the heater blew up and killed the whole family? The property manager said the tenant had waived liability but anything could happen in court. He couldn't advise the tenant on legal or civil issues.

The property manager called the landlord and told him the tenant broke his leg and was threatening to sue. The landlord said he had never given permission to use the ladder. The property manager said the tenant could sue for anything, any time. He just wouldn't win in court if the landlord had a good attorney. The property manager asked the landlord to send him something in writing denying liability based on the lease and the law. The landlord asked if the tenant would sue him or the property manager. The property manager said he would sue both. The tenant could go to small claims court without an attorney, or hire an attorney and go to general district court.

The landlord pointed out that the property manager was not an attorney. The property manager said no, he was not an attorney, but he knew some attorneys. He hired one recently when a tenant sued over a fallen chandelier. No one was hurt but they went to court. The landlord won the case easily with a summary judgement. The tenant had no case. But the landlord had six hundred dollars in legal fees. No one really ever wins in court, he said.

The landlord threatened to sue the property manager for not telling him to get rid of the ladder.

285. Three Million Dollar Drug Bust

A tenant was arrested for drug trafficking. The police raided his house and confiscated three million dollars worth of marijuana. Two male tenants were jailed and held pending trial. The female tenant was not a flight risk, had toddlers, and posted a lower bail. She and her children remained local. The lease was terminated unilaterally by the landlord based on a lease clause prohibiting criminal activity on the premises. The police tore up cabinets, walls and opened every possible hollow cavity. They found hidden stashes. They removed large trash bags full of marijuana. They removed guns and computers. The house was secured and watched by the police for several days. Tow trucks hauled away three sports cars, a motorcycle and a van. After the house was clear and the dogs smelled nothing more, the landlord and the property manager were allowed back in. They brought in contractors, who estimated repairs of nearly a hundred thousand dollars. A hazmat team tested air and surfaces, in case of meth. Insurance agents came and shook their heads. Neighbors gathered and gossiped. The locks were changed. Doors and windows were locked. Motion sensors were installed. After the police were gone there were nightly break-ins by people, maybe former drug customers, maybe people who read about it in the papers, searching for hidden drugs or money. The contractors working on the house pried up floorboards and searched the ductwork for drugs. The cleaning company looked in every nook and cranny for contraband. When the house was restored it was put on the sales market. The landlord never wanted to own a rental property again. The male tenant was convicted and sentenced to ten to twenty. The female tenant was convicted and sentenced to house arrest. The house sold below market value. During the following two years there were occasional attempted break-ins. Some holes were dug in the yard at night. The house was sold again. The new buyer brought in a backhoe and dug up the back yard. He said he was putting in a pool.

286. Get Out

The property manager went to inspect a rental property at an appointed time. He had made the appointment with the husband, who had not told his wife. He knocked and rang the bell. After a minute with no answer he entered with his key. In the foyer he heard footsteps upstairs.

A woman yelled, "GET OUT!"

He yelled, "PROPERTY SERVICES."

She yelled, "GET OUT."

He yelled, "I AM IN!"

She yelled, "NO. GET OUT!"

He yelled, "OKAY." He walked to the door and stepped just outside the threshold. He leaned into the foyer and yelled, "I'M OUT!"

She yelled, "GET OUT."

He yelled, "I'M OUT. I'M STANDING OUTSIDE. I'M JUST YELLING WITH MY HEAD INSIDE."

She yelled, "GET OUT."

He yelled, "I HAVE AN APPOINTMENT. CALL YOUR HUSBAND."

She yelled, "WAIT. CLOSE THE DOOR AND WAIT."

The property manager waited outside the front door. After several minutes the tenant came to the door and opened it a few inches. She was wearing a towel on her torso and a towel on her head. She must have been in the shower when he entered. She handed him her cell phone and said, "TALK TO HIM!"

He answered the phone. The husband asked, "What are you doing in my house?"

The property manager replied, "I made an appointment with you on the phone on Monday."

The husband said, "My wife is home alone. You can't go in."

"I can, by contract and by law, but I'm willing to back down if you will meet me here tomorrow, same time."

"No, no. I have to work."

"So do I. This is my work. I go into your house for a living."

"I'm not comfortable."

"I'm uncomfortable too. Your wife is uncomfortable. Everybody is uncomfortable."

"Please don't come into my house."

"It's my house too. I manage it."

"Who are you?"

"I work for Property Management Services. I met you when you moved in."

"Oh. You. I remember. The real estate agent. "

"Who did you think I was?"

"I had no idea. I feel much better now. Put my wife back on the phone."

287. Bedroom Door Locks

During a routine annual inspection the property manager saw keyed locks on the bedroom doors. He told the tenant they might keep people from escaping during a fire. He also said interior bedroom door locks made it look like a boarding house, a lease violation. He asked to see all the rooms. The tenant did not have keys for all the doors, furthering the suspicion of a boarding house.

The property manager said he would return in one week. If the locks were not gone he would remove them himself. If he had to, he would remove the doors from their hinges. All for the safety of the occupants. He also said he required a list of the occupants in each room, and which bed belonged to whom. He would not seek an eviction if the tenant could comply with the lease, building code and fire code requirements.

The tenant agreed. One week later the property manager entered. The house had been cleaned. The original door knobs were returned to their doors. A list was provided of the occupants, their bedrooms, and beds.

The property manager left. He saw three men sitting in their car watching him. He drove away, then doubled back and watched. The three men entered the house. He assumed they were the unauthorized occupants.

The property manager had done his due diligence, corrected the situation, and witnessed the corrections. He would not report his suspicions yet. He would wait until the next inspection and bring up the three men at that time. Any liability in case of fire on the part of the landlord would be mitigated by the inspection, warning, correction, and compliance. He would not threaten and demand again until next time.

288. The Translator

The tenant sued the property manager because he didn't do necessary repairs. A big hole in a ceiling. A broken stair step. Issues that could be safety-related. She had a winnable case, but the landlord was cheap and didn't believe his house needed repairs. It was fine when he left.

When their case was called, the tenant stated her claim in broken English, with a thick accent. The judge asked if she needed a translator. She didn't answer. He instructed the clerk to find a translator. Her case was moved to the back of the docket.

Two hours later, after all the day's cases were called, a translator was found. The case was called. The judge asked the translator to state the tenant's claim.

The tenant bypassed the translator and said, "I don't need a translator. He's no good."

The judge said, "You're speaking English now?"

The translator asked if he could leave.

The tenant said, "Let him go. I will speak for myself."

The defendant's attorney objected and requested dismissal.

The judge said, "We waited for two hours for a translator. I will ask again. Do you speak English? Do you need a translator?"

The tenant said, "I never said I didn't speak English. The translator was your idea."

The judge said, "Yes, you're right. My mistake. Case dismissed."

289. Garage Full of Food

A neighbor of the tenant called the property manager and reported the tenant was receiving large deliveries. It appeared he ran a business out of the house. The property manager arranged an appointment with the tenant to investigate.

"A neighbor said you are shipping or receiving lots of boxes."

"Which neighbor?"

"They want to remain anonymous."

"I own a restaurant. When it's full I store boxes of dried and canned foods here."

"The association is very picky about it. Let me look."

They opened the garage. It was full of boxes. Cases of tomato sauce. Crates of produce.

"This kind of thing is not allowed. It's in the lease. There are also community rules and health department and zoning regulations. Can you move this stuff to the restaurant?"

"That's not really practical. Can't you make an exception?"

"If you didn't have trucks and vans coming and going, no one would have complained. It's my job to enforce compliance, even for things you think are normal. I don't want to seem like the bad guy."

"You should come to my restaurant for dinner. There is no charge."

"You'll move this stuff out?"

"Free dinner for your wife too."

"Please understand that the neighbors' complaint can be enforced by other authorities."

"The neighbors can come. Authorities too. Everyone can come."

290. The CLUE Database

A rental property had a burst pipe and a flooded basement. The landlord filed a claim with his homeowner's insurance. Walls, floors and personal property were replaced. Another pipe leaked a year later. Another claim was filed. A third leak occurred ten years later. The landlord's insurance company dropped him. The landlord could not get insurance with other firms. He was told about the C.L.U.E. Database. Comprehensive Loss Underwriting Exchange. The insurance companies track water damage and other claims. Three strikes and you're out. Blacklisted. Call Lloyd's of London. Pay the big bucks. Get a "Cadillac" policy.

Water damage claims became a high risk when the mold scare began. A news report of deaths due to mold had circulated. Insurance companies took note. The CDC later refuted mold as the cause of the deaths, but the damage was done.

The Federal Credit Reporting Act allows participating insurance companies to track insurance claims through Nexislexis, and be alerted to excessive claims and high risk. It is possible for a homeowner to file ONE CLAIM and be dropped due to previous claims by previous owners of the same house.

The landlord contacted federal regulatory agencies and was told the practice was perfectly legal and acceptable. He consulted an attorney who said the same thing. He ultimately got insured by an exclusive and expensive insurance company. The rates were so high it may have been cheaper to just go uninsured, but the mortgage holder required he have insurance.

The landlord asked the property manager why he hadn't been warned about CLUE. The property manager said insurance was a contract between parties outside the property management process. Property managers are not allowed to provide insurance or make representations about the insurance industry. Property management and insurance are separately licensed and do not have expertise outside their own licenses. Similarly, a property manager cannot give legal advice without a law license. State licensure boards also prohibit plumbers from doing wiring and painters from laying bricks.

The landlord said he should have been warned. He fired Property Management Services and hired another firm.

291. Flooded Basement

The basement flooded. The property manager called a plumber. The plumber said it wasn't a pipe leak. The tenants had left the basement door open and rain water had flooded in. The back yard was graded improperly so that water runoff went directly down the rear basement stairway and into the house.

The drywall, insulation and carpet were removed from the basement. It was treated for mold and mildew. A dehumidifier was installed. The tenants were told it was their fault and they would have to pay for the repairs. They asked why. Why couldn't they leave their door open? Why were they being blamed? It was so unfair.

The plumber told the property manager it might not have flooded if the stairway drain wasn't clogged, or if the backyard sloped away from the house instead of toward it. The landlord discretely paid the plumber to unclog the drain at the bottom of the stairway. He had the back yard re-graded without explaining why to the tenant. He continued to blame the tenant. The property manager knew it was unfair but the owner told him not to talk. He consulted an attorney, who advised him to represent the owner's interests and not the tenants. He would have no liability if he documented that he had informed the landlord truthfully in all matters and not willfully deceived the tenants. The tenants didn't know what to think, so they paid for everything.

292. Bedroom Break-In

It was sub-zero temperature. The power was out in an empty rental that was on the market. A neighbor saw the For Rent sign and called to warn the property manager about the power outage and frozen pipes in the neighborhood. He grabbed his coat and went to drain the pipes. He planned to open the drains and faucets and let all the water in the house drain down to the main drain in the basement. So there would be nothing left to freeze.

His key wouldn't turn the deadbolt. The locks were frozen. His fingers were so cold he could barely hold on to the key.

He walked around the house looking for a loose screen or an unlocked window. It was locked up tight. Usually people lock their main level windows but neglect to lock the top level. They never heard of a breed of burglars called "second-story men." He found a ladder under the deck in the back yard. He climbed up and looked in the bedroom windows. One was unlocked. He pried the screen off, breaking it in the process. He opened the window and crawled in, falling head-first onto the carpeted floor. He opened all the tub and sink faucet valves, opened the drains, and went downstairs. In the basement he opened the laundry deep-sink faucet. All the water in the house drained out into the deep sink. Hopefully it would go out the main drain to the street. Mission accomplished.

He put the ladder away and went back to his office. He bragged about his clever ladder-climb and drain-opening adventure. He bragged about his breaking and entering skills. He had saved the house from expensive repairs. No one was impressed. He called the owner and told him. The owner was not impressed.

Weeks later the owner called. He had received his monthly statement. He demanded to know why he had to pay twenty-five dollars for a new screen. What the hell could go wrong in an empty house?

The property manager mentally moved the account from his imaginary Heroic Accomplishment File to his overstuffed Unappreciated Sacrifices file.

293. Kitchen Break-In

The cleaning company called the property manager. The key didn't work. The tenant would move in the next day. He had to get the house opened today.

He went to the house. The windows had older sliding metal frames. He took a screwdriver and painstakingly pried out the outer lip of the track, all the way around the slider, without making noticeable dents or scratches. He popped out the slider and crawled into the kitchen, over the sink and counter, head first down onto the vinyl floor, and opened the front door from the inside.

The cleaners gave him their key and said it didn't work. He tried it. It didn't work. He wiggled it. He wiggled the knob. No luck. He sprayed WD-40 in the key hole. Then the key and lock worked fine. It was a common problem. Locksmiths often got paid lots of money for just spraying oil in a key hole. He had pried open the window and crawled in for no reason.

He put the window back in place and carefully pried the frame and track back around it. He left no mark. No one would know there was a break-in. A police car pulled up. A neighbor had seen him crawl into the window. See something, say something.

The next day the new tenant tried to move in. They called the property manager. They couldn't get in. The key didn't work.

294. Family Room Break-In

The tenant locked himself out. He had changed the locks so the property manager's key would not work. He called the property manager for help. The property manager met him at the house and told him he couldn't change locks without permission and giving him a key copy. The property manager grabbed the tire iron from his trunk and went around back. He put the prying end of the tire iron under the sliding glass door and lifted it out of the track just enough to put his hands underneath, lift the whole door, and set it to one side on the patio. He entered, got the tenant's new key copy from the kitchen counter, and opened the front door. The tenant thanked him profusely and apologized for changing the locks without permission, then demanded he hire someone to fix the sliding door so it couldn't be opened by anyone with a tire iron and half a brain. The property manager agreed, and said he was taking the new key to the hardware store to make a copy and would then give the original back to the tenant. The tenant objected, but the property manager held the key.

295. Break-In and Fix-Up

A potential new client called from overseas. He had left the U.S. in a hurry because was a diplomat in an international hot spot. His house was locked up, the grass was long, the utilities were off, and it needed painting, cleaning, carpet, and repairs. He would pay for everything the property manager had to do to fix it up. The property manager called a locksmith, a landscaper, a painter, cleaners, carpet installers, a handyman, the water company and the power company. The house was fixed up in thirty days, rented out in ten more days, and collected ample rent for a lease term of five years, with few repairs and expenses. The landlord thanked the property manager profusely. When he returned from overseas, he gave the property manager a box of Cuban cigars worth two hundred dollars stateside. The property manager accepted it, and reported the gift to his employer/broker. Any gift worth over fifty dollars could be construed as payment subject to commission rules and taxes, or else it could be an improper kickback. All such gifts were reported to the broker, recorded and reported. His boss split the cigars with him, listed it as a commission, and put it on their 1099 forms at the end of the year.

296. The Museum

A tenant moved in. He stopped paying rent. The property manager couldn't reach him. He went to the house to see if the tenant had skipped town. The house was furnished impeccably. It was spotless. Every picture on the walls was level. The magazines on the coffee table were arranged in a perfect semi-circle. It was like a museum. He talked to the neighbors. They never met the tenant. They never saw him come or go.
The property manager called the landlord.

"The house is like a museum. He's taking great care of your house."

"That's great news."

"But he's not paying rent and I can't reach him."

"How much does he owe us?"

"Two thousand."

"Let's give him another chance."

A month later they spoke on the phone again.

"The house is still like a museum. I still can't reach the tenant. He still doesn't pay rent."

"We'd hate to lose a tenant who cares for our house so much. Let's give him more time."

"He owes four thousand now. I'm not comfortable. Maybe we should evict."

"No, give him another chance."

A month later they spoke again. Still a museum, still no contact, still no rent.

The landlord asked, "What should we do?"

The property manager said, "You have to evict. He owes six thousand dollars. If we start the eviction process now it will take two months and he will owe you over ten thousand by the time the courts get him out."

"What if we just let him stay until the end of the lease term? A few more months. And then he will move out at the end of the lease."

"Why would he move out then?"

"His lease would be up."

"He never has to move out."

"What do you mean?"

"He has a free house. He is stealing two thousand dollars a month from you. Why would he ever move out? The end of the lease doesn't mean a thing if the lease is never enforced."

"That doesn't make sense. Won't he have to move out at the end of the lease?"

"By contract, yes. By law, you can't touch him without a court order."

"It's not fair."

"You found this tenant on your own. Not through our advertising. Can you tell me anything about him? Did you get references, employment, or a credit check?"

"Oh, no. He's a family friend. We trust him."

297. The Property Managers

A group of property managers, from different firms, met for lunch once a month to discuss business. First, they discussed regulatory hurdles, accounting practices, and marketing strategies. Next, they talked about greedy landlords and whiny tenants. Eventually the conversation degenerated into bitching about eviction, mold, hoarders, and sewage backups. No one wrote those stories down. The stories might invite accusations of libel and slander by previous clients. The property managers didn't want potential new clients to read about worse-case scenarios. It might be bad for business.

298. The Prostitute

The property manager was processing a rental application from a twenty-seven-year-old female. She had applied to rent a condo for two thousand dollars per month. He pulled her credit, which was excellent. Her credit card balances had been paid on time for all of her adult life. Her previous landlord said she had paid rent on time and had taken good care of his rental property. The only thing she lacked was a good employment reference. The property managers disagreed on whether she was a good risk or not.

"She has great credit. That's what matters. We should accept her application."

"Not so fast. We need to verify she has a job."

"We rent to retired people. They don't have jobs."

"That's different."

"Your mother has no job."

"Don't go there."

"Maybe she's a trust-fund baby."

"Okay, let's let the landlord decide."

The property manager called the landlord and told her that the applicant had no job, but was otherwise a great candidate—on paper.

The landlord asked, "Does she need a job to rent my house? Is that required, if she has money?"

The property manager replied, "I prefer employment to money in the bank. A regular income is better than a big bank account. It's more reliable."

The landlord asked, "What would you do if you were me?"

"I would wait and find a different tenant. But my co-workers disagree. They say money is money, and I'm being overly cautious."

The landlord asked, "Did you ask her? Did you call her on the phone and ask her where her money comes from?"

"Oh, I should have thought of that."

"Please, call her. If she works from home, or drives Uber, accept her."

"Yes. I should have thought of that."

The landlord clarified, "But not if she's a prostitute or a drug dealer."

"Oh, I should have thought of that."

"I hesitate to ask. Have you ever rented to a prostitute?"

"Once, but she had great employment references."

299. The Trampoline

A rental property had a trampoline in the back yard. A child bounced off it, landed on solid ground, and broke his arm. The tenants sued the property manager. The attorneys agreed that the property manager's firm would pay the hospital bills, and the trampoline would be removed. Six months later the tenant's child fell out of his bedroom window and landed on the ground, on the exact spot where the trampoline had been. The tenant called her attorney again.

300. Concrete

A disgruntled tenant stopped paying rent and was evicted. Just before he moved out, he poured bags of cement down all the drains and toilets in the house. The cement set up and all the pipes were turned to concrete. After the eviction, after the tenant left town, the landlord and property manager discovered the damage. Plumbers and home inspectors were brought in. A structural engineer was consulted. Insurance adjusters and their attorneys weighed in. The house was condemned. The mortgage holder was informed. The only property value left to the owner was the market value of the lot, minus the cost of demolition. The landlord asked his attorney about arson and was told that if he did that, he would be the prime suspect. The landlord hired a collection agency, which hired a skip-tracer. The tenant was found. He was unemployed and bankrupt.

The house and land were sold for twenty-five percent of the original purchase price. The buyer demolished the house, subdivided the lot into two parcels, erected two single-family homes, and sold them both for a five hundred percent profit.

301. The Big Boat

A tenant received permission from the landlord, neighbors, and local municipality to build a boat in his back yard. He completed the cabin cruiser in two years. At the end of the lease term he tried to move the boat around the house to the street. It was too big. It wouldn't fit between the houses. Disassembly, removal, and reassembly would cost more than a new boat. The landlord met the tenant and property manager at the house. The owner could sue the tenant, but the tenant had no money. The landlord forgave the tenant and said he would break the boat down and sell it for scrap, or sell its parts to a boatyard. The tenant moved out, lost his security deposit, and paid a token undisclosed amount as a settlement.

After the tenant moved out, the landlord terminated the property management contract, and moved into the house. He waited a few months before hiring a crane from a boatyard. The crane picked up the boat, hoisted it over the house, and set it down in a boat trailer in the street. He named the boat Finders Keepers.